Simon & Schuster's
Guide to
HOUSE PLANTS

Alessandro Chiusoli
and Maria Luisa Boriani

Photographs by Enzo Arnone
Illustrations by Vittorio Salarolo

U.S. Editor Stanley Schuler

A FIRESIDE BOOK
PUBLISHED BY SIMON & SCHUSTER INC.

Simon and Schuster/Fireside Books,
Published by Simon & Schuster Inc.
Simon & Schuster Building
Rockefeller Center
1230 Avenue of the Americas
New York, New York 10020

SIMON AND SCHUSTER, FIRESIDE and colophons are registered
trademarks of Simon & Schuster Inc.

Symbols by Daniela Carli

Originally published in Italian by Arnoldo Mondadori Editore S.p.A.,
Milan

11   Pbk.

Printed and bound in Spain by Artes Gráficas Toledo, S.A.
D.L. TO: 195-1999

Library of Congress Cataloging in Publication Data

Chiusoli, Alessandro.
  Simon & Schuster's guide to houseplants.

  Translation of: Piante d'appartamento.
  Bibliography: p.
  Includes index.
  1. House plants.   2. House plants--Pictorial works.
I. Boriani, Maria Luisa.   II. Title.
SB419.C48313 1986   635.9'65   86-22018
ISBN 0-671-63218-3
ISBN 0-671-63131-4 (pbk.)

CONTENTS

NOTE

Plants are listed alphabetically by their scientific Latin name; common names are given where applicable. In botanical classification plants are grouped into families, within which different genera may be identified. The genus name is given first. Each genus may include one or more species. The name of the species is indicated by a capital letter (e.g. *Anthurium andreanum*, where the first name denotes the genus and the second name the species). A species may include several varieties that differ in size and characteristics, or in the color of flowers and leaves.

Botanical varieties are by convention given in italics and come after the genus and species names (e.g. *Anthurium andreanum album*). There are also cultivars, that is varieties produced by means of cultivation of hybrids. These are indicated by a capitalized name, given in inverted commas, which comes after the genus and species names (e.g. *Anthurium andreanum* 'Guatemala.')

Many ornamental plant varieties are hybrids, obtained by cross-breeding different species or varieties or, more rarely, different genera (for example, X Laeliocattleya). Crosses between different species are often indicated by the name of the genus followed by the capitalized name of the cultivar in inverted commas. This is the case, for example, with most orchids, since hybrid cultivars are more readily available commercially than original species (e.g. *Cymbidium* 'Minuet,' *Cymbidium* 'Peter Pan').

EXPLANATION OF SYMBOLS

Decorative use

decorative flowers

ornamental foliage

Temperature

cool or fresh
(13–18°C/55–
64°F)

medium (18–24°C/64–75°F)

warm (24–27°C/75–80°F)

Position

full sun

filtered light

shade

Watering

moderate watering

normal watering

generous watering

spraying of leaves

INTRODUCTION

Many of us who do not possess a garden and feel the need to be surrounded with flowers and greenery can derive great fulfillment and pleasure from the cultivation of indoor plants. The opportunity to practice a form of indoor gardening, no matter how limited the space available, provides a necessary feeling of perspective and calm amid the turmoil of everyday life, and the results we achieve can help to brighten up our surroundings.

Plants have various needs of their own and it is pointless to fill every room indiscriminately with greenery without taking these needs into account. We have to make certain, first of all, that we are keeping our plants happy. The secret of success is to appreciate that plants react to their surroundings and sometimes even to their owners.

It is important to look after them properly, being neither too fussy nor too negligent. Plants live and grow in accordance with their individual biological rhythm which is related to the environmental conditions of their country of origin. Alterations to their normal vegetative cycle can be effected only with special structures and methods that will guarantee the best possible conditions for development and flowering, such as greenhouses that enable plants to be forced so their beauty can be enjoyed at particular times of the year. A greenhouse is indispensable not only for forcing, but also for the straightforward cultivation of the majority of house plants as these, coming from tropical or subtropical climes, have special requirements, notably light, temperature, water, soil and atmospheric humidity; all of which must be met to ensure good results. In cities, however, particularly for people living in apartment houses, a greenhouse is out of the question, but this does not mean having to give up the idea of growing plants. The important point is to choose correctly those species, varieties and hybrids that possess the characteristics likely to ensure luxuriant growth and, where applicable, fine flowers in existing surroundings. Because heat, light and humidity are likely to vary from room to room, special factors have to be considered when making the initial choice of plant. Where light is concerned, for example, it is essential to remember that north- and west-facing windows let in less light than south- and east-facing windows. For that reason it is advisable to select plants that have different lighting requirements; and in summer, plants in the brightest rooms may have to be moved away from windows in order to avoid scorching and fading of foliage.

Well-lighted surroundings make it possible to grow many plants with attractively colored leaves but that are highly demanding. For example, the *Cordyline* species require very bright light whereas the *Dracaena* species, although belonging to the same family, need little light. In this case it is important not to confuse the two, as often happens.

Various types of plant
Broadly speaking, house plants are divided into two main groups: those with flowers and those with decorative foliage. Flowering pot plants may include both greenhouse and garden plants. As a rule they are bought in bud, ready for flowering. Newly purchased plants do not need much attention apart from the right position, sufficient watering and the continuous removal of faded flowers which, in the case of many species such as *Kalanchoe*, ensures the growth of new buds and hence prolonged flowering. More problems are likely to arise in subsequent years if the plant is a perennial, which generally calls for considerable care over such matters as temperature, lighting, feeding, pruning and so forth. Less demanding species like certain begonias, for example, adapt in various ways to indoor surroundings; but others like poinsettia, cyclamen and azaleas need additional protection under glass.

Plants that flower indoors for many months or at intervals, but every year, give the most pleasure and understandably form the basis of most collections. Obvious examples of plants that produce splendidly varied color in summer are the fuchsias, whose delicate, hanging blooms in a mixture of shades against the same background make a wonderful dissplay. Then there are also the bulbous plants such as *Hippeastrum* (amaryllis) and sweetly scented hyacinths for winter.

Foliage plants are usually distinguished by their green or variegated leaves. Their beauty, however, does not reside in coloration alone but also in the shape, structure, pattern and veining of the individual leaves. The wavy leaves of *Asplenium* (bird's nest fern) are soft and delicate, whereas the palmate leaves of *Chamaerops* (fan palm), on long, stiff stalks, give a more formal, austere effect. The markings on the shiny leaves of *Calathea* look as if they were created by the exuberant brush of a painter, and the veining of certain agaves give the impression of being built up on strictly geometric principles.

While such features help dictate the choice of particular plants to suit the decor of the home, they should not be the sole guide to selection, for as a rule the plants with colored foliage tend to be more demanding and delicate, often needing conditions of temperature, light and humidity that are hard to obtain indoors. *Croton, Maranta* and *Cordyline*, for example, are very beautiful and decorative, but only for a short time if they lack the proper environmental conditions.

For this reason it may be wise not to be too ambitious and to leave these and other "difficult" plants to the pro-

Popular house plant choices include, among many others, Dracaena deremensis, Dracaena marginata tricolor, Philodendron *and* Cordyline.

fessionals, while concentrating instead on species that may be less spectacular and rare but more satisfying overall, such as *Begonia rex, Tradescantia variegata, Peperomia* and *Chlorophytum.* The *Coleus* species, too, although generally used for decorating beds and borders in the garden, do very well indoors, making showy pot plants of red, green, yellow, purple and pink coloration.

Plants with wholly green foliage have fewer environmental needs and exceptions such as the maidenhair fern and the paradise palm (*Kentia*, which, though they may survive for a long time, may not grow and even take on a stunted appearance.

ORIGINS AND HISTORY

Man's wish to surround himself with ornamental plants, even in his indoor habitat, dates from earliest times. Much archeological evidence, from Greek, Chinese, Egyptian and Roman excavations, reveals an interest not only in plants that could be used for food but also for decorative purposes, such as roses and hyacinths. But it is in more modern times, in the wake of the great explorations to tropical countries that

The genus Rhododendron comprises a large number of species, many imported from the East. R. simsii, commonly misidentified as Azalea indica, is grown as a house plant, as is the less familiar R. obtusum. Indoor azaleas are almost always hybrids derived from different families, and are cultivated for just one season.

an enthusiasm for new plants on the part of botanists, flower-growers, missionaries and traders alike began to develop. Most of these "researchers" were in the service of botanical gardens, royal families or aristocrats all competing for possession of the rarest plant.

England played a prominent part in the importation of exotic plants (George III and his mother founded the celebrated Kew Gardens) that were subsequently cultivated under protected conditions. These were initially large heated huts, that developed into the famous Victorian hothouses. In 1800 the trade in exotic plants was big business, and each new plant imported unleashed a race to acquire an example of it. There was thus a cactus fever, a fern fever and at the close of the nineteenth century, a vogue for orchids.

Among the major difficulties botanical researchers had to contend with here was not merely that of collecting orchids, African violets, dracaenas, from the most distant parts of the world, but of keeping specimens alive during the long homeward sea voyages involved.

Plants were generally transported in wooden chests that did little to guarantee their survival. It was thanks to an English physician, Nathaniel Bagshaw Ward, who ingeniously devised a glass case (subsequently known as the Wardian case) that plants could be transported successfully all over

13

the world. These Wardian cases proved so popular that they found their way, with various embellishments, into many European drawing rooms whose owners favored exotic plants.

Many of the species displayed in these cases are still cultivated today, but most have undergone changes through the process of hybridization which botanists and nurserymen carried out as new plants were discovered in order to meet the public's increasing demand for different plants. Many botanical researchers and hybridization experts are remembered through the names of genera and species created or discovered by them. Thus, the Frenchman Michel Bégon, following a stay in the Antilles around 1680, brought back begonia specimens. Poinsettias were introduced to the United States from Mexico by one Joll Poinsett, who had been the first U.S. Minister there. Other species bear the names of scientists, botanists and seafarers who made a contribution to natural history through their work. The Columnea, for example, recalls the Italian Fabio Colonna, author of botanical treatises; and the genus Bougainvillea was named after the seaman Louis Antoine de Bougainville and fuchsias after the German physician Leonhard Fuchs.

Arrangement and composition

In arranging indoor plants it is important to bear in mind that the chosen species must be suited to the particular room conditions. Thus in normal houses and apartments it is impossible to grow plants such as *Calathea,* some bromeliads, and certain orchids that cannot survive if the temperature drops too low at night or if the difference between the day and night temperature exceeds 9°C (16°F). Indeed, if there is a greater temperature range, vegetative activity ceases and the plants quickly die unless both watering and feeding are curtailed or even halted. Rooting activity, respiration and photosynthesis are slowed down in such a way that if watering and feeding are continued, the resulting conditions are ideal for the development of physiological diseases and molds.

"Difficult" plants can be grown only where an independent heating system is available. Good lighting is also essential. In south- and east-facing rooms the greenery can consist of *Cissus, Coleus, Peperomia magnoliaefolia, Aphelandra, Capsicum, Hippeastrum,* etc. Yet these plants, which love the sun, can also be harmed by direct radiation; so they need the protection of curtains, especially when the weather is very hot. Alternatively, to avoid the scorching of plants placed near south-facing windows, they should be moved. This should also be done on winter nights if windows are not double-glazed because of the sharp fall in temperature close to the glass.

Plants can be effectively displayed by being grouped into geometric compositions which are echoed in an appropriate shape of container. In choosing plants for such a display, it is important to check that they will happily adapt to these conditions.

Humidity also plays a significant role in the development of house plants and may prove a restricting factor in homes where the air becomes too dry for the proper growth of many species. Thus some of the loveliest and most elegant ferns find their ideal habitat only in the bathroom, where there is plenty of warmth and humidity.

When plants are arranged indoors as decorative items designed to blend with the rest of the furnishings, thought must also be given to their shape and height. If correctly combined, such plants can provide special effects, even of perspective, so that the room itself may appear to be altered in size. As a rule, large plants that grow tall need to be placed in a position where a smaller specimen would be over-whelmed and its ornamental qualities lost. But large plants in a small room simply create a sense of confusion, and limit the available space. Groups of small plants, perhaps put into unusual and elegant containers, can give the impression of forming a rare collection.

Positioning species with soft, light green leaves, such as maidenhair fern, next to dark-leaved species like *Cissus*, with a light placed behind them, creates highly effective interplays of color.

The color of the walls, in addition to the style of furnishing, should be considered when introducing a plant as an integral part of the decor. A white or pale-colored wall, which has a positive influence on the plant's development by reflecting light, can be used successfully as background for both foliage and flowering plants. Dark walls do not adequately show off dark-foliaged species such as *Ficus elastica* and *Aspidistra*, whereas they can highlight plants with pale flowers or white-veined foliage such as some forms of *Syngonium, Fittonia* and *Aechmea fasciata.*

If a room has colored or highly patterned wallpaper, or if the furniture includes chairs and sofas in ornate fabrics, avoid going for dramatic effects and choose plants that bring a touch of lightness and simplicity, like *Schefflera* or *Cyperus*. Never underestimate the decorative effect of containers: if tastefully chosen, they enhance plants that are normally little appreciated. Some people feel that plants look best in natural materials such as rush, cane or natural wood. But ceramic and metal containers are also used to create interesting effects.

If you are growing tired of certain plants that you have had for some time, you might strive for a new look by adding small flowering bulbs, or even a climber or an epiphyte, to the same pots. This is an excellent idea for enlivening a *Ficus elastica, Dieffenbachia* or *Philodendron* that may have lost its basal leaves.

Provided the individual needs of the plants you grow are given priority, your final choice is a matter of personal taste.

With a little imagination, by taking full advantage of the enormous variety of shapes and sizes in which house plants come, you can achieve a pleasing match between greenery and existing decor.

There are, however, two basic rules that must be followed when grouping house plants: First, you must be sure that they have similar cultural needs. Second, you should try to avoid too many contrasts in a single composition.

If the only difference in the requirements of the chosen plants is the amount of water to be given, this problem can be overcome by placing each plant in a separate pot but putting them all together in one container. (In fact, by adopting this procedure in any type of composition, many problems can be eliminated.) A layer of pebbles in the bottom of the large container will provide extra drainage for the smaller pots and prevent too much water from damaging the roots.

Another advantage of a large container is that you can easily and quickly replace plants that are unhappy and whose growth may be stunted. This is especially useful when a single plant shows signs of disease, perhaps affecting the root system, in which case speedy removal will keep the other plants from becoming infected.

It is sensible to arrange the plants in the container by adopting the same rules as for planning a border or a flower bed: the tallest plants at the back, the bushy ones in the center and the hanging plants at the front edge of the container.

In order to create a microclimate ideal for growth, it is advisable to place the plants as close as possible to one another, burying each pot in moist peat to increase humidity since, in most rooms, this will be lower than the normal requirements of the plants.

Many arrangements (particularly of prize specimens) will acquire greater decorative effect if the beauty of the constituent plants is accentuated by means of an artificial light source, such as a spotlight. An unusual effect can be achieved by illuminating from behind a group of plants in different shades of green. A suitably positioned spotlight will throw into relief both the shapes and the patterns of leaves. Such artificial light sources should not be considered as substitutes for natural sunlight as there is a risk of weakening the plants.

In making plant arrangements we are most likely to proceed along one or other of the lines so far described, but there are alternative methods which concentrate on a vertical effect. These are ideal solutions for breaking up a large area, and may take the form of small groups of plants, terrariums and glass cases, or even a live dividing wall composed of

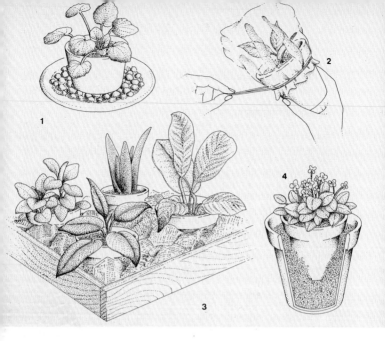

climbing plants clinging to sections of trellis or bamboo cane partitions.

If the room is not sufficiently large, such supports can even be placed against a wall. Since plants suspended in this manner require frequent spraying and the canes periodic cleaning, the walls should be protected with a washable paint or vinyl wallcovering.

A dividing wall can also be created without the aid of a trellis by using plants of different heights and with very dense foliage. Climbing and hanging plants which adapt well to such situations include *Philodendron, Syngonium, Cissus* and *Hedera.* To achieve a curtain effect, the climbing species should be placed in pots at the base of the trellis and the hanging species on a shelf above.

Plants that can be affixed directly to the trellis are the epiphytes, which do not need to be grown in pots with compost. In nature these plants live attached to the branches and trunks of trees, not as parasites (i.e. not to derive nourishment from them) but simply as forms of support, essential for them to grow nearer the most luminous zones of the forest. The commonest epiphytes are certain bromeliads (for example, *Aechmea fulgens,* but not *Billbergia nutans* which is spite of being a bromeliad is a ground plant and is unsuitable for such purposes), the epiphytic orchids, and some fleshy plants such as *Epiphyllum, Platicerium,* etc, and all these can be used for special arrangements.

Natural conditions can be reproduced indoors for these plants by giving them the support of a branch or piece of cork-oak bark. The shape of the branch or trunk is sometimes important. Certain plants live happily in clefts or forks where in nature they are helped to grow by deposits of slowly decomposing organic matter.

CULTIVATION METHODS

General problems

For luxuriant growth and flower production plants must be kept in the right conditions.

We have already seen that such requirements include the correct amount of light, heat, water, food and air. Since most house plants are of tropical origin, they have to be provided with conditions as similar as possible to those of the original natural surroundings. If only one of these factors is lacking, a plant is likely to wilt or perhaps die. Highly adaptable as many species are, they have limits. We must never forget that no plant will flourish in every environment. Plants that love light, for example, will never display all their beauty if confined to dark corners, and vice versa.

Understanding the fundamental processes that take place inside plants enabling them to live, helps us to satisfy their needs. Knowledge of photosynthesis, respiration and transpiration, even in superficial terms, may help to explain why, for example, watering (perhaps daily) is a necessity, or why shutters or curtains should be opened even when nobody is at home, or why fertilizers have to be applied.

In order to grow, plants produce sugars and proteins from natural substances contained in water and air. The fundamental process of photosynthesis is due to the carbon dioxide present in the atmosphere, mineral elements which are, or should be, present in the soil, water and light. The energy furnished by photosynthesis permits the raw, simple elements to be transformed into a mixture of sugars which in their turn are utilized as nutritive substances. Following a closed cycle, these sugars are once more transformed into energy, also essential for all other vital processes.

Light plays an indispensable part in the process of photosynthesis by affecting the chlorophyll that is present in the leaves and green stems. By absorbing oxygen present in the atmosphere, plants bring about the decomposition of the sugars, releasing energy. This creates the conditions for respiration, which goes on not only in the light but also in darkness, culminating in the plant's emission of carbon dioxide.

The process of transpiration, whereby the plant "loses" water, is regulated by the opening and closing of the stomata or slits situated in the lower surface of the leaves. These are utilized in all processes, to absorb carbon dioxide in the course of photosynthesis and oxygen during respiration.

The opening mechanism of the stomata is closely related to the amount of humidity in the air. Therefore, in order to limit excessive loss of water through transpiration, the atmosphere around the plant has to remain humid. This is why plants should be arranged in groups rather than placed in various parts of the room.

Plants need careful and understanding owners. Above all, to ensure photosynthesis we have to give them the right amount of light.

The temperature for each plant must also be suitable, and here too it is useful to know more about the processes that occur at the various temperatures likely to be encountered in natural surroundings with the alternation of the seasons and of day and night.

A plant grows luxuriantly at what is called optimum temperature (characteristic of each species). There are different levels of optimum temperature: that which is ideal for germination, that which is ideal for rooting, and that which is ideal for growth. Every phenological phase of the plant (i.e. in which climate is an influencing factor) is marked by different temperature levels that determine whether or not cultivation will be successful.

Apart from these ideal temperatures, there are others, recommended for the various species, which do not directly affect the development of the plant but which help to keep it alive and healthy. These are known as the biological maxima and minima. Below and above these temperatures all the metabolic processes of the plant will cease.

In nature such extremes may be encountered at precise times of the year, for example in winter and, for a short while, in summer. In winter plants from temperate zones go into vegetative dormancy, their vital processes all being slowed down, so that the absorption of water and nutritive elements is reduced to a very low level and, in some species, curtailed completely. This behavior also occurs in house plants originating in other latitudes, with the important difference that their seasons cannot always be called winter and summer and do not coincide with ours. That is why it is essential to know from where our indoor plants come.

In the case of flowering plants there is a further consideration; not only do we need to know the thermoperiod (the period of exposure to a particular temperature) but also the photoperiod, namely the number of hours of light indispens-

able for getting the plant to flower. Many plants do not flower once they come indoors. There may be different causes: perhaps failure to pay attention to their period of dormancy, or because they require fewer hours of daylight than are given to other plants. A classic instance is the chrysanthemum. Originally from the Far East, this is a "short-day" plant; i.e. the flower buds develop as the days grow shorter. To get them to flower in October – November, nurserymen must keep the plants in darkness for several hours of the day in order to reproduce their original conditions. Similar behavior occurs in *Euphorbia pulcherrima* (poinsettia), another very beautiful short-day species: flowering and the red color of the bracts come about only under conditions where light and temperature are strictly controlled.

The growth cycle

Every species has its precise growth cycle. In temperate latitudes, the most familiar cycle is that of deciduous plants. Most people know at what time of year a rose becomes dormant and when it grows and blooms. But matters are more complicated in the case of an evergreen. Many people believe that the term "evergreen" means that the plant has no annual rest period and, since evergreen house plants retain their leaves throughout the year, it is easily forgotten that in the regions where they originate their growth is seasonally arrested.

Certain species from temperate climes, also keeping their foliage in winter, grow more vigorously if allowed a period of dormancy. Indoor plants of tropical and subtropical origin will, in their natural habitat, continue to grow without interruption because of the minimal seasonal differences of outside conditions. So it is often claimed that such plants are easy to cultivate during winter in heated apartments or houses, but this belief is the cause of the most frequent failures. Although temperature conditions are optimal in our latitudes, nevertheless, outside conditions vary with the seasons and the amount of light, whether daylight or artificial indoor lighting, becomes the limiting factor. Thus, in order to get a species such as *Saintpaulia ionantha*, which has no resting period in nature, to flower indoors, even though the temperature may be the same as that to which it is accustomed, it must be provided with a supplementary amount of artificial light.

Leafy plants also react to inadequate lighting in winter. The stems grow longer and the leaves lose their typical hue and take on a faded color, finally becoming diseased as a result of weakness.

Even plants which in nature do not need to rest in winter should in the home be subjected to enforced dormancy to slow down development until conditions are again ideal for the resumption of vegetative activity.

Nothing complicated is needed to induce a plant to rest. In the case of tropical plants reduce watering to a minimum and avoid fertilization.

Temperature and humidity

All house plants need warmth, except in the case of those very rare species that give good results only if kept at a low temperature. The rule applies to all bulbs, many annuals and all those plants requiring a period of vegetative rest. Once again, however, care should be taken not to give too much. Although intense cold can be fatal, so can excessive heat. What must be remembered is that house plants should be kept, as far as possible, in constant temperatures, even cooler than the optimal; what must be strictly avoided is abrupt temperature changes at different times of day.

The ideal temperature range for plant growth is around 18–24°C (64–75°F); the variation between day and night temperature should not be more than 4–5°C (7–9°F). Greater variations will soon do damage, causing flowers and leaves to fall, foliage to turn yellow, etc. With central heating, these temperature ranges are easy to achieve and maintain. In spite of this, house plants often develop yellow leaves that soon drop off, together with the flowers and buds. There are different reasons for this. Various rooms may have particular spots unsuitable for plants or at least for delicate plants especially sensitive to temperature changes. A plant placed too near a radiator or an open fire may be exposed to a current of warm, dry air, causing its leaves to wrinkle. Equally harmful are drafts from windows and doors not properly closed. Other danger points may be shelves situated in front of windows: there is a sharp drop in temperature close to glass during winter. Dark, warm corners lead to elongation of stems but also to weak and straggly plants. Finally, it is important to give special treatment to those plants in the colder rooms of the home, since there is minimal loss of water through evaporation, and therefore less watering is needed.

Whereas a little ingenuity will easily achieve such conditions, the problem of atmospheric humidity is more difficult to deal with. The relative air humidity, i.e. the amount of water vapor in the atmosphere, regulates some of the plant's fundamental activities. Transpiration, the loss of water through the stomata when these open to absorb gases, is restricted when the air is moist. Conversely, when the air is dry transpiration increases, so that if the plant does not make up for the lost water, the leaves wilt and the flowers fall.

Any rise in temperature should be accompanied by an increase in relative humidity. Central heating creates air that is too dry for plants accustomed to places where atmospheric humidity approaches the point of saturation.

Humidity is therefore the vital factor in the cultivation of most ornamental plants. There are various methods of increasing the humidity in the air, such as spraying the leaves to create water vapor, but the disadvantage is that this does not last long. The best solution to ensure an almost constant presence of humidity around the foliage is to place the plants in containers with a layer of gravel that is kept wet at all times on the bottom. Single plants can also be kept moist by setting the pot in a bigger container filled with wet peat.

In addition to such homemade expedients, there are, on the market, automatic electric humidifiers provided with sensors that activate them when the air humidity drops below fixed levels appropriate for the plants. Humidity is measured on a scale ranging from 0% (absolutely dry) to 100% (saturated with humidity). For good results with indoor plants, it should never go lower than 55–60%. This figure should be increased for plants with light, soft foliage such as maidenhair fern. Conversely, plants with thicker, leathery leaves can more easily thrive in drier air.

To regulate temperature and relative humidity it is essen-

tial to have to hand a thermometer and a hygrometer. The thermometer must be one that registers the minimum and maximum temperature, so that the day and night levels can also be controlled.

Light

Plants have different light requirements, depending on the growth conditions in their countries of origin. Even plants of the tropical forest have diverse needs, for some grow at ground level while others live attached to tree trunks. So while being guided by esthetic considerations in selecting house plants, we should also consider the amount of light that we can provide indoors.

The quantity of light varies in different corners of a room. The light level drops rapidly away from windows. This decrease cannot usually be measured precisely by the human eye, and to get an exact reading one would have to resort to photoelectric cells. Contrary to what might be supposed, such instruments will reveal that the areas near the windows are not the brightest in the room.

If the corner picked out for a plant is not right, the reaction will be swift. The adult leaves gradually turn yellow while the young ones remain small and pale. Plants with variegated foliage will fail to keep their characteristic color and become completely green.

The amount of light entering any environment depends on numerous factors. The size and number of windows is important but so too are the season, the direction the room faces and outside factors such as the presence of buildings, trees and so forth.

South-facing windows get the most light, followed in order by those facing east, west and north. The amount of light coming in varies according to the position of the sun, so that there are differences during the course of the day and at various seasons. North-facing windows furnish dimmer, but more constant and continuous light. South-facing windows are not only brighter (getting direct light for more hours a day) but also warmer. During summer few plants can survive on these windowsills unless provided with some shade. Ideal positions for shade-loving plants are those close to east-facing windows which get direct sunlight only in the morning, this being less strong and hot than that which comes in at noon through west-facing windows.

In the open, plants receive light from every direction, but this rarely happens indoors where light usually comes from only one direction and obliquely – never from above. This causes an imbalance in growth, which occurs mainly in the direction of the light source. This phenomenon – known as heliotiopism – will be less acute if plants are placed in front of a white wall. Another method to keep plants growing vertically rather than at a slant is to keep turning them around; but this expedient (to be adopted only in extreme cases) should be avoided with flowering plants in bud since there is a risk of the flowers falling.

The quantity of light has been mentioned, but the importance of its quality should be remembered. There is a great difference between summer and winter sunlight, and a further difference between natural and artificial light. Artificial illumination is used by nurserymen for many valid reasons, not only to lengthen the hours of light and thus encourage blooming in "long-day" plants, but also to stimulate the photosynthetic processes and hence the plants' development. Recourse to artificial light also makes it possible to cultivate plants in dark corners. Species that give excellent results when exposed to artificial light include some cacti, *Saintpaulia* (African violet), which then flowers continuously, *Begonia rex,* etc.

To obtain the best results, the form of artificial light used should be similar to that of the solar spectrum. This is not easy to achieve, but preference should be given to lamps in which the proportions of red and blue-violet radiations are not very different from those in nature. The principal kinds of lamp used are incandescent lamps, fluorescent lamps (or

Bromeliads and crassulas are cultivated for their decorative foliage and rosettes. The leaves are fleshy, and these plants can therefore tolerate dry surroundings. The flowers are usually short-lived.

tubes), metal-halide lamps, self-ballasted mercury-vapor lamps and a combination of two or more different lamps. Incandescent lamps are most often used just for simple illumination, although the red light they emit is excellent for flower development. Their main disadvantage is that they give off a large part (70–75%) of their energy in the form of heat and therefore must be placed high above plants to prevent scorching.

Metal-halide lamps produce brilliant white light and are useful for plant lighting; but since they are mounted high above the plants, they are largely restricted to public and commercial buildings with high ceilings. They are rarely used in homes.

Conventional mercury-vapor lamps are popular in Europe for plant lighting but not in the United States. However, a new self-ballasted mercury-vapor lamp that can be screwed into a conventional lamp socket is becoming rather widely used in the U.S. for lighting individual potted plants. All mercury lamps give off a light more like sunlight and emit less heat than incandescents. They are expensive to buy and operate.

Fluorescent lamps are by far the most popular light source among gardeners. They consume less electricity while emitting more light with less heat than most other lamps. And they last a long time – roughly 7,000 hours (as compared with about 750 hours for incandescents). Furthermore, fluorescents give off light of many different colors so that you can provide plants with almost exactly the light they need – blue-white light for root development and reddish light for flowering. Today, most U.S. gardeners use one Cool White lamp with one Warm White lamp. But you can use any combination of fluorescents you find successful. For example, you can use nothing but the so-called Grow lights, which give off a purplish light; or nothing but Daylight tubes, which give off a cold blue-white light; or a mixture of Grow light and Day light tubes; or any other mixture you prefer.

(Fluorescents are so efficient and offer so many opportunities for mixing light colors that the old practice of combining incandescent lamps with fluorescent lamps has largely been forgotten.)

Whichever kind of lamp you use, it is important to hang them at the proper height above the plants. For incandescent lamps the distance should be increased in relation to their power; thus a 100-watt bulb should be placed 50–60 cm (20–24 in) away while a 75-watt bulb is placed 40–45 cm (16–18 in) away. In the case of other lamps, which produce less heat, the ideal distance is determined by the needs of the plant. For example, flowering plants such as *Saintpaulia* that require a moderate amount of light, should be about 25–

30 cm (10–12 in) away. Plants such as orchids, bromelids and the like, which require more light, should have the benefit of stronger lamps.

If you decide on artificial lighting, be sure to follow all safety procedures. All wires must be waterproof and every part of the installation must be grounded (earthed). To avoid risks, it may be advisable to have an electrician make the installation.

Watering
Whenever you buy a new plant, give thought to the amount of water you give it weekly. It may not be enough to follow literally the instructions of the florist or garden center from which you bought it. Conditions at home are different from those in a nursery and vary with the season, so watering must depend on the microclimate that is created indoors. Watering is usually regarded as the simplest of growing operations, but this is not so. One of the most frequent reasons for failure in keeping house plants is incorrect watering. With too little water the plant wilts, but with too much the effect is worse because the air present in the soil is driven out, causing suffocation of the roots. The right amount of water depends on the plant's demands, and on surrounding conditions. The outward appearance of the plant is not a

27

reliable guide as to when water is needed. The most sensible course of action is to control the moisture content of the soil. This needs to be done weekly during cold periods and daily in the heat of summer. If the surface of the soil is dry, it does not always mean that water is called for. The only sure guide is to check the soil in depth by inserting a finger; if it feels completely dry, lose no time in watering plentifully.

There are moments in the course of the vegetative cycle when plants require more water, namely when they are about to bud and when, during active growth, they show new shoots and flowers.

The proper interval between successive applications of water is also determined by other factors. The type of container and the soil in which the plant is being grown are important. House plants are usually kept in clay pots, because they look better; but nowadays nurserymen tend increasingly to grow plants in plastic pots. If you buy plants in this form, remember to water them less frequently than those in clay pots. Unlike clay, plastic is not porous; consequently, there is no water loss by evaporation through the sides of the pot.

The type of soil also has a considerable influence on frequency of watering. Peat and loamy soil lose water more slowly than sand or a highly porous soil. It is important to remember that if the medium consists only of peat, it should never be allowed to dry out completely. Water should be given when the layer just below the surface is still moist. Peat, compared with other mediums, retains a large amount of water that cannot be used by the plant.

The size of the plant in relation to the diameter of the container must also be taken into account. The bigger the plant, the quicker the soil dries.

Having resolved the problem of how much water to give, decide on how to apply it and think about its quality. Opinions are divided on whether plants should be watered from above, or provided with water from beneath. Both methods are acceptable, but it is important to measure the quantity of water. When watering from below there is no risk of drenching the leaves, which may result in spots or mold, especially in the case of downy leaves and rosette-shaped plants. But there is the danger of an accumulation of salts in the topmost part of the soil; and another risk is that the water may stagnate in the container beneath the pot, suffocating the roots.

If watering from above, choose a can with a long, narrow spout so that water is able to reach the surface of the soil hidden by the leaves and yet not drench them. Apply water so that it does not flow out of the drainage hole in the bottom of the pot because here too excess water should not be

For some plants, such as bromeliads, water should be poured into the center of the plant as well as into the pot (1); to create a moist microclimate set the pot into peat (2) or lay it on pebbles (3); it is also useful to set the plant on a support over a receptacle containing water (4); the simplest method to maintain moisture is to spray the leaves with water.

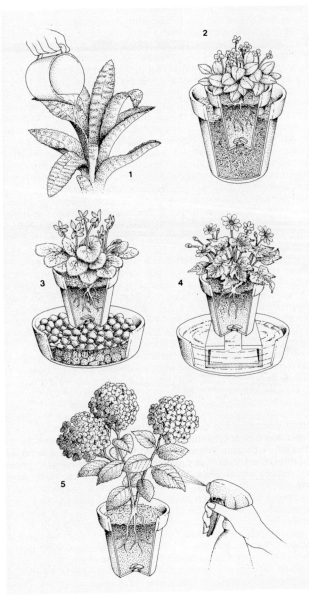

allowed to collect in the container.

The best water to use is soft and at room temperature. To determine the lime content (hardness) of water, use a pH indicator, sold in most garden centres. If the water is excessively hard, you will have to buy a softener. The simpler solution is to use rain water, though in large urban areas this may not be advisable because of the dangers of pollution. If you have only a few plants you can boil the water, causing some of the lime to form a deposit. Another way of neutralizing the lime is to put some peat overnight in a tub containing the water to be used on the plants; the following day the water will be ready for application.

In the case of lime-hating plants, such as camellias, it is absolutely essential to neutralize the calcium, for the latter prevents the assimilation of iron and causes a disease known as ferric chlorosis. This is manifested by the yellowing of the leaf surface between the veins. The remedy, apart from the use of soft water, is to apply specific preparations such as Sequestrene.

Feeding

Plants need not only water but also nutriment. There is a close connection between water and fertilizers because the roots absorb the food in the water. As well as the substances existing in the soil, plants have to find additional food, mainly during their vegetative period, from March to September.

There are various types of plant food suitable for different types of cultivation, but in their case too, the basic rule is not to overdo it. A plant that is growing rapidly as a result of stimulation by nitrogen fertilizers is not strong enough to withstand privation and parasites.

On the market there are natural fertilizers and chemical fertilizers in soluble, liquid, granular and powdered forms. Chemical fertilizers for house plants are effective and easy to use when the instructions are followed; they contain the three elements essential for the balanced development of plants: nitrogen, phosphorus and potassium. Nitrogen (given the symbol N in preparations) helps the development of leaves and stems and is essential for producing chlorophyll; it is applied in the form of nitrates. If abused, it causes etiolation (whitening) of the plants and retards flower formation. Phosphorus (P), administered in the form of phosphoric acid or phosphates, plays a decisive role in root development. Potassium (K) stimulates the formation of flowers and fruits. Plants with colored foliage also derive benefit from the application of the macroelement.

These are the three elements required in greatest quantity, but there are others that are needed in small amounts. These

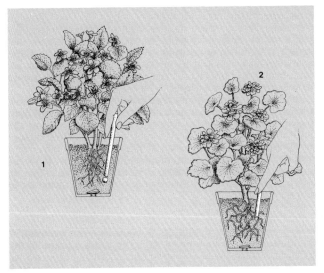

are known as microelements or trace elements. All general preparations on the market should contain the proper balance of macroelements and trace elements.

There are many commercial preparations, including those for particular types of plants and cultivation stages. Thus foliage plants need nitrogen-rich food, which is valuable for other plants as well during the early phases of growth, after the winter rest, when the development of new shoots is to be encouraged. Preparations with a high phosphorus content are recommended for slow-growing plans, stimulating root development. Flowering plants, once they have finished blooming, need to prepare for the next flowering period, and can do with applications of food with a high content of potassium. Special fertilizers for particular plants include specifics for orchids and for acid-loving plants.

You may decide to use organic as well as chemical fertilizers. The former furnish the necessary substances to the plants after a certain time lapse, and have the advantage of not increasing the concentration of salts in the soil.

Chemical products, in the form of capsules or granules, also have a slow and prolonged effect, being designed specifically to release their nutriment over a period of three to six months. More practical to use are liquid fertilizers or powders soluble in water, which have the advantage of being applicable at the time of ordinary watering. They have an immediate tonic effect on the plants and are especially useful, when sprayed on the leaves, for those plants that absorb little nutriment through the roots, like many epiphytes. Other fertilizers in the form of powder, granules, etc. are not immediately efficacious but require two or three weeks for the constituent elements to be released.

Before administering any type of plant food it is advisable to check that the soil is moist, otherwise the food might burn the roots. Other rules to follow: avoid feeding during the dormant period (November to February); wait three or four months before feeding repotted plants because new compost contains mineral elements. Finally, feeding is of no use for diseased plants as fertilizer is not a medicine; in fact, in order to assimilate nutritive elements the plant must be in prime condition.

Repotting

This is an essential operation. A plant in a pot necessarily occupies a limited volume of soil. The roots quickly fill the space at their disposal and soon find no more nutriment for the plant's development. The only solution is to give it new soil and a larger container.

Initially plants should be reported every year, at the beginning of the growth season, whenever this occurs. When they have reached a fair size they can be repotted at longer inervals: obviously they cannot be given bigger pots indefinitely.

The plant must be examined carefully to decide when repotting is due. The roots are the guide. In many species thinner roots will protrude from the drainage hole of the pot, but this is not necessarily a sure sign since many plants thrust their roots out of the pot in search of moisture which for some reason cannot be found inside. To be quite certain, remove the plant from the pot. To make sure the ball of soil stays intact, place the palm of the hand against the surface of the soil and hold the stem tight between the fingers. Then turn the pot upside down and tap it gently but firmly against a table edge. If the roots are tightly twisted around the soil, you should certainly repot. They need not, in fact, get to this stage, for the repotting can be done when the tips of the roots show all over the surface of the compost: There are exceptions: *Clivia* (Kaffir lily) and certain shrubs flower more rapidly if the root system is kept slightly pot-bound.

Having decided to repot, choose the new container and soil very carefully. The pots should not be very much larger than the previous ones. If the plant was in an 8-cm (3-in) pot, give it a pot 1 cm (½ in) bigger. If the original pot is over 12 cm (5 in) and up to 40 cm (16 in), increase the measurement by

2 cm (1 in); thus a pot with a 12-cm (5-in) diameter should be replaced by one with a 14-cm (6-in) diameter. The new pots, made of clay, should be rinsed or soaked in water for a few minutes prior to use, otherwise they may absorb part of the moisture from the soil. If you reuse pots that have previously contained plants, be sure to wash them thoroughly in warm water, using a brush, to get rid of all traces of soil and possible deposits of calcium; then clean them with a disinfectant soap or with a diluted solution containing water and chlorine bleach. Before putting soil and plants into the new pots, pour a 2 cm (1 in) layer of gravel or crocks into the bottoms for drainage.

In addition to the standard clay or plastic pots, there are also containers with self-watering systems which, if properly handled, can be very convenient. These provide water for the plants according to their needs. In theory they are simple to use, but incorrect handling frequently results in failures. To avoid disappointment, certain rules have to be observed: (1) Use such containers mainly for species that grow fast; (2) immediately after repotting and for a couple of months thereafter water from the bottom in order to allow the roots to grow down to the base of the pot, where they can best utilize the water that rises through capillary action; (3) later, water not only from the self-contained supply but also from above so that the soil remains uniformly moist; (4) keep a regular check on the water level at all times.

Whether you use such a container or one of the standard types of pot, success will ultimately depend on the correct choice of soil. Plants have different requirements so you cannot use the same soil for repotting all of them – and fortunately there is no need to since there is a considerable range of ready-to-use potting soils on the market. Some are meant for foliage plants; some for flowering plants; and some for plants with special needs such as orchids, azaleas, cacti, etc. These are generally preferable to ordinary garden soil because the essential ingredients (loam, humus and gritty material) are well balanced. In addition, they retain moisture while at the same time being sufficiently porous to encourage good drainage; they have the correct pH value for the plants for which they are specifically designed; and they are free of weed seeds, insects and other harmful organisms.

Despite these advantages of ready-mixed potting soils, however, many people like to prepare their own. If you are so inclined, you will have to collect the diverse ingredients and mix them in varying proportions according to the requirements of the plants.

The commonest ingredients are:
clayey-calcareous garden soil: never used on its own because it is too compact and heavy.

Leafmold: derived from the decomposed leaves of trees and shrubs. The leaves of deciduous plants are most often used, but conifer needles are also widely used, especially when a fairly coarse composition and high acid content are sought, as for azaleas.

Peat: there are two types, differing in structure and acidity; for pot plants the type with larger pieces, more fibrous and light in color, is preferable.

Sphagnum moss: can be used to stimulate the roots of orchids immediately after division, or mixed with other ingredients such as bark to maintain humidity and yet ensure sufficient porosity.

In addition to these organic ingredients there are other, inorganic components that help to make up the soil, such as sand, perlite, vermiculite, etc. These are used to lighten and improve the porosity of soils that are too compact or that may become too heavy after watering, such as garden soil or peat.

Hydroculture

One of the major headaches in keeping indoor plants is the worry of finding someone to water and perhaps feed them, when you go away on holiday. This problem vanishes if you decide to grow plants by the hydroponic method. In this way

34

Repotting. Remove the root ball from its container, with your hand over the soil; spread a layer of new soil in the bottom of the new pot, and place the root ball on top of this (2); fill in the sides with soil, pressing down well with your fingers (3); immerse the pot in a container full of water (4). Another repotting method is to place the original pot into the larger one and fill the sides with moisture (5); remove the old pot and place the root ball in the space thus created (6).

the roots develop in water containing the necessary fertilizing elements, appropriately dissolved; furthermore, you virtually do away with the need for repotting and choosing soil.

For hydroculture a water-holding container is needed (there are suitable appliances on the market consisting of two containers), and some inert material for anchoring the plants. In theory, almost any plant will flourish if grown by this method; but success can be guaranteed only if you use plants raised from cuttings made to root in water: in this way the plant is already provided with roots adapted to live only in water. It is also possible to use hydroculture for plants previously grown in soil. In such cases you must first eliminate all traces of soil from the roots by washing them, if need be, under gently running water. The plant is then ready to be put into the hydro-container. It will suffer a shock initially, but this can be lessened by keeping it at a constant temperature of about 20°C (68°F) and sufficiently moist. After a couple of weeks the root system can be washed again to get rid of old, dead roots and thus leave plenty of room for those "transformed" by their aquatic life. The method commonly used today for hydroponics calls for a double container consisting of two pots, one holding water with the fertilizing solution, and the other, smaller in size, which rests on the first and accommodates the plant, which is held firm by an inert material. The material most favored is clay granules, notable for their porosity which allows them to retain humidity that can be used by the plants if the need arises. There is one disadvantage, however, in that normal feeds, once absorbed by the clay granules, are difficult to wash away. This creates a risk of salts accumulating, which is harmful to the roots. To prevent this there are special fertilizers that furnish the plant with food only when it is required.

Bonsai

Bonsai, or the cultivation of certain trees or shrubs by dwarfing them by means of pruning, pinching the branches and so on, is of Chinese origin but the technique was developed in Japan from the 13th century onward, in which country it has acquired a cultural and spiritual significance alien to Western people.

A bonsai certainly helps one to understand nature and to rediscover and appreciate the change in the seasons, so often neglected in modern living.

Many species lend themselves to the bonsai technique, but it is important to bear in mind the proportions of the plant. Leaves, for example, should not be excessively large. Choose among laurels, pines, oak, gardenia, hibiscus etc. For a bonsai to be healthy, certain rules must be observed. The

Hydroculture: place a layer of charcoal at the bottom of the container, followed by a layer of sand, and set up the plants, holding them up by means of pebbles (1 and 2). Containers for hydroculture are made up of two receptacles: an inner one to house the plant, and an outer one containing the nutritive solution (3). Several plants can be grown in a wide container half-filled with fertilizer; if the level drops, distilled water should be added.

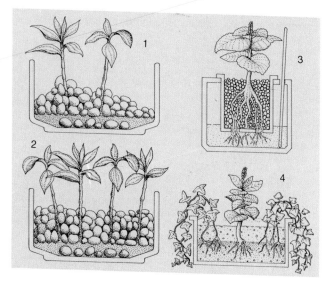

container should be of the appropriate size and should also, by tradition, be compatible with the style of cultivation (vertical, slanting, cascading, etc). The choice of soil is also very important; it should be porous, with a draining layer at the base of the container. In addition to watering and feeding, a bonsai will also require further more delicate care which is vital for its well-being.

Repotting should be carried out once a year for young plants and every two or three years for more adult plants. The main purpose of such regular repotting is to eliminate part of the roots that have developed which could block the small container, and suffocate each other. Always repot a bonsai during its rest period. In summer, pinch or remove any branches that are growing into an awkward shape.

Bottle Gardens

These are more or less direct descendants of the original Wardian cases, whereby plants gathered in equatorial forests could be conveyed to Victorian drawing rooms.

Many glass containers for plants are available nowadays, the most practical ones having wide necks. Tinted glass is not recommended in that it shuts out the light. Having chosen your container, the soil should be prepared carefully. Using a paper funnel, pour a layer of gravel (2–3 cm/1–2 in)

Juniperus rigida, an example of bonsai. The most suitable plants for bonsai are those already used to an indoor life.

Miniature gardens. Cover the base of the container, including the drainage holes, with pieces of terra cotta (e.g. broken up plant pots) and 2 cm (1 in) gravel (1); add a layer of soil, arrange the plants in this, mounding up the mixture all around them (2); add more soil, pressing down well; water and feed as each species requires (3). The final result is extremely effective (4).

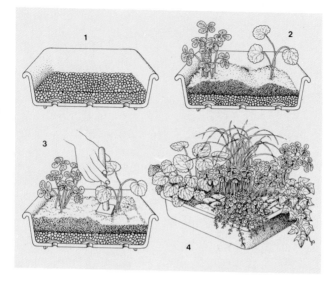

into a bottle, and then 7–10 cm (3–4 in) of soil. The quantity will of course depend on the size of the container.

Using little sticks or similar implements to help you, lower the plants into the bottle. Plants with slow-growing leaves are best for this kind of display. Ferns and bromeliads are a good choice.

Miniature Gardens

Small plants and young ornamental plants can be displayed in miniature gardens. Suitable choices are small flowering plants such as begonias, Campanula isophylla and *Saint-paulia ionantha*. The orange colored berries of *Neivera depressa*, for example, provide the composition with a long-lasting touch of color.

Particularly attractive effects may be obtained by displaying cacti and succulent plants with pebbles and sand to suggest rocks and desert. The containers can vary in shape and size and be as unusual as you like. The most important thing to remember is to have adequate drainage in the container, and to choose the soil with care.

Pruning

House plants, like garden plants, sometimes need judicious pruning of shoots and woody branches, although this opera-

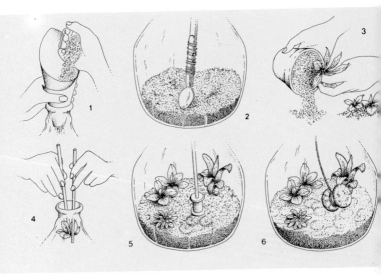

tion is not absolutely necessary, as it is for most roses, flowering shrubs and fruit trees. It is useful for indoor plants to check the growth of over-vigorous specimens, and for forming more compact, bushier plants if they have been damaged or seem stunted as a result of age. Making a cut above a node will stimulate the development of new shoots from the latent buds in the leaf axils.

The two principal types of pruning adopted for indoor plants is to stop the shoots and cut away the woody branches. Stopping means cutting or pinching the tip of the shoot above a node; and it is often advisable for newly rooted cuttings in order to encourage the development of new shoots – especially side shoots. It can also be done on adult plants, with the same intention, but in the case of fast-growing plants with delicate stems, such as *Tradescantia* and *Impatiens*, for example.

Pruning which involves removing branches that have already grown must be done in such a way that the cut quickly heals. It is therefore best to make the cut above a side branch at an oblique angle so that water will run off and disease is less likely to set in.

The ideal time for pruning is when growth resumes. But stopping can be carried out from the spring right through the summer, as the need arises. These are general rules. But

Calliandra twedyi, *an ornamental plant with showy red and white stamens. In South America these plants are used to provide coffee plantations with shade.*

there are certain ornamentals that must be pruned at particular times to give of their best. This is the case with some flowering shrubs like *Hydrangea, Fuchsia, Hibiscus,* etc., which require various types of pruning at specified times in order to produce their finest blooms. *Fuchsia* is pruned at the beginning of spring since the flowers form on the shoots that grow after the pruning operation. *Hydrangea,* however, benefits from the pruning of old (two- or three-year) branches, which should be removed every year to ventilate the foliage and stimulate the growth of the younger branches that will carry the flowers. In the case of *Hibiscus,* you should remove any branches that become entangled with new growth.

The flowers of *Passiflora* grow on new branches, so the plants should be shortened to 10–15 cm (4–6 in) before growth resumes. *Bougainvillea* also flowers on young branches, but on those produced during the previous growing season. So if pruning is necessary, it should be done after flowering, otherwise this will be ruined for the next season (pruning will eliminate many flower buds).

Given the different methods of flowering, it is essential to dertermine, before pruning, on which branches the flowers are carried. If there is any doubt, the plant should be left to grow freely.

Supports and props

Bushy and single-stemmed plants sometimes need support, especially plants such as *Dizygotheca* and *Impatiens*, whose stems may be so long and straggly that if unsupported they will droop, or even break, under the weight of vegetation.

Supports are often necessary during the flowering period alone, to bear the weight of large inflorescences produced on thin stems. For this purpose short stakes can be used and the stems tied with string, raffia or special bands. Ties must not be attached so tightly that they might prevent the stems from growing freely; a figure-of-eight knot is best.

Climbing plants need special supports to grow normally and develop aerial roots and tendrils, or simply entwine themselves, according to the characteristics of the species. Climbing forms of *Philodendron*, *Pothos* and *Hedera* have aerial roots that attach themselves only to rough, wet surfaces and these grow best if firmly supported by poles of moss or props of highly porous foam rubber. For these species it is also useful to tie the shoots.

It is essential to provide ties for plants such as some varieties of *Bougainvillea* which, although climbers, have no special organs for attachment but which in nature find support from the surrounding vegetation. For other plants furnished with tendrils, ties are beneficial but not essential, since the tendrils alone are sufficient to allow the plant to grow independently.

In addition to stakes, canes and moss-covered poles, there are trellises, hoops and the like, which can be bought but are also simple to make at home.

Propagation

Plants are able to reproduce in two basic ways: by sexual means (utilizing seeds) or by asexual means (agamic or vegetative), whereby portions of the plant are used, from which other parts develop.

By seeds. Seeds are used for propagating many ornamental plants, especially for flowering annuals, such as petunias, zinnias, calendulas, and alyssum. Perennials, too, can be propagated by seed but these are generally better reproduced by vegetative multiplication, which has the advantage of creating individuals that are the same as the mother plant and which is also faster. Furthermore, sowing may present some difficulties: the seeds of many species will germinate only under controlled conditions of temperature and humidity, obtainable only with the aid of a greenhouse or at least a hot-bed.

If you decide to propagate with seeds, apart from observing certain general principles that apply to the method as a whole, you may have to adopt special procedures for some

Propagation by seed. Fill a shallow container up to 2 cm (1 in) from the rim with suitable mixture, keeping the seeds well apart. Cover with soil and lay a sheet of glass over the container. Put in a warm place; when the seedlings sprout, move the container into the light and remove the glass.

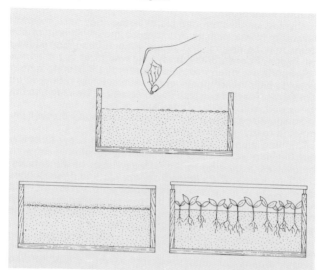

seeds that are difficult to germinate.

The sowing container must not be too deep and should be furnished with drainage holes: among the main causes of failure are molds and other fungal diseases that may develop as a result of excessive moisture. Seed trays are the commonest form of container, but there are others consisting of numerous alveoli or small pits, each of them accommodating one or two seeds. Other types of container, mainly used by growers, include plastic pots etc.

Having chosen your container, fill it with suitable soil (for many species sand and peat in equal quantities are fine) and press down gently with a flat piece of wood to get the surface level. Then sprinkle the seeds. Methods of sowing differ according to the size of the seeds. Small seeds are the hardest to distribute and there is a risk of sowing too densely. Very large seeds may require treating, otherwise they will not germinate at all or germinate too late. This treatment consists of immersing them in warm water for 24 hours or more (for seeds of over 5 mm in diameter) or of making a knife cut or abrasion in the skin (for seeds with hard coverings).

After sowing, cover the seeds with a layer of sand; the very tiniest, however, can be settled by spraying. The depth of sowing should be roughly twice the diameter of the seed.

To ensure results, keep watch on the seedbed, making certain that the soil never dries out but is never too wet. The ideal temperature for the germination of seeds of most house plants is around 18°C (64°–65°F). To keep these conditions more or less constant, cover the tray with glass or plastic.

When the seedlings show at least two proper leaves, transplant them into single pots, diameter 5–6 cm (2–2½ in), using light soil (half sand, half peat). During this period the seedlings should be kept in moist, shady surroundings until they get stronger. Then they can be moved gradually to brighter areas. The pots can be placed near a window so long as the seedlings do not receive any direct sunlight, which they are still too tender to withstand.

The seeds of some fruits can be sown indoors. Oranges, lemons, grapefruit, apples and pears are easy to propagate and quickly form healthy seedlings. The seeds of rarer species such as peanuts, coffee (not roasted) and palms are also easy to work with. Coffee, for example, can be planted in spring by putting the beans in sand at a temperature of 23°–26°C (73°–79°F). The seedlings that sprout are transplanted into normal soil and are then repotted some months later.

Asexual reproduction This is the method used for the majority of house plants. It is done in various ways, using portions of the plant. A common method is to take cuttings of stems, leaves, side shoots or the plantlets that some species produce on their stems and leaves. Other reproductive methods are by division, layering and air-layering.

Taking cuttings. This is a very simple method that entails removing a section of plant and rooting it in moist soil or, in some cases, in water. Herbaceous cuttings root most easily and at any time of year; woody cuttings root with more difficulty and have to be taken in spring or early summer. There are no fixed rules as to the length of a cutting; but it is important to make sure it has at least one node. If the cutting has leaves, remove those nearest the cut tip, which has to be stuck into the soil. Portions of very big leaves can be cut off or, as in the case of *Ficus elastica*, rolled up. Leaf removal helps to reduce loss of water by transpiration.

To encourage the development of the root system of species that do not produce roots easily, it is advisable to immerse the cutting in a hormone preparation (or rooting powder) to stimulate rooting. These preparations are easily available in plant shops or garden centers. Once the roots form, the new seedlings should be transplanted into individual pots containing the soil in which they will grow.

A cutting can be from the tip of a stem or from a stem section provided with one or two nodes. Strong, woody stems like those of the *Cordyline* and *Dracaena* species can be broken into a number of segments and partially buried horizontally in peat or sphagnum: new shoots will grow from the nodes. Certain plants such as *Saintpaulia*, foliage begonias and fleshy plants are normally propagated by leaf cuttings.

Multiplication by **lateral shoots** is possible for species, such as bromeliads, that produce new shoots from the main or secondary stems or even from the base of the mother plant. Once they are of a reasonable size, these shoots can be detached.

Propagation by **division** is used for plants that grow in clumps. Remove the plant from the pot and look for one or more points where separation comes easily. Plants with rhizomes can also be divided in this manner. Use a sharp knife to make the break easier.

Layering and air-layering (see Glossary) are methods used for propagating plants whose cuttings will not take easily. Layering involves attaching the stem or a branch to the potting soil without detaching it from the mother plant: roots will eventually appear at the point of contact with the soil. This method can be used indoors to accelerate the rooting of climbing or hanging plants. **Air-layering** is used for plants with stiff, upright stems that do not bend easily and that are therefore unsuitable for layering. It is a very satisfying method, useful for saving or rejuvenating plants that have

in a shaded position until the cuttings have taken root (4). Turn the pot upside down and separate the rooted cuttings (5); repot these separately in pots of 8–10 cm (3–4 in) in diameter (6); water (7) and then put in the shade for several weeks.

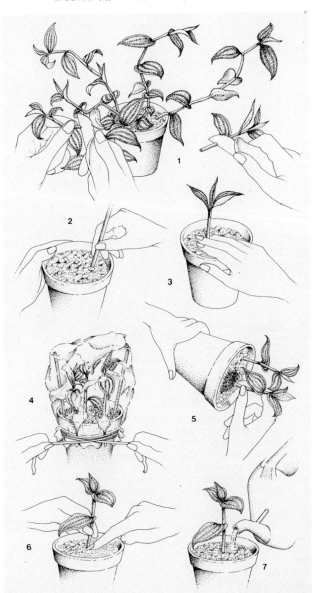

Air-layering. This method is suitable for plants which have grown on long, leaf-bare stems, such as the philodendron, and is carried out in spring and summer. Tie the top leaves together and make an incision in the stem (2); apply hormone rooting powder to the incision, where the roots will grow, and insert some damp moss into it to keep it open (3). Alternatively cut off some of the bark around the stem (4); prepare a ball of

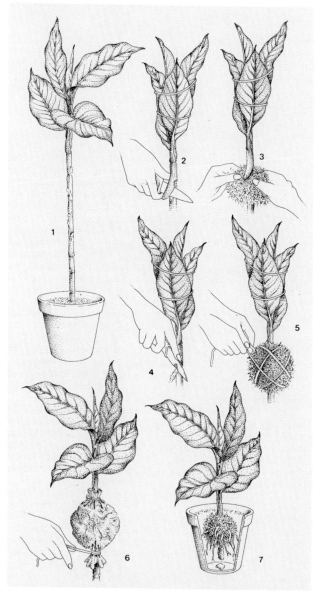

*moist sphagnum moss and potting mixture and tie it on to the stem (5). Cover the
moss with plastic securing it top and bottom with string and undo the leaves (6).
Return the plant to its usual position. After 6–8 weeks the roots will grow through the
moss (7).*

lost their basal leaves, as often happens with *Ficus, Dracaena, Dieffenbachia*, etc.

Pests and diseases

Ailments that may occur among house plants are not always the result of errors of cultivation in non optimum conditions; there are numerous outbreaks of disease caused by fungi, bacteria, viruses and insects. Whereas problems associated with cultivation can be easily resolved once the cause is identified, defense against actual disease is often more complicated.

Parasites are the most virulent enemies of plants grown in the open or under glass; house plants are also prone to the attacks of fungi, insects, etc. They must be carefully protected, particularly those that have just been bought: most parasites are introduced only in this way. In such cases the plant must first be isolated well away from others until you are sure the disease has been wiped out. Quick intervention will simplify matters. This is one of the fundamental reasons why, whenever you water or feed plants, it is wise to inspect them, especially the hidden parts such as the under surface of the leaves, where harmful insects such as red spiders, scale insects, aphids, etc., commonly nest. By frequent and careful cleaning you will avoid much harm to the plants as well as the necessity of bothersome treatment.

Cleaning plants is important because it improves their appearance and also prevents obstruction of the stomata through which occur the gaseous exchanges that are indispensable to healthy plant growth. The leaves can be effectively cleaned by frequent dusting (every week) with a damp cloth and, when necessary, washing (if the leaves are very dirty) with a wet sponge. It is not advisable to use milk, beer, oil and similar substances, which are likely to be more harmful than effective.

Apart from attending to the leaves, be sure to keep the surfaces of pots and the soil clean. Green algal deposits often appear on clay pots and this is a clear sign of excess moisture. Another unmistakable sign is the presence of white crusts on pot and soil due to excessively hard water (it can also point to over-fertilizing, although as a rule this does not occur in house plants).

The truly worrying diseases are those caused by fungi, bacteria and viruses that invade the plant cells. Often they spread as a result of faulty care. Gray mold, caused by *Botrytis cinerea*, a microscopic fungus, usually develops when the environment is too wet; and rotting of the stem, which leads to decay of the affected tissues, is also the result of incorrect cultivation.

Other frequent diseases of indoor plants include leaf

47

Aphids with sucking mouth part (1) and with chewing mouth part (2); others with licking-sucking mouth parts (3). Scale insects attack flowering and fruit-bearing plants, leaving a white secretion (4). Mites, which ruin flower petals (5). Anthracnose, disease caused by a fungus (6). Mealy bug, an insect with a white secretion, attacks flowering and fruit-bearing plants (7). Cockchafer, a root-attacking beetle (8). Root rot, a disease

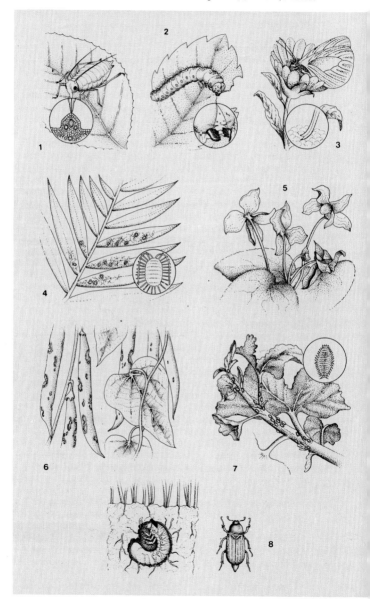

that attacks plant roots (9). The effects of mealy bug attack on foliage (10). Mildew, a white powdery mold (11). Scale insect, which attacks ornamental plants (12). Whitefly, a prolific insect that preys on most plants (13). Red spider mite, which attacks many plants (14). Plant lice attacking a rose (15).

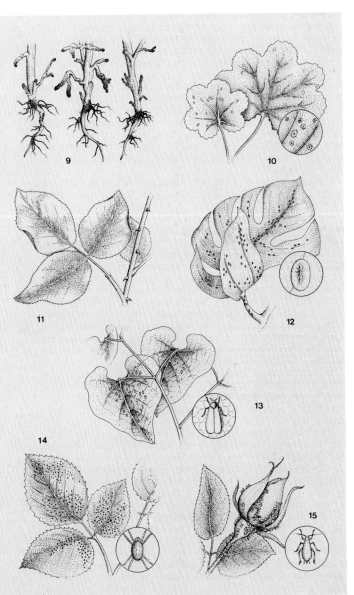

yellowing or shriveling, caused by fungi and bacteria, and sooty mold, a blackish deposit that covers stems and leaves. The latter, however, can easily be dealt with by washing, and since it is caused by insects that suck the sap (aphids, scale insects, etc), the plant should be treated against such insects.

Viruses are by far the most serious causes of disease. Whereas with fungal attacks you can often act quickly by removing the affected leaves and flowers, in the case of viruses the whole plant must be thrown out. The most common symptoms of viral disease are discolored streaks and spots on the leaves, curling and wrinkling of the leaf blade, arrested plant growth, etc. Viruses are transmitted by insects that suck the sap, thus passing the infection from one plant to another.

Animal parasites often attack house plants, but since these are easily detectable it is sensible to keep them under control and treat the plants as soon as the parasites appear to prevent them from multiplying rapidly. The symptoms here are different, depending on the various types of insect mouth parts. Insects with sucking mouth parts cause the leaves to turn yellow or otherwise become deformed; chewing insects make holes in the leaves, eat the edges and gnaw the stems and growing tips. The roots, too, can be damaged by nematodes and other worms, and also by the larvae of insects which, when adult, do no harm to the plants. One example is the larva of the owlet moth, which spends its life underground, doing serious damage to seeds, bulbs and tubers with its chewing mouth parts. The adult, however, does no damage because it has a licking and sucking apparatus for feeding on flower nectar.

The fight against insects must therefore be based on the form of the particular mouth parts. For aphids, which suck the sap, you will need to use an insecticide that circulates through the system (these preparations are called systemics). Others work by contact and work only on the parasites concerned when applied directly to the plant. Trade preparations give all the necessary information about how to use the product correctly. Do not forget to follow to the letter the instructions for proper dosage; many insecticides, apart from damaging plants, may also be harmful to those applying them.

Chemical products, the so-called fungicides and bactericides, can be used for diseases caused by fungi and bacteria respectively. These, too, work either by the systemic method or by simple contact.

When insecticides, fungicides and bactericides are used in the home, it is advisable for effective results, to place the plant under a sheet of sealed plastic in order to create a closed environment. The product can then be sprayed through a hole. There are many preparations on the market in the form of sprays, dusts and granules. If a spray is used be careful to follow the instructions regarding the minimum distance from which it is to be applied. Failure to do so risks seriously damaging the leaves.

However, if you remember that plants are very responsive to the treatment they receive, and if you give them proper care your indoor garden will flourish, and enhance your home.

1 ABUTILON MEGAPOTAMICUM 'Variegatum'

Family Malvaceae.
Origin Brazil.
Description An evergreen shrub of drooping habit with slender stems bearing ovate, pointed, toothed and sometimes lobed leaves 6–10 cm (2–4 in) long. The leaf blade has yellow blotches. The pendulous flowers are bell-shaped and grow singly or in pairs from the leaf axils. Each flower has a red calyx which partially enfolds the yellow corolla, from which dark anthers project; length of flower is 4–5 cm (2 in). The flowering season is from May to October.
Care The species can be grown outside in warm regions. Indoors it needs plenty of bright light, even direct sun for several hours daily, and can be kept at medium temperatures of 18–22°C (64–71°F). Water regularly while growing, letting the surface of the soil dry out before repotting. Reduce amount of water during rest period. Feed with standard liquid fertilizer fortnightly from April to October. Soil made of organic matter, peat and sand in equal proportions. Replace the plants every 2–3 years with new specimens, preferably obtained from cuttings. Prune vigorously in March–April, reducing length of branches by one third.
Propagation The species itself can be propagated from seed or from cuttings; the cultivar 'Variegatum' only from cuttings. Take 10 cm (4 in) tip cuttings from April to June, planting them in mixture of equal parts peat and sand. Wrap in plastic bag and put in cold greenhouse.
Pests and diseases Frequently attacked by scale insects.

---

2 ACACIA RETINODES
Wirilda

Family Leguminosae.
Origin Australia.
Description Also known as *A. floribunda*. Shrub or small tree, up to 9 m (30 ft) tall; in natural environment has light green or bluish evergreen leaves, 8–10 cm (3–4 in) long. May grow to height of 120 cm (4 ft) in pot. Small, round, scented yellow flowers, in loose clusters. Flowering continues from spring to October. The fruits are flat pods.
Care Grows well in all soils, even lime soil. Soil must be well drained. Can be used as stock for compound-leaved acacias which are calcifuges. Cultivated outdoors in temperate climates; grown indoors in colder areas. The plant needs plenty of light. Water abundantly in spring–summer, moderately in winter. Feed with liquid fertilizer every two weeks from May to August. The best growing medium is a mixture of 2 parts organic soil, 1 part peat, 1 part coarse sand. Repot annually, in March, using gradually larger pots up to 30 cm (12 in) in diameter. Pruning unnecessary, but to keep the plant small, cut back branches after flowering.
Propagation From seed. Sow in April at 16°C (61°F). As soon as seedlings are a few centimeters in height prick out in 8 cm (3 in) pots; repot in 5–10 cm (2–4 in) pots. Can also be propagated from cuttings, taking 5–10 cm (2–4 in) twigs from part of an old branch. Plant in mixtures of peat and sand, in equal parts, in hot-bed at temperature of 16–18°C (61–64°F). Rooting takes several months.
Pests and diseases A fairly resistant plant, not subject to any particular diseases.

3 ACALYPHA HISPIDA
Red-hot cat's tail, chenille plant

Family Euphorbiaceae.

Origin India, Java.

Description Shrub growing to height of 75 cm (30 in), with large, ovate, bright green leaves, hairy underneath, up to 25 cm (10 in) long. The inflorescences are long, drooping spikes, 20–50 cm (8–20 in), bright red, growing from July to October in the leaf axils.

Varieties A. hispida 'Alba' has pinky-white flowers.

Care The plant needs bright light, otherwise it will fail to flower and will grow too tall, but it dislikes direct sun. It does well at high temperatures, never below 16°C (61°F). It cannot stand dry air; place the pot in holder filled with damp gravel and spray the foliage daily in spring–summer until flower buds appear. Water plentifully. Reduce amount of water during winter dormancy. Cultivate in mixture of 1 part organic soil, 1 part peat and 1 part coarse sand. Give liquid fertilizer fortnightly during growth. Very decorative in first year; prune and repot or replace annually in early spring if too big.

Propagation In March–April prune the branches, taking 8–10 cm (3–4 in) tip cuttings, or detach young lateral shoots with a piece of bark and woody stem, planting them in small pots containing moist soil. Wrap in plastic bags and place in indirect sunlight at a minimum temperature of 21°C (70°F). When cuttings resume growth, roots have developed.

Pests and diseases Scale insects and red spider attack.

4 ADIANTUM CAPILLUS-VENERIS
Southern maidenhair fern, Venus's-hair

Family Polypodiaceae.

Origin Subtropical and temperate zones.

Description Rhizomatous fern of modest size, maximum 30 cm (12 in) tall. Delicate, pale green triangular leaves, with fan-like pinnules on black leaf stalks. Species suitable for growing under glass or indoors.

Varieties Adiantum capillus-veneris 'Mairisii.' There are no other varieties of this species. There are, however, varieties of related species (A. raddianum, A. hispidulum, A. tenerum) which are also commonly known as maidenhair fern.

Care Grows well in warm, humid sheltered spots, even in the open provided the temperature does not fall below 12°C (53°F). Needs bright but filtered light and a very humid atmosphere. Not always easy to grow indoors because of the difficulty of maintaining the right measure of humidity. The roots should always be slightly moist, and must not be allowed to dry out nor be drenched. Water frequently but in moderate amounts, letting the surface of the compost dry between successive waterings. Spray the foliage daily, especially in warm, dry surroundings. Grow in a mixture of 1 part organic soil and 1 part coarse peat. Feed monthly or more often during the growing period with liquid fertilizer.

Propagation In spring divide the clumps, leaving a piece of rhizome attached to each, and pot. Place in the shade and water carefully.

Pests and diseases Subject to animal parasites: root scale insects, leaf miners which cause black spots on the leaves, and soil lice which feed on the roots.

5 AECHMEA FASCIATA
Urn plant

Family Bromeliaceae.
Origin Brazil.
Description Height 50 cm (20 in). The leaves, 35–40 cm (14–16 in) long, form a funnel-shaped rosette which retains water; they are curved, spiny gray-green with silvery transverse strips. The plant flowers in the adult state (3–4 years), in late summer, once per rosette. The flowers, initially blue and then red, in a compact inflorescence, 15 cm (6 in) tall, fade rapidly, with spiny pink bracts which remain decorative for many months. The rosette dies 1–2 years after flowering.
Varieties A. fasciata, 'Variegata' has leaves longitudinally streaked creamy-white; 'Albo-marginata' has leaves with ivory-white edges.
Care Prefers direct exposure to sunlight. The correct temperature is above 18°C (65°F); for short periods the plant can even withstand lower temperatures. Organic acid soil, without calcium, made up of partially rotted leaves or conifer needles, peat and sand in equal quantities. The plant needs much moisture; do not let soil dry out. The rosette should be kept full of water. If possible use rain water, but not lime water. Apply liquid fertilizer to soil and spray leaves every fortnight in spring. In autumn and winter the rosette and the earth should be kept slightly damp.
Propagation In spring cut the base of side shoots when they are roughly half the size of the parent plant and place them in a pot of sand for rooting.
Pests and diseases Not subject to any particular diseases.

6 AESCHYNANTHUS LOBBIANUS
Lipstick plant

Family Gesneriaceae.
Origin Indonesia.
Description The plant is prostrate in habit and has long, drooping stems which bear elliptic, slightly toothed leaves, dark green with purple margins. The tubular flowers, about 5 cm (2 in) long, have an almost black, bristly calyx, and a red corolla of which the throat and part of the lobes are creamy-white. The flowers appear in pairs during the summer.
Care Very suitable for growing in hanging baskets, the plant enjoys bright light but will not tolerate direct sun. It needs a high level of atmospheric humidity. Does well at normal room temperature throughout the year, and does not require a winter rest period. Water plentifully while in flower and spray the plant with tepid water; at other times water sparingly. Growing medium should be acidic and porous, consisting of 3 parts peat and 1 part moss or, alternatively, of peat, vermiculite and perlite in equal proportions. Give liquid fertilizer monthly in spring-summer. Repot every 2–3 years.
Propagation Cuttings can be taken at any time of year. Cut the stems into 10 cm (4 in) sections and plant them in growing medium. Wrap the pots in plastic bags and expose them to filtered light at room temperature. After rooting, in 4–7 weeks, remove the bag and keep the mixture and the air moist.
Pests and diseases Very prone to attack by aphids.

7 AESCHYNANTHUS SPECIOSUS
Basket plant

Family Gesneriaceae.
Origin Indonesia.
Description Climbing plant. Height 20–35 cm (8–14 in), diameter 30–40 cm (12–16 in). Green, ovate, pointed leaves about 10 cm (4 in) in length, paired or in groups of three. A tuft of bright yellow-orange tubular flowers, surrounded by 4–8 leaves, appears at the tip of the stem from July to September. The flowers are 7–8 cm (about 3 in) long and slightly downy. Each flower lasts only a few days.
Varieties There is a hybrid *Aeschynanthus × splendidus,* which is derived from an interspecific cross.
Care Bright light but not direct sun, and high surrounding humidity. Minimum winter temperature 9°C (48°F). If kept indoors, the plants should have no winter rest period and should be watered continuously, abundantly in summer while flowering, moderately at other times. During the flowering period spray the plants with water at room temperature. Grow in acid, porous soil made up of 3 parts porous peat and 1 part moss, or peat, vermiculite and perlite in equal parts. Avoid water collecting. Liquid food monthly in spring and summer. Repot every 2–3 years, preferably using 12–15 cm (5–6 in) bowls or hanging baskets.
Propagation By cuttings, at any time of year. Cut 10 cm (4 in) lengths of stem and plant in pot in the previously described mixture. Cover with a plastic bag and expose to filtered light at 21°C (70°F). Rooting takes 1–2 months.
Pests and diseases Very prone to aphid attack.

8 AGAVE AMERICANA
Century plant

Family Agavaceae.
Origin Mexico.
Description Height up to and above 2·5 m (8 ft). Stemless succulent with hard, thick gray-green leaves, spiny along edges and at tip. The leaves, up to 2 m (6½ ft) in length, are ascendant, sometimes with downward-turned tip, and arranged in an open rosette. The plant flowers only after 10 years, in summer; then the plant dies. The yellow-green flowers form clusters on scapes, themselves 5–6 m (16–20 ft) long. Note, however, that measurements given here apply to old specimens, grown in the open.
Varieties *A. americana* 'Marginata,' with yellow-edged leaves; 'Medio-picta,' central yellow stripe down length of leaf; *A. americana* 'Striata,' with longitudinal stripes.
Care Easy to cultivate. Very frugal and resistant to drought. In mild climates it grows in the open; in colder latitudes, in a greenhouse or indoors. During the resting period it must be kept at a temperature of 10–12°C (50–54°F). Likes direct sunlight but can also live in shade. Water little in the growing period, letting the soil dry out to about two thirds between successive waterings; water even less during dormancy. Feed with a liquid preparation once a month, leaving off in rest period. Grow in a very porous mixture made up of 2 parts organic soil, 2 parts coarse sand and 1 part peat. Repot every year in spring.
Propagation The species produces basal shoots which, cut off in spring, root easily in pots.
Pests and diseases Highly resistant to parasites.

9 AGAVE VICTORIAE-REGINAE
Queen Agave

Family Agavaceae.
Origin Mexico.
Description Very decorative species with rosette of oblong–triangular green leaves, edged with bright white lines. The leaves have smooth edges and terminate in a sharp spine. The plant grows to a height of 15–20 cm (6–8 in) and is 20–40 cm (8–16 in) in diameter. Growth is slow and only 2–3 new leaves form every year. The outer leaves tend gradually to dry up and should be cut off at the base. The plant produces a spiky inflorescence. There are varieties with longer or shorter leaves and with white lines that are fainter or completely lacking.
Care Cultivation requirements are similar to those of *A. americana*. It can also live in the open if winter temperatures do not drop below 10°C (50°F). Likes direct sunlight but also tolerates shade. Water sparingly during the growing period, once a month, and also feed with a liquid preparation. Water very little during the resting period, allowing the soil almost to dry out between waterings, and do not feed. Grow in mixture of 2 parts humusy soil, 2 parts coarse sand and 1 part peat. Because the plant grows slowly, it can be repotted every 2–3 years. Easy to grow.
Propagation Unlike *A. americana*, does not normally produce shoots, so that propagation must be by seed. Rare varieties produce lateral branches or stolons.
Pests and diseases Highly resistant to parasites.

---

10 AGLAONEMA MODESTUM
Chinese evergreen

Family Araceae.
Origin China.
Description The genus comprises diverse plant species grown for their very decorative foliage, which is almost always variegated more or less with white or gray. In *A. modestum* the very long ovate leaves on a long stalk are wavy and covered with a waxy sheen. The inflorescence is similar to that of the Arum lily, with a central spadix, about 5 cm (2 in) long, enclosed by a spathe. Flowering occurs in summer and the flowers are followed by red berries.
Varieties There is one variety with green leaves and another with variegated leaves, *A. modestum* 'Variegatum.'
Care Easy to grow. It does well in warm, moist and shady surroundings. Does not like direct sunlight so can be a useful plant in dimly lit rooms. The ideal temperature is around 25°C (77°F) by day and should not drop below 16–20°C (61–68°F) at night. Requires a lot of moisture so watering should be regular, both on soil and foliage, at room temperature. Place the plant in a bowl filled with constantly wet gravel. During the very short winter rest period, give the soil a little water but stop feeding with the liquid fertilizer that should be applied once a month at other times. The potting medium should be a mixture of 1 part organic soil, 1 part peat and 1 part sand. Young growing plants should be repotted every spring, adult plants only every 2–3 years. Average diameter of pot 10–12 cm (4–5 in).
Propagation Use the method described for *A. crispum*.
Pests and diseases Aphids; red spider if air too dry.

11 AGLAONEMA CRISPUM
Painted drop Tongue

Family Araceae.
Origin Philippines.
Description The leathery leaves, up to 30 cm (12 in) long, are borne on long stalks developing from the central stem. As the leaves fall progressively, circular scars appear on the stem. In the typical species the leaves are gray-green with darker green central veining and margins. The inflorescence consists of a spadix enfolded by a bract.
Varieties A. crispum 'Silver Queen' has gray-green leaves strongly marked with silver.
Care Requirements for cultivation are the same as those described for A. modestum.
Propagation Can be done from seed in spring at temperature of 27°C (80°F), but asexual methods are preferable indoors, and essential for the variety. The plant produces basal shoots which are cut from the parent in April–May; these should bear 3–4 leaves and, if possible, some roots. Plant them in a pot with damp mixture of peat and sand in equal parts. Wrap the pot in a plastic bag and set to root in an average bright place or in the greenhouse at a temperature of 18–21°C (64–70°F). After about 2 months the rooted plant can be treated as an adult. It can be propagated by cutting the stems of old, soon to be discarded plants into segments, which thus constitute cuttings, or by layering.
Pests and diseases Red spider if surroundings too dry; scale insects.

12 ALLAMANDA CATHARTICA
Golden trumpet

Family Apocynaceae.
Origin Tropical America.
Description Climbing evergreen plant, highly decorative, which can grow to a considerable size, 3.5 m (11½ ft) tall and 2–2.5 m (6½–8 ft) long. The narrow, oval, glossy green leaves are 10–12 cm (4–5 in) in length. They are in opposite pairs or in whorls of 3–4. Funnel-shaped, golden-yellow flowers with 5 petals. Flowering from July to September.
Varieties Cultivated varieties are 'Grandiflora,' large yellow flowers; 'Hendersonii,' orange flowers; 'Schotti,' which has yellow flowers with brown streaks on neck; 'Williamsii,' yellow flowers with pinkish neck and sometimes bushy habit.
Care Needs plenty of light but not direct sun; temperature of at least 18–20°C (64–68°F), in winter not less than 13°C (55°F), and high humidity. During the growing season it should be thoroughly watered and fed every three weeks with a liquid fertilizer. Water sparingly and suspend feeding during rest period from October to March. Grow in mixture consisting of 3 parts organic soil, 2 parts peat and 1 part fine sand, repotting every year until it is in a container of maximum 40–50 cm (16–20 in) diameter, sufficient for accommodating the sturdy root system.
Propagation Cuttings in April–May from nonflowering branches, about 8 cm (3 in) long. Place in pots with equal parts sand and peat. Enclose pots in plastic bags (or keep in greenhouse) and expose to filtered light at 21–23°C (70–74°F).
Pests and diseases Aphids, red spider.

13 ALOE ARBORESCENS
Candelabra aloe

Family Liliaceae.
Origin South Africa.
Description Succulent with bare, woody, unbranched stem which bears a tuft of leaves at the tip. In its native environment it may grow 4–15 m (13–16½ ft) or more, but as a house plant it seldom exceeds 1 m (3 ft). The fleshy green leaves are up to 50 cm (20 in) long, narrow with toothed edges. The tips tend to bend downwards. When the plant is 2–3 years old, shoots begin to appear at the base. The clusters of red flowers are borne on a long, simple or branched stem. Flowering period is May–June.
Care Like all species of the genus *Aloe*, this is easy to look after. In mild climates it can be planted in the open provided the minimum winter temperature is not below 15°C (59°F). In cold areas the plants can live indoors during the winter and be put outside in the summer, exposed to the sun. For good flowering results it is advisable to rest the plant in winter at a temperature not exceeding 10°C (50°F). Water plentifully in the growing season, but while the plant is dormant it is enough not to allow the potting medium to dry out. Feed every fortnight in spring-summer with a liquid fertilizer. Grow in a medium consisting of 3 parts organic soil, 1 part peat and 1 part sand, repotting every April. When the container has reached a diameter of about 30 cm (12 in), do not repot any more but replace part of the potting medium each spring.
Propagation Remove the lateral shoots with some roots and pot in medium which must be kept damp.
Pests and diseases Same as for *Aloe variegata*.

Family Araceae.
Origin Malaya.
Description Cultivated as a house plant for its decorative foliage. The leaves, up to 35 cm (14 in) long, are heart-shaped at the base so that the 2 lobes almost touch, and are borne on long stalks. Leaf color is bronze with metallic reflections on the upper surface, purple below. The veins are darker in color. Plants grow from an underground rhizome.
Varieties The genus *Alocasia* comprises several highly decorative species and hybrids. One such hybrid is *Alocasia × Amazonica* (illustrated opposite below). This has leathery leaves, 60 cm (24 in) long and 30 cm (12 in) wide, with distinctive white veining.
Care Being a plant of tropical origin, it must have warm, moist surroundings. It grows well in dim light but does not respond to bright light, especially direct sun. Minimum temperature in winter and at night is 18°C (64°F). Water regularly, but sparingly with tepid water during growth, and do not let pools form in the pot-holder. Spray the foliage daily. Give low-concentrate liquid fertilizer every fortnight in growing season, decreasing amount of water. Potting medium should consist of 1 part garden soil, 1 part peat and 1 part coarse sand. Easy to grow.
Propagation By division of the rhizome. In spring cut the rhizome into sections, taking care to leave some roots and leaves on each portion. Pot in mixture of peat and sand, and after a while repot into standard growing medium.
Pests and diseases Red spider and scale insects.

15 ALOE VARIEGATA
Partridge-breasted aloe, tiger aloe

Family Liliaceae.
Origin South Africa.
Description A succulent plant, growing to a height of about 30 cm (12 in), with thick, fleshy leaves which are lanceolate, with toothed margins and a sharply pointed tip. They form a basal rosette and grow from a very short stem in 3 overlapping rows; the color is green with irregular white stripes. The tubular red flowers are in racemes 30 cm (12 in) long, blooming March–April. In addition, when the leaves are cut, they reveal an almost transparent gelatinous substance, not white, hard and fibrous, as in the agave.
Varieties *A. variegata ausana* (origin S.W. Africa) with a rosette of thick bluish-green, deeply toothed leaves, and white stripes.
Care Easy to cultivate, its requirements are similar to those of *A. arborescens.* It needs plenty of light but, unlike the latter, it does not like direct sun. Water plentifully in summer, particularly if the plant is outdoors, but sparingly in winter and in such a way that water does not get into the rosette. To prevent the basal leaves from rotting by becoming buried in the potting mixture, it is best to cover the surface with coarse sand or perlite.
Propagation In spring-summer detach lateral shoots with a few roots. Pot in damp mixture used for adult plants and keep moist, though not too wet, to prevent them rotting.
Pests and diseases Mealy bug may attack rosette leaves or surface roots.

16 ANANAS COMOSUS 'Variegatus'
Pineapple

Family Bromeliaceae.
Origin Brazil and Colombia.
Description This plant has leaves measuring up to 90 cm (3 ft), which are curved, spiny and arranged in a rosette 60 cm (2 ft) or more in diameter; they are green with long, creamy-white marginal stripes. The flowers, blue with pink bracts, are on an inflorescence 7–8 cm (about 3 in) long which grows in the center of the rosette. The fruit may also form but in temperate latitudes it seldom grows to maturity.
Varieties Another small variety is *A. comosus nanus* which grows to a height of 30 cm (12 in).
Care Needs strong light and direct sun. The optimum temperature is 18–24°C (64–75°F) in spring and not less than 16°C (61°F) in autumn and winter. Water once or twice a week in summer, once in winter, and allow to dry out between waterings. The environment should be kept humid and the leaves sprayed twice a week. Feed with liquid fertilizer every fortnight. This plant has virtually no resting period. Repot in spring until container's diameter is 20 cm (8 in).
Propagation Any time, but preferably in April, from basal shoots. Cut them at the base when they are 10–15 cm (4–6 in) long and plant them in a 10 cm (4 in) pot with soil made up of equal parts of peat and coarse sand. Keep in shade at 23°C (74°F), keeping the pot just damp. Repot every 6 months. The plant can also be propagated by cutting the tuft of apical leaves and getting it to root.
Pests and diseases Not subject to particular ailments.

17 ANTHURIUM ANDREANUM
Painter's palette

Family Araceae.
Origin Colombia.

Description Evergreen plant about 50 cm (20 in) tall, with decorative leaves and flower spathes. It has a reduced root system. Cultivated hybrids have large dark green leaves, sagittate, heart-shaped and leathery, up to 40 cm (16 in) in length, on long stalks. The inflorescence is a cylindrical, creamy-yellow spadix, 7–8 cm (2¾–3¼ in) long, set off-center of a flattened spathe, waxy and shiny in appearance, colored red, pink or white. The plant flowers indoors from May to September or, under glass, almost all year.

Varieties *A. andreanum album* with rounded, cordate, white spathes; *A. andreanum* 'Guatemala' with glossy, reddish-purple and yellow spathes; *A. andreanum rubrum* with crimson spathes.
Care Bright but filtered light and constant temperatures of 18–21°C (64–70°F). Tolerates a minimum winter temperature of 12°C (54°F). As it needs a moist environment, the pot should be placed in a bowl of wet gravel and the plant sprayed daily. Plentiful watering and liquid feeding in spring and summer. Refrain from feeding during dormant period. Grow in 3 parts coarse peat, 1 part chopped sphagnum and a little organic soil. Repot adult plants every 2–3 years, young plants every year. Some hybrids of *A. andreanum* are suitable for growing by hydroculture.

Propagation Same as described for *A. crystallinum*.
Pests and diseases Aphids, red spider.

18 ANTHURIUM CRYSTALLINUM
Strap flower

Family Acaceae.
Origin Colombia, Peru.

Description Unlike *A. andreanum* and *A. scherzerianum*, which are cultivated for their spathe, *A. crystallinum* is grown for its ornamental foliage, the inflorescence being quite insignificant. The heart-shaped leaves, 40–50 cm (16–20 in) long and up to 30 cm (12 in) wide, are extremely decorative. In young plants the foliage color is a metallic violet; later it turns dark green with white streaks along the veining of the upper surface; on the lower side the color varies, however, from pink to purple. Flowering period from May to September. The inflorescence, in the form of a spadix, is surrounded by a pale green bract. The plant is about 50 cm (20 in) in height.

Varieties *A. crystallinum illustre* with large, velvety leaves brightly veined with white and yellow.
Care Difficult to grow indoors. Growing temperature 18–21°C (64–70°F); winter minimum 13°C (56°F). Requires bright but diffused light. Potting medium and general care are the same as those described for *A. scherzerianum*.

Propagation By division of clumps in April. Remove clumps from pots, clean off the soil and separate them, taking care to leave each section with a little root or at least a shoot. Plant each portion in a pot full of peat and keep at a constant temperature of 22°C (72°F) in moderate light. keep the peat moist, avoiding water accumulation. It can also be propagated by stem, leaf and root cuttings in June.
Pests and diseases Subject to aphid attack.

19 ANTHURIUM SCHERZERIANUM
Flamingo plant, Pigtail plant

Family Araceae.
Origin Central America.
Description The species has leathery, lanceolate dark green leaves on long stalks, 30–40 cm (12–16 in) long. Numerous hybrids are grown more often than the pure species. The plant is about 50 cm (20 in) in height. The inflorescence has a shiny spathe, red, pink, yellow or white, according to the variety. The spadix is curved or hooked, red or orange-yellow, and set off-center of the spathe. Flowering period May to September.
Varieties A. scherzerianum 'Rothschildianum' has a light or dark red spathe, speckled white; A. scherzerianum nebulosum has a double spathe, white with red specks.
Care A. scherzerianum is the species best suited as a house plant. Water generously during the growing period. In winter, when the plant is resting, allow the surface of the soil to dry out between successive waterings. Sprinkle the foliage daily and keep the pot in a bowl of damp gravel. The normal temperature for growth is 18–21°C (64–70°F). The minimum temperature can be 10°C (50°F) for short periods. Feed with liquid fertilizer fortnightly from May to August. Grow in very porous medium composed of 3 parts coarse peat and 1 part sphagnum mixed with a little loam. The pot should be one-third full of drainage material like gravel. Young plants should be repotted every April, adult plants every 2–3 years.
Propagation Methods as for A. crystallinum.
Pests and diseases Very subject to aphids.

---

20 APHELANDRA SQUARROSA
Zebra plant

Family Acanthaceae.
Origin Brazil.
Description Species grown for its large ovate leaves, up to 25 cm (10 in) long and 10 cm (4 in) wide, shiny dark green with ivory-white veining. The plant flowers in summer, producing spikes of yellow blooms 8–10 cm (3–4 in) long. The plant can grow to a height of 30–40 cm (12–16 in).
Varieties A. squarrosa 'Louisae,' Saffron Spike, with narrower white-veined leaves; 'Dania,' with silvery veins.
Care Needs bright indirect lighting. Lives at room temperature indoors but after flowering requires a resting period at a lower temperature, not below 13°C (55°F). During the growing period water plentifully, always keeping the soil wet; during winter dormancy water very little, allowing the soil to dry between waterings. Spray the leaves and keep the plant in a bowl full of wet gravel. Feed every week during the growth season with liquid fertilizer, fortnightly for the rest of the year. Grow in medium composed of 1 part organic soil, 1 part peat and 1 part coarse sand. Repot every spring; before doing so prune the plant drastically, retaining only a few leaves. Cutting off the spike after flowering helps the production of side shoots.
Propagation In spring, from lateral shoot cuttings planted in a pot with equal parts of peat and sand, covered with a plastic bag and placed to root in an environment that is warm, at least 21°C (70°F), bright but shaded.
Pests and diseases Aphids and scale insect attack.

21 ARDISIA CRENATA
Coral Berry, Spice Berry

Family Myrsinaceae.

Origin East Indies, Malaysia, China.

Description Formerly known as *A. crenulata*, this elegant bush grows indoors to a height of 1 m (3 ft). The erect stem bears alternate, oblong-lanceolate leaves up to 15 cm (6 in) in length, dark green with a shiny, leathery, undulating blade. The plant flowers in June, producing clusters of small white blooms, flushed bright pink. Each flower is star-shaped, 1.5 cm (½ in) in diameter. The flowers are succeeded by decorative berries, first green then bright red, which last until the next flowering.

Varieties There are one or two varieties of this species and of related species such as *A. japonica*.

Care Needs bright light but cannot stand direct sun. Demanding in terms of temperature and moisture, it is not easy to grow indoors and does much better in the greenhouse. The plant prefers cool temperatures, around 15°C (59°F). At a higher temperature place the pot in a bowl full of damp gravel and spray the plant every day. Minimum winter temperature should be 7°C (44°F). Water plentifully during growing season; let the soil almost dry out between successive waterings in resting period. Apply liquid fertilizer fortnightly in spring. Medium composed of 1 part loam, 1 part peat and 1 part sand. Repot every spring; young plants in pots of up to 12 cm (5 in) diameter. As the plant ages it loses its beauty and should therefore be replaced or pruned drastically in February 10 cm (4 in) from base. New branches will form, the best of which can be selected.

Propagation From seed or cuttings, or by air-layering. Indoors the first method is simplest. Sow in March at a temperature of 18°C (64°F) and prick out once or twice according to need.

Pests and diseases Mealy bug and scale insects generally. If grown in too dry an environment it may lose berries prematurely and be attacked by red spider.

22 ARAUCARIA HETEROPHYLLA
Norfolk island pine

Family Araucariaceae.
Origin Norfolk Island (Australia).
Description Known also as *A. excelsa*. Evergreen conifer which in its native habitat may grow to a height of 60 m (almost 200 ft) but indoors only to 1–1.5 m (3–5 ft). It grows very slowly. The branches normally grow horizontally; the narrow, sharp, needle-like leaves form a fan. The color of the new foliage is light green, becoming dark in autumn.
Varieties *A. heterophylla glauca* has blue-green foliage; *A. compacta* is more compact in habit.
Care The species needs moderately bright light but not too dim, otherwise it loses its leaves. It lives happily at room temperature but not below 5°C (41°F). Above 23°C (73°F) it requires a high degree of atmospheric humidity, spray the foliage every 3–4 days. In summer it can usually be kept in the open, watering abundantly without letting water collect in the pot and applying liquid fertilizer once a fortnight. During the resting period suspend feeding and water little. Grow in medium consisting of 1 part organic soil, 1 part peat and 1 part coarse sand, repotting every 2–3 years, in spring. Pots should normally be 20–25 cm (8–10 in) in diameter.

Propagation From seed or cuttings, but the latter procedure requires very exact temperatures hard to obtain except in the greenhouse. Sow seed in March at a temperature of 10–15°C (50–59°F). When the seedlings have developed, transplant them into pots.
Pests and diseases Root rot, avoid standing in water.

---

23 ASPARAGUS DENSIFLORUS 'Sprengeri'
Sprengeri fern

Family Liliaceae.
Origin South Africa.
Description Species with thread-like, curving and drooping stems, up to 2 m (6 ft) long, suitable for growing in hanging baskets. The thorny stems are covered in needle-like phyllodes (pseudo-leaves). The plant produces insignificant flowers and red berries; it grows to a height of 50 cm (20 in), with a diameter of up to 1 m (3 ft).
Varieties In addition to the variety 'Sprengeri' there are two other forms: *A. densiflorus* 'Sprengeri nanus,' of smaller size; 'Sprengeri robustus,' of particularly rapid growth.
Care Easy to cultivate indoors, using techniques as described for *A. setaceus*; bright but not direct light. Minimum winter temperature 7°C (44°F). Water abundantly in spring–summer, very little in winter. Give liquid fertilizer fortnightly during growth period. It is best to grow the plant in a hanging basket containing a mixture made up of 1 part loam, 1 part peat and 1 part sand. The average size of the basket should be 20–25 cm (8–10 in). Repot every spring, or replace with fresh mixture. Remove the older, yellowed branches to encourage formation of new shoots.
Propagation In spring divide clumps, leaving a piece of rhizome and some fronds on each portion, then pot in fresh soil mixture. Seeds can also be sown in spring or autumn at a temperature of around 16°C (61°F), but the procedure is lengthy.
Pests and diseases Scale insects; red spider causes white spots on foliage.

24 ASPARAGUS SETACEUS
Asparagus fern

Family Liliaceae.
Origin South Africa.
Description Also known as *A. plumosus*. Bushy plant which when adult may grow to a height of 3 m (10 ft). The delicate, highly ornamental foliage is made up of green needle-like leaves known as phyllodes. The true leaves are mere scales. The plant is much used for floral decoration. There are insignificant flowers and red berries. The plant grows from an underground rhizome.
Varieties In addition to the species, varieties are *A. setaceus* 'Nanus,' smaller in size, and *A. s.* 'Robustus,' with strong, climbing stems.
Care Easy to grow indoors, the species can also live in the open in temperate zones provided the minimum temperature does not fall below 7°C (44°F); outside in the summer, it should be kept in shade, for although it likes bright light it does not respond to direct sunlight. During spring and summer indoor plants should be watered plentifully, not letting the potting soil dry out completely. Feed with liquid fertilizer fortnightly during summer. The medium should consist of 1 part organic soil, 1 part peat and 1 part sand. The plant needs repotting every spring, increasing the size of the container. Keep the soil level in the pot fairly low.
Propagation Easily done indoors by dividing dense clumps in spring and potting in above medium, or sow in spring or autumn.
Pests and diseases Red spider and scale insects.

---

25 ASPIDISTRA ELATIOR
Cast-iron plant

Family Liliaceae.
Origin China.
Description Also known as *A. lurida*. Plant with strong dark green leaves, 40–50 cm (16–20 in) long, the stalks of which sprout from a half-buried rhizome. Total height of plant 40–60 cm (16–24 in), diameter 60 cm (24 in). The insignificant opaque purple flowers appear in August at ground level.
Varieties *A. elatior* 'Variegata' has creamy-white striped leaves.
Care Easy plant to grow indoors, usually kept in areas where few other house plants can survive. It can stand deep shade, temperature fluctuations, dust and dry air. The better it is looked after, the better it will grow. An ideal position as regards natural or artificial light is in a north-facing window. *A. elatior* 'Variegata' needs somewhat brighter light, but not direct sun. Water moderately throughout year, letting the soil half-dry out between successive waterings. Wash the leaves from time to time and feed fortnightly during spring and summer with liquid fertilizer. Grow in medium of 1 part loam, 1 part peat and 1 part sand. Repot every 3–4 years in spring, but add fresh soil every year.
Propagation By division of clumps in spring. Cut the rhizome into sections, each with roots and at least two leaves, and repot in fresh soil. No feeding necessary in early months. Afterwards adopt the same cultural methods as for adult plants.
Pests and diseases If the plant is overwatered brown marks may appear on the leaves.

26 ASPLENIUM NIDUS
Bird's nest fern

Family Polypodiaceae.
Origin Tropical Asia, tropical Australia, Polynesia.
Description Belongs to the group of ferns, grown for their foliage in greenhouses, in the home and in gardens. Their size, shape and habit vary greatly. *A. midus* is an epiphyte in its native habitat and resembles a bird's nest, hence its common name. This fern has undivided, shiny, bright green foliage, arranged in rosettes. Each leaf, slightly wavy and with a central vein, may be up to 1 m (3 ft) long. When formed, the new leaves are very fragile and should not be touched. On the lower side of each mature leaf are rounded formations called sori which contain the spores, resembling a fine yellow-brown dust.
Care Like all ferns it must have complete shade and needs little light. It grows well at room temperature but this must not drop below 13–15°C (55–59°F). Water plentifully during growing period and spray the foliage, but reduce amount of water in winter dormancy, simply making sure the soil does not dry out. Feed once a month with liquid fertilizer, except in resting period. The potting medium must be well drained and porous, formed of 2 parts fibrous peat, 1 part fibrous soil and 1 part coarse sand. Repot only when roots fill pot, in spring. Clean the leaves periodically.
Propagation This can only be done by sowing the spores. It is a difficult, highly specialized technique.
Pests and diseases Aphids, scale insects.

---

27 AUCUBA JAPONICA 'Variegata'
Gold dust plant, spotted laurel

Family Cornaceae.
Origin Himalayas to Japan.
Description Hardy evergreen shrub with opposite, ovate-elliptic, shiny green leaves with golden-yellow spots. Produces insignificant red flowers in summer, followed by bright red, persistent berries. It can be grown either as an outdoor plant, up to 4 m (13 ft) tall and 3 m (10 ft) across, or as a house plant, up to 1 m (3 ft).
Varieties *A. japonica* 'Variegata'; *A. japonica* 'Crotonifolia' with lighter, blotched yellow or ivory leaves; 'Goldieana' with golden yellow leaves, light green on the margins.
Care Very easy plant to grow either indoors or out. Indoors it prefers a shaded position but can even be put in direct sunlight. Cultivated house plants do best at maximum 24°C (75°F); if hotter they need a great deal of moisture. Water them abundantly throughout the year but do not allow water to collect in the bowl under the pot. Feed once a month, from May to September, with diluted liquid fertilizer. Grow in medium made up of 1 part organic soil, 1 part peat and 1 part sand, or in ordinary garden soil. Repot in March if the size of the plant warrants it, otherwise add fresh soil. Prune old or straggly plants in March.
Propagation In spring take 10–15 cm (4–6 in) cuttings and plant them in mixture of peat and sand. Wrap each pot in a plastic bag and keep in bright but shaded surroundings. The plant will start to grow in a few months. The plastic bag can then be removed and when the plant is 30 cm (12 in) tall it can be repotted in the normal medium.

28   BEAUCARNEA RECURVATA
Pony Tail

Family Liliaceae.
Origin Mexico.
Description Small tree which grows, in its native habitat, to a height of 10 m (33 ft). The base of the house plant's stem is swollen and bears a terminal rosette of straight, narrow leaves up to 1 m (3 ft) long and 1–2 cm (½–1 in) wide. The leaves are rough and slightly leathery, blue-green or gray-ish. Clusters of small whitish flowers are produced.
Care Needs plenty of light and even direct sun. In winter it should be kept in sheltered surroundings, bright but not too hot, and in summer it can stand in the open. Coming from arid regions, it withstands drought, needing little water in summer, its soil being allowed almost to dry out between successive waterings. In winter watering can be reduced even further. During spring and summer feed with a liquid fertilizer every 3 weeks. Grow in a fairly compact lime medium comprising garden soil, leafmold and fine sand in equal parts. Repot every 2–3 years.

Propagation The stem sprouts lateral shoots used for propagation. As a rule they have to be rooted in a heated greenhouse at 21–23°C (70–73°F). If trying it indoors cut the shoots in spring, dry them off for 7–8 hours and pot them in a mixture of 2 parts peat and 1 part sand. Moisten the potting medium and cover the pot with a plastic bag, placing it in a bright spot. When the cuttings have rooted, expose them gradually to dry air and repot them in growing medium.
Pests and diseases Scale insects, mealy bug.

29   BEGONIA COCCINEA HYBRID

Family Begoniaceae.
Origin Brazil (for true *coccinea*).
Description Belongs to the group of fibrous-rooted begonias. It has a few bamboo-like stems, over 1 m (3 ft) long, bearing unequally-sided, elongated, ovate leaves with wavy and slightly toothed margins, measuring 10–15 cm (4–6 in) long and 6–8 cm (about 3 in) wide. The upper surface is green with silver spots and red borders, the underside is dark red. The deep red flowers, 1 cm (½ in) across, are borne in hanging clusters on a red stalk. They bloom in summer and continue until mid-autumn.
Varieties *B. Coccinea* 'Pink,' has pale pink flowers.
Care The species thrives at medium temperatures and needs bright, filtered light. It can also stand direct sun, if not too strong, morning and evening. During the growth period it should be watered plentifully, without flooding, and sprayed. Watering can be reduced in winter. Growing mixture consists of 1 part organic soil, 2 parts peat and 1 part sand. Repot in spring.
Propagation From cuttings in early summer. Take 10 cm (4 in) sections of nonflowering stems and plant them in mixture of equal parts peat and sand. Wrap the pot in a plastic bag and place it in medium, filtered light.
Pests and diseases Plant parasites: mildew, grey mold, root rot, leaf bacteria. Animal parasites: leaf miners, thrips, mites.

30 BEGONIA REX HYBRIDS
Rex begonia

Family Begoniaceae.
Origin Assam (India) (for the species).
Description Begonia with large, fleshy rhizome bearing tufts of roots. It grows to a height of 30 cm (12 in) but there are varieties which do not exceed 10 cm (4 in). The *B. rex* group, comprising a very large number of hybrids, has very showy, ornamental leaves which are asymmetrically heart-shaped, up to 30 cm (12 in) long and 25 cm (10 in) wide, on long stalks arising from the rhizome. The leaves often exhibit splendid colors (light green or copper, pink, red, silver) in a variety of patterns. Flowers are produced rarely, and only by adult plants, in June–September.
Varieties Three varieties suitable for indoor cultivation are: 'Merry Christmas,' with reddish-yellow leaves marked with pink, silver and green; 'President,' with dark green and silver leaves; 'King Edward IV,' purple leaves marked with pink.
Care Fibrous-rooted and rhizomatous begonias are cultivated by the same methods. The *B. rex* hybrids, grown for their foliage, require bright but filtered light; in contrast, the *B. cucullata* varieties and hybrids, cultivated for their flowers, need several hours of direct sunlight daily. Minimum winter temperature is 13°C (55°F). When indoors they should be sprayed. Liquid fertilizer applied fortnightly from May to September. Growing mixture formed of soil, peat and sand in equal parts. Repot annually in spring.
Propagation In April, when repotting, divide the rhizomes, making certain that every section has a few roots and at least one shoot. Can also be multiplied from leaf cuttings in May–June.
Pests and diseases See *B. coccinea* hybrid.

31 BEGONIA SEMPERFLORENS-CULTORUM
Wax begonia

Family Begoniaceae.
Origin Brazil (for the species).
Description The genus comprises approximately 1,000 species of perennial plants as well as a vast number of hybrids and cultivated forms, differing greatly in color, form and development. Some are evergreen, others have deciduous leaves. They are grown for their flowers, their foliage or both. Female and male flowers develop on the same plant. Cultivated begonias are divided into three groups based on root form: fibrous rooted, tuberous or rhizomatous. *B. semperflorens* is fibrous rooted, a dwarf species of 15–30 cm (6–12 in) with many branches, its shiny, waxy leaves green or bronze-red. The flowers, red, pink or white, are borne in loose clusters. The male flowers are 2–3 cm (about 1 in) across, their petals simple or in 2–4 whorls, appearing from June to September–October; the female flowers are produced all year round. There are many hybrids of the species which are commonly grown outdoors in summer.
Care As for *B. rex.*
Propagation From May to August with nonflowering shoot cuttings; each cutting should be 8–10 cm (3–4 in) long, taken below a leaf, which should be removed. Treat with root hormone preparation and plant cutting in mixture of peat and sand in equal parts. Place in bright but diffused light at 18–21°C (64–70°F). Once rooting has occurred, transplant. Propagation can also be done by seed, in February–March, at 16°C (61°F).
Pests and diseases See *B. coccinea* hybrid.

32 BEGONIA X TUBERHYBRIDA
Tuberous begonia

Family Begoniaceae.
Origin *B. x tuberhybrida* belongs to the large group of tuberous begonias characterized by a thickened root. All the tuberous begonias are deciduous; some, like the *B. x tuberhybrida* forms, have a long period of winter dormancy, others flower in winter and rest in summer. The 'varieties' of *B. x tuberhybrida* have fleshy stems, erect or prostrate, green leaves that are ovate and pointed, 15–20 cm (6–8 in) long, and, most noticeably, large flowers that bloom from June to September.
Varieties The many hybrid forms include 'Diana Wynyard,' with big white flowers; 'Mary Heatley,' pale orange; 'Rhapsody,' pink; and 'Olympia,' with crimson flowers.
Care In winter the plant is dormant and only the tuberous root survives, which should be kept at around 7°C (44°F). In summer the plants live happily outdoors in the shade or indoors. Water copiously when growing, taper off in autumn and stop when leaves start turning yellow. Give liquid fertilizer fortnightly in spring and summer. Grow in pots, bowls or hanging baskets, using a highly porous medium: 1 part organic soil, 2 parts peat and 1 part sand. The roots of *B. x tuberhybrida* are planted in April in shallow boxes containing moist peat, placing them concave side upwards. After 3–4 weeks, having been kept in dim light, they should be transplanted in pots containing the growing medium.

Propagation In spring cut a tuberous root into two or more sections, each provided with a bud. Disinfect with sulphur dust and pot.
Pests and diseases Mildew, gray mold, root rot, leaf bacteria. Leaf miners, thrips, mites.

---

33 BELOPERONE GUTTATA
Shrimp plant

Family Acanthaceae.
Origin Mexico.
Description Evergreen shrub grown for its strange clusters of flowers covered with pinkish-brown bracts which look like shrimps. The pendulous flower spikes, 10–12 cm (4–5 in) long, bloom from March to December. The delicate green leaves are ovate and slightly hairy, 2–4 cm (1–2 in) long.
Varieties There is a cultivar, *B. guttata* 'Yellow Queen,' with yellow bracts.
Care For successful flowering the plant must have bright light and direct sun for several hours a day. It flourishes at a temperature of about 18°C (64°F). Minimum winter temperature is 7°C (44°F). In summer it should be kept in a well-ventilated spot, protected from hot sun. Water abundantly from March to November, but very little in winter. Feed weekly from May to September with liquid fertilizer. Grow in medium consisting of 1 part organic soil, 2 parts peat and 1 part sand. Repot every spring until container is about 15 cm (6 in) in diameter; then give it fresh soil each year.

Propagation In spring take stem cuttings of 5–8 cm (2–3 in) and pot them in mixture of peat and sand in equal parts. Wrap the pot in a plastic bag and put it in a bright but shaded spot, at a temperature of 18°C (64°F). After rooting, repot in growing medium, taking care for some months not to expose them to direct sunlight.

Pests and diseases If kept in proper conditions of light, temperature and humidity, the plant is reasonably resistant to the attacks of parasites.

34 BLECHNUM GIBBUM

Family Polypodiaceae.
Origin New Caledonia.
Description The genus *Blechnum* contains many species of variously sized ferns, some small and creeping, others erect and up to 1½ m (5 ft) tall. *B. gibbum* has pinnate, deeply divided fronds 50–60 cm (20–24 in) long and 30 cm (12 in) wide, set on stems with a scaly black base, up to 90 cm (3 ft) in height. The fronds form a compact, asymmetrical group and have slightly curved pinnules. Some leaves are sterile, others are fertile, bearing the sporangia.
Care The plant likes bright light but not direct sun. It is not easy to raise indoors, for it prefers temperatures of 16–18°C (61–64°F) and air that is not too moist. It also does well in warm surroundings of 21–24°C (70–75°F) and above, but in such cases it requires moisture, with a bowl of wet gravel under the pot, and must be watered plentifully. In winter it remains dormant (November to March) at 15°C (59°F) but can be kept even at 10°C (50°F), so needs little watering. Feed weekly from April to October with a solution that is not too concentrated. The growing medium should not contain much lime and can be made up of organic soil and leaf mold in equal parts, or of organic soil and peat in the same proportions. Repot every 2 years providing adequate drainage layer.
Propagation From spores, with a highly specialized technique. Sometimes the plant sprouts basal shoots which can be removed and repotted separately.
Pests and diseases Aphids, mealy bug, scale insects.

35 BOUGAINVILLEA GLABRA

Bougainvillea, paper flower

Family Nyctaginaceae.
Origin Brazil.
Description Woody climbing shrub. As a house plant it grows to a height of 2.5 m (8 ft) and in open ground to more than 8 m (26 ft). The branches are thorny and bear deciduous ovate leaves which are not particularly decorative. The creamy-white flowers are insignificant but are surrounded by papery bracts in bright purple or violet. The bracts appear in spring and summer and persist for several months.
Varieties *B. glabra* 'Sanderana variegata,' mauvish-pink bracts and white-bordered leaves; *B. glabra* 'Alexandra,' bright purple-violet bracts.
Care Difficult to grow indoors. For flowering it needs bright light and direct sun during the growing season for at least 4 hours a day. The plant does well at room temperature while growing, but when dormant prefers a cooler temperature, though not less than 8–10°C (46–50°F). Do not water too much, allowing much of the soil to dry out before watering again. In winter reduce watering even further. Feed every fortnight, from spring to end-summer, with a liquid fertilizer. Grow in mixture of organic soil, peat and sand in equal parts. Repot young plants every spring. Prune in February, shortening branches by one-third.
Propagation From cuttings in spring and summer.
Pests and diseases The plant, if not provided with suitable light and temperature conditions indoors, soon loses its leaves. It may be attacked by aphids.

36 — BOUVARDIA X DOMESTICA

Family Rubiaceae.
Origin Mexico.
Description Hybrid obtained from crossing various species of *Bouvardia*. It is an evergreen shrub with oval, opposite leaves which grows to a height of 60 cm (2 ft). The flowers, red, pink or white, according to variety, are tubular with four terminal lobes on a stalk, arranged in terminal clusters. Flowering lasts from June to November.
Varieties 'President Cleveland' with crimson flowers which are sometimes double. Some varieties are cultivated for their cut flowers.
Care Indoor growing is not easy because the temperature has to range around 13°C (55°F) both in winter and summer. Shady positions. Water abundantly during spring and summer and spray to keep atmosphere moist. Reduce watering after flowering. Feed with liquid fertilizer once a week from May to September. Use a mixture consisting of 1 part organic soil, 1 part peat and 1 part sand, repotting every year in March. Drastic pruning can be done in February by cutting down the stems to within a few centimeters of the base. As the plant ages it loses its beauty and should therefore be replaced every 2 years.
Propagation From cuttings in spring. Cut portions of young twigs, about 8 cm (3 in) long, and plant in mixture of peat and sand in equal parts. Keep at 21°C (70°F) in moist atmosphere. In optimum conditions rooting will occur in 3 weeks.
Pests and diseases Sensitive to unsuitable conditions.

---

37 — BRUNFELSIA PAUCIFLORA CALYCINA
Yesterday-today-and-tomorrow plant,
Franciscan nightshade, Franciscea

Family Solanaceae.
Origin Brazil.
Description Evergreen shrub, 60–90 cm (2–3 ft) tall, with glossy, ovate elliptic leaves. The plant will flower throughout the year, especially if a temperature range of 13–16°C (55–61°F) is maintained. The attractive, scented flowers, developing from the leaf axils, are 5 cm (2 in) across; their color is successively violet, blue and white, lasting 3–4 days.
Varieties *B. calycina* 'macrantha' has bigger flowers.
Care Does well in bright surroundings but not in direct sun; in summer it can go outside in shady positions. During growth it needs plenty of humidity. When flowering is over, water sparingly and keep the plant at a temperature of around 12°C (53°F), minimum 10°C (50°F). Feed once a month during the growth season with a diluted liquid fertilizer. Potting mixture should consist of organic soil, peat and sand in equal proportions; repot once a year, after flowering or in spring.
Propagation From February to August from half-woody cuttings of previous year's shoots. The base of each cutting should be dipped in a hormone rooting preparation. Plant the cuttings in 8 cm (3 in) pots with equal parts coarse sand and peat. Wrap pot in plastic bag and keep at 21°C (70°F). After one month, remove the bag and water in moderation, feeding once a fortnight. After about 3 months transplant into standard 12–16 cm (5–6 in) pot.
Pests and diseases Mites, if surroundings are too dry.

38 BROWALLIA SPECIOSA

Sapphire flower, amethyst flower

Family Solanaceae.

Origin Colombia.

Description Grown for its beautiful flowers, which bloom from June to September. The slender, erect or slightly pendulous stems, up to 60 cm (2 ft) long, bear ovate, pointed bright green leaves. The tubular flowers, with a corolla opening into a star shape, are 5 cm (2 in) in diameter and grow in the leaf axils; they are very lovely, violet-blue with blue veining along the petals and often a white throat.

Varieties *B. speciosa* var. 'major' flowers throughout the year and is ideal as a house plant for growing in autumn and winter; the flowers are dark blue. *Alba* has white flowers.

Care Indoors the plant is cultivated as an annual and discarded after flowering. It needs light, even direct sun if not too strong. The ideal temperature for growing is 13–15°C (55–59°F); it can live at rather higher room temperatures but this shortens the flowering period. Water sparingly, letting part of the mixture dry out between applications. Feed with liquid fertilizer every fortnight from the time the plant is at least 5 cm (3 in) high and right through flowering season. Pot plants should be grown in a mixture made up of 1 part organic compost, 1 part peat and 1 part sand. Can also be grown in hanging baskets.

Propagation From seed in early spring for flowering in autumn and winter. The technique is complicated and difficult indoors.

Pests and diseases Aphids attack young shoots and buds; these may be followed by gray and sooty molds.

39 CALADIUM BICOLOR
Angel's Wings

Family Araceae.
Origin Tropical America (of species).
Description Deciduous plant with thick subterranean stem (tuber). Can grow to a height of 40 cm (16 in). Grown for its large, ovate heart- or arrow-shaped leaves, varying in size up to a maximum of 35 cm (14 in), borne on long stalks set directly into the stem. The leaves, especially of the hybrids, are particularly striking, variously colored (green, pink, red and white) and so blended as to form contrasting effects, patterns and markings.
Varieties C. 'Candidum,' white leaves with green tracery; C. 'John Peel,' leaves with red veining; C. 'Pink Cloud,' leaves variegated dark green with transparent marbling of lavender rose, white and pink along main veins; C. 'Sea Gull,' leaves, greenish white centers, bluish green toward the margin with white veining in relief.
Care Needs a very moist environment. In winter the tubers can be kept for at least 5 months at a temperature of 15°C (59°F) in a dark corner, buried in dry peat. Pot them in spring and keep them at 21°C (70°F) to allow leaves to develop. During this period the plant needs plenty of humidity, so it should be sprayed daily and the pot placed in a bowl full of damp gravel. It needs a lot of light but cannot stand direct sunlight or drafts. Potting medium: 1 part organic soil, 3 parts peat and 1 part sand, with a thick drainage layer.
Propagation The tuber of the parent plant produces small tubers which are removed in spring and planted.
Pests and diseases Mites if air too dry.

---

40 CALATHEA CROCATA

Family Marantaceae.
Origin Brazil.
Description Unlike other plants of the genus Calathea which are cultivated for their decorative foliage, the species C. crocata also has splendid flowers. The leaves are ovate, metallic dark green with purple tints and grayish spots scattered along the veining. The flower heads are enfolded in yellow-orange bracts.
Care Needs more exposure to brighter light than other Calathea species grown for foliage, but dislikes direct sun. Thrives at temperatures of 15–21°C (59–70°F). At levels of over 18°C (64°F) spray the plants daily with lime-free water to avoid white marks forming on the leaves, and place the pots in layers of wet gravel. During spring-summer water the mixture plentifully; in winter reduce amount of water, letting the surface of the mixture dry out before repeating. Give liquid fertilizer every fortnight from spring to autumn. Potting medium should consist of 1 part organic soil, 3 parts peat and 1 part sand. Repot every June.
Propagation In May–June divide the thicker clumps into sections, each containing a piece of rhizome, a few roots and some leaves. Repot each portion in damp compost, wrap in plastic bag and set in medium light at temperature of 16–18°C (61–64°F) until rooting.
Pests and diseases Red spider if surroundings too dry.

41 CALATHEA MAKOYANA
Peacock plant

Family Marantaceae.
Origin Brazil.
Description The plant grows to an overall height of 40–50 cm (16–20 in). The ovate oblong leaves are 15 cm (6 in) or more in length, on long stalks growing from a short, often inconspicuous stem. The leaves have very thin V-shaped lines running from the center vein to the margins, and other elliptical streaks. The upper side of the leaves is pale green with dark green patches, and the underside is chestnut-pink with purple markings.
Varieties There are no horticultural varieties of this species. Related species (*C. metallica, C. picturata*) and varieties known in the trade simply as *Calathea*.
Care Shaded positions and average lighting. Temperature 15–21°C (59–70°F). If the temperature is high, the plant should be sprayed every day with rain water to avoid the formation of calcareous marks, and the pot placed in a bowl full of moist gravel. Water plentifully but during winter dormancy reduce. Feed with liquid fertilizer every fortnight during growth season. Grow in medium formed of 1 part organic soil, 3 parts peat and 1 part sand. Repot every year in June.
Propagation In May–June the clumps can be divided into sections, each with a few roots and leaves. Repot each portion in a moist soil, cover with a plastic bag until rooting occurs and keep in moderate light at a temperature of 16–18°C (61–64°F).
Pests and diseases Scale insects, mealy bugs, red spider.

42 CALATHEA ORNATA 'Sanderana'

Family Marantaceae.
Origin Northern South America.
Description Very decorative appearance with leathery, upright leaves on long stalks attached to a short stem. The leaf blade is dark olive-green with parallel and strongly contrasted veining in pink or white, the streaks curving away in pairs or large numbers from the central rib. The underside of the leaf is purplish-red.
Care Shaded positions in medium light are best, with temperatures of 15–21°C (59–70°F). If the temperature is high the plant should be sprayed daily with rain water to prevent spotting and the pots placed on beds of wet gravel. Water the plants generously during the period of growth and reduce the amount during winter dormancy, allowing the surface of the soil to dry out between successive waterings. Feed every fortnight in the course of growth. Potting medium formed of 1 part organic soil, 3 parts peat and 1 part sand. Repot every year in June.
Propagation In May–June divide the clumps into sections, each containing a piece of rhizome, roots and a few leaves. Plant each portion in damp mixture, wrap in plastic bag until rooting occurs and keep in medium light at temperature of 16–18°C (61–64°F).
Pests and diseases Scale insects, mealy bugs, red spider.

43 CALCEOLARIA X HERBEOHYBRIDA
Slipper wort

Family Scrophulariaceae.
Origin Chile (for species).
Description Hybrids of *Calceolaria* come from the crossing of many species. They are biennial plants which grow to a height of 30–40 cm (12–16 in), with vivid flowers that bloom for one season. Flowers are red, yellow or orange, often with speckles of contrasting color. In the greenhouse the plant flowers from May to July, in the open from June to August. The ovate, soft and slightly hairy leaves are up to 20 cm (8 in) wide and grow in groups at the base of the plant.
Varieties Among the many cultivars the one best suited to indoor cultivation, C. 'Multiflora nana,' is a dwarf form, up to 20 cm (8 in) tall. It produces numerous flowers in various shades of yellow and red, with crimson spots.
Care For prolonged flowering indoors the plants must be kept in a cool position and with bright indirect lighting. Acid growing medium of organic soil, peat and sand in equal parts. Water generously and place pot in bowl of moist gravel.
Propagation A complex operation done by growers only. Seeds are sown in June (for flowering the following spring) at a temperature of at least 18°C (64°F) in seedbed soil. When seedings are a few centimeters high they are pricked out and transplanted into 7–8 cm (3 in) pots filled with growing soil. They have to spend the winter at a temperature of 7–10°C (46–50°F). In March of the second year they can be brought indoors or put out in the open, where they will flower in the summer. After flowering they are discarded.
Pests and diseases Very subject to aphids.

44 CALLISIA ELEGANS
Striped inch plant

Family Commelinaceae.
Origin Mexico.
Description Plant with recumbent stems suitable for growing in hanging baskets. Height 8–10 cm (3–4 in). The stems are up to 60 cm (2 ft) long, with very close-set, alternate, stalkless leaves. The leaves are ovate and pointed, 3–4 cm (1½ in) long, dark green, with white lines running lengthwise along the upper surface. The underside is reddish-purple. The plant produces insignificant white flowers.
Care Easy to cultivate. Likes bright but filtered light in warm surroundings. Grows fast at average room temperatures. In winter it prefers a rest period of 1–2 months at temperatures of 10–15°C (50–59°F). Water generously while growing, keeping the mixture permanently wet but not allowing water to collect. Water very little during dormancy and let surface of mixture dry out before repeating. Feed every fortnight with liquid fertilizer when plant is growing. Potting medium formed of 1 part organic soil, 2 parts peat and 1 part sand. The plant lasts about 2 years and should then be replaced.
Propagation In spring-summer take 5 cm (2 in) stem cuttings, planting several in a single pot with standard growing mixture. Place in bright, indirect light and water moderately. After 2–3 weeks the cuttings will root. In about 2 weeks begin feeding and treat as adult plants.
Pests and diseases Fairly resistant to parasites.

45 CALLISTEMON CITRINUS
Lemon bottle brush

Family Myrtaceae.
Origin Australia.
Description Shrub or small tree of spreading habit, up to 2–3 m (6–10 ft) in height in native environment; may grow to more than 1 m (3 ft) as potted plant but can be kept shorter if pruned. The gray-green leaves, smelling faintly of lemon, are straight and lanceolate. The small flowers, without petals, have large numbers of protruding red stamens in cylindrical spikes at the tip of the stalk, 5–10 cm (2–4 in) long, which look like bottle brushes. Flowers appear in July.
Varieties The variety C. citrinus 'Splendens' has crimson stamens 4 cm (2 in) long.
Care The plant likes direct sunlight and is best kept outdoors in summer. In winter it needs a rest period at 8–10°C (46–50°F). When growing again, water plentifully, not allowing water to collect in the pot. During dormancy water only to prevent soil from drying out. Feed every fortnight with liquid fertilizer, except in resting period. Growing medium of organic soil, peat and sand in equal parts. Repot each spring in progressively bigger pots. Prune after flowering.
Propagation From June to August take 10 cm (4 in) cuttings of current year's shoots, each with a piece of root. Plant in pots with moist mixture of peat and sand in equal parts. Enclose in plastic bags and place in bright, indirect light at 21°C (70°F). After rooting, uncover the plant, water moderately and when the roots have filled the pot, transplant into growing soil.
Pests and diseases Fairly resistant to parasites.

46 CAMELLIA JAPONICA
Camellia

Family Theaceae.
Origin Japan, Korea.
Description Evergreen shrub, cultivated for its magnificent flowers. The strong, shiny leaves are ovate with a pointed tip, alternate, 10 cm (4 in) long and 5 cm (2 in) wide. The flowers may be single with 5 petals and yellow stamens, double with stamens transformed into petals or semi-double. Size of flowers ranges from 5 cm (2 in) to 14 cm (6 in). Most varieties flower in spring.
Varieties 'Adolphe Audusson,' semi-double crimson flowers, 10 cm (4 in) wide; 'Albo plena,' double white flowers, 10 cm (4 in) wide; 'Pink Perfection,' double pink flowers, 8 cm (3 in) wide; 'Alba simplex,' single white flowers, 8 cm (3 in) wide, flowers in winter.
Care Grows well in indirect light; although it dislikes direct sunlight, neither the atmosphere nor the soil should be too dry, but avoid standing in water. Keep cool; at temperatures above 18°C (64°F) it does not live long and produces few flowers. Flowering buds develop in autumn-winter at temperatures of 8–16°C (46–61°F). Indoors the pot should be placed in a pan or bowl full of moist gravel and sprayed every day. Water well in growing season and infrequently during winter. Feed fortnightly with standard liquid fertilizer while growing. It needs well-drained, acid soil of leaf mold, organic soil and peat in equal amounts, and a little sand. In spring repot small plants or replace part of the soil of larger plants.
Propagation From cuttings, but difficult indoors.
Pests and diseases Mildew; aphids and scale insects.

47 CAMPANULA ISOPHYLLA
Star-of-Bethlehem

Family Campanulaceae.

Origin Northern Italy.

Description The genus *Campanula* comprises many species of annual, biennial and perennial plants *C. isophylla* is a dwarf perennial with trailing or recumbent stems, up to 30 cm (12 in) long. Leaves are heart-shaped with dentate edges. The blue star-shaped flowers, 3 cm (about 1 in) across, appear June–July in very large numbers.

Varieties *C. isophylla* 'Alba,' white flowers; Cisophylla 'Mayi,' variegated, slightly hairy leaves, blue flowers.

Care Easy to cultivate indoors in hanging baskets. Needs plenty of light, direct or diffused. Adapts to a wide temperature range, but needs a cool environment for prolonged flowering. Above 18°C (64°F) place pot in layer of moist gravel and spray daily. In winter rest the plant at 5–10°C (41–50°F). Keep soil damp during growing season and water little during dormancy. Feed every fortnight from spring to end of flowering period with liquid fertilizer. Grow in mixture of organic soil, peat and sand in equal parts. Repot every spring.

Propagation Take cuttings, each with 3–4 pairs of leaves, in March–April. Dip the base in rooting preparation and plant in pot with moist mixture of peat and sand in equal parts. Enclose in plastic bag and place in filtered light. After about 3 weeks, when rooted, transplant into growing medium.

Pests and diseases Subject to gray mold if kept in too wet conditions.

---

48 CAPSICUM ANNUUM
Christmas pepper, ornamental chilli

Family Solanaceae.

Origin South America.

Description Cultivated for its decorative fruits. It is a shrub, 30–40 cm (12–16 in) tall, with slightly woody stems and long, faintly hairy, ovate leaves. Insignificant white flowers emerge from leaf axils from June onwards. These are followed in October by prominent berries in various shapes and colors. There are three types of variety: cone-shaped fruits in green, creamy-white, yellow, orange and red; rounded fruits in yellow or violet; and bunches of red fruits in groups of 2–3. These fruits last 2–3 months.

Varieties 'Christmas Greeting,' cone-shaped, green, violet, yellow or red fruits; 'Fiesta,' pointed fruits which change, as they ripen, from yellow to orange and red; 'Rising Sun,' rounded red fruits.

Care Easy to grow, the plant is usually kept indoors in winter for decorative purposes and outdoors in summer. It likes bright light, if possible direct light several hours a day. Does well at room temperature but fruit lasts longer if at 13–15°C (55–59°F). Water abundantly, not letting water stand in pot. To increase humidity place pot in bowl of moist gravel. Give liquid food fortnightly. Grow in normal garden soil or in equal parts of loam, peat and sand. Cultivate as an annual, throwing out plant after fruiting.

Propagation From seed, but the technique is rather difficult indoors. It is usual to buy seedlings in autumn when fruits have already formed.

Pests and diseases Red spider, whitefly, aphids.

49 CAREX MORROWII 'Variegata'
Sedge

Family Cyperaceae.
Origin Japan.
Description The genus contains a very large number of species which live in the most diverse habitats: wet or dry locations, seashores and mountain zones. Only the species *C. morrowii* and its variety 'Variegata' are cultivated indoors. This plant grows to a height of 20–30 cm (8–12 in); it is a tufted perennial, similar to grass. Its straight, slender leaves grow in tufts from a rhizomatous root. In *C. morrowii, variegata* the leaves have white streaks. It does not need a rest period. The plant is highly suitable for use with other broad-leaved species, particularly those with similar requirements.

Care It does well in bright but shaded places. In winter it prefers cool temperatures of 10–15°C (50–59°F) but also thrives at higher levels, up to 21°C (70°F). In the latter case the air must be kept moist. Spray the plant and set the pot in a holder filled with wet gravel. Water with moderation, letting the surface of the soil dry out between waterings. Give liquid fertilizer monthly in spring and summer. Growing medium formed of organic soil, peat and sand in equal parts. Repot in increasingly big containers when leaves completely cover pot.

Propagation In spring divide the tufts into 2 or 3 sections, each with leaves and roots, and pot them in growing mixture. The portions must be big, otherwise the plant will have difficulty in taking root.
Pests and diseases Red spider if surroundings too dry.

50 CARYOTA MITIS
Clustered fishtail palm

Family Palmae.
Origin India, Indonesia, Philippines.
Description This is a palm with compound, bipinnate leaves. Each leaf consists of a stalk with a secondary axil to which are attached leaflets or pinnules, deeply divided and wedge-shaped, with fringed borders. The leaves grow very long and wide from a short stem, forming a corona around the plant. The plant grows slowly (a few centimeters a year) and indoors can reach a height of 2.5 m (8 ft).

Care It likes sunlight – preferably slightly diffused. Needs warm surroundings with a temperature not lower than 13°C (55°F). At temperatures above 21°C (70°F) it is best to place pot in bowl of damp gravel. Water plentifully, allowing no water to collect. There is no resting period so growth should be slowed down in autumn-winter by reducing amount of water. Feed once a month from March to September with liquid fertilizer. Grow in mixture of organic soil, peat and sand in equal quantities, with a good drainage layer. It is advisable to use small pots in which the roots can be fitted quite compactly. Repot only every 2–3 years.

Propagation From seed. The palm may also grow lateral suckers which, if detached with their roots when 30 cm (12 in) long, can be planted in pots of moist soil.
Pests and diseases If grown in surroundings where air is too dry, the leaf tips may shrivel and the plant be attacked by red spider.

51 CATHARANTHUS ROSEUS
Madagascar periwinkle

Family Apocynaceae.
Origin Malagasy Republic (Madagascar).
Description Small shrub grown for its ornamental flowers. Shiny green leaves with white line along central vein, in opposite pairs. The tube-shaped flowers, 3 cm (about 1 in) wide, are pale pink and open star-like singly or in clusters at the tip of the stems. Flowering period April–September.
Varieties In addition to the species there are two varieties: C. roseus 'Albus,' white flowers; 'Ocellatus,' red-centered white flowers.
Care Perennial plant but often thrown out in autumn after flowering because as it ages it loses its decorative quality. Needs plenty of light and several hours of direct but not too strong sunlight daily in order to flower at its best. Can be kept indoors or outdoors in summer. Minimum winter temperature 10°C (50°F). Water plentifully but do not let water collect in pot. Feed fortnightly for entire flowering season with liquid fertilizer. Growing medium consists of 1 part organic soil, 1 part peat and 1 part sand. Do not overdo repotting; large plants only should be transplanted into bigger pots in spring. Average diameter of pot 10 cm (4 in).
Propagation From seed at start of spring; place containers (in greenhouse or plastic bag) at 20–24°C (68–75°F) in indirect light. If dry uncover the plant and water moderately. At 3 cm (about 1 in), repot and treat like adult plants.
Pests and diseases Because it is kept indoors for a short period and then discarded, it is not attacked by parasites.

52 CATTLEYA HYBRIDS

Family Orchidaceae.
Origin Horticultural hybrids of tropical American and West Indian species.
Description Epiphytic orchid with cylindrical or club-shaped pseudobulbs, 25–30 cm (10–12 in) long. The pseudobulbs develop from a rhizome and when immature are covered with green leaves: the lower leaves turn papery and enfold the mature pseudobulb, while the 1–3 upper leaves grow into proper strap-shaped leaves, 20–25 cm (8–10 in) long. The flowers, single or in groups, are borne by a terminal stalk. Waxy-looking, they are pink, purple and lilac, often streaked. Each flower is 10–18 cm (4–7 in) across. Flowers normally in winter.
Varieties C. 'Johnsoniana,' yellow flowers; 'Alba' is white; 'Dioniae' is pink.
Care Set in bright but filtered light at a temperature above 15°C (59°F). Does well at 18–24°C (64–75°F) but cannot tolerate fluctuations or dry air. Set pots on layers of wet gravel and spray every day if above 21°C (70°F). Water plentifully while growing but let the soil dry out completely before repeating. After flowering, plant has 6 weeks dormant period; water only to prevent pseudobulbs drying out. Apply a liquid preparation for orchids every 2–3 weeks during growth. Potting medium formed of 2 parts osmunda fiber and 1 part sphagnum moss. Repot after flowering.
Propagation Cut the rhizome into halves and repot separately in fresh mixture. Keep in medium light for several weeks.
Pests and diseases Sometimes scale insects and mealy bug.

53 CEROPEGIA WOODII
Rosary vine, String-of-hearts

Family Asclepiadaceae.
Origin South Africa.
Description Herbaceous plant with long, trailing stems which may grow to more than 2 m (6 ft). These stems develop from a large, gray, woody tuber lying at the soil surface and bear, at intervals of about 7 cm (3 in), pairs of fleshy, heart-shaped leaves; these are dark green, the upper side patterned silvery-white, 2–3 cm (about 1 in) long. Pink and purple tube-shaped flowers grow at the axils during August–September.
Care The species is cultivated in hanging baskets or can be made to climb on supports. It requires bright light and even direct sun if this is not too intense. It grows well throughout the year at room temperature of 18–22°C (64–71°F). Water moderately, not wetting the soil too much and allowing about two-thirds of it to dry out before watering again. Give liquid fertilizer once a month from spring to autumn. The very porous potting mixture should be made up of 1 part organic soil, 1 part peat and 2 parts sand. Drain the bottom of the pot thoroughly. Repot small plants only in spring and set several specimens in each container 4–5 cm (about 2 in) apart from one another.
Propagation In spring or summer detach the tubers forming on stems and group them at the surface of a pot filled with a thin layer of sand. Set in filtered light and water sparingly. Rooting occurs in about 8 weeks.
Pests and diseases Subject to rot if overwatered.

---

54 CHAMAEDOREA ELEGANS
Parlor palm

Family Palmae.
Origin Mexico, Guatemala.
Description Small, slow-growing palm which may reach a height indoors of 1.20–1.50 m (4–5 ft). Upright stem, parallel-veined green leaves, arranged in slightly irregular pairs on stalk. Each leaflet is about 15 cm (6 in) long and 2 cm (1 in) wide, with a tapering tip. In autumn adult plants may produce branched stems of small yellow flowers, and later fruits, from leaf axils.
Varieties *C. elegans* 'Bella' is a smaller, slower-growing variety of the original species.
Care Easy to grow indoors. Needs bright but not direct light. Does well at room temperature, 18–23°C (64–73°F), but can also stand lower temperatures, down to 13°C (55°F). In summer it can be put outdoors in the shade. Tolerates dry but prefers moist surroundings, so spray foliage frequently and place pot in container of damp gravel. Water plentifully in growing season. During winter dormancy allow surface of soil to dry out between waterings. Feed once a month in growing period with liquid fertilizer. Growing medium: 1 part organic soil, 2 parts peat and 1 part coarse sand. Repot, when roots fill the pot, in increasingly large containers, up to 25–30 cm (10–12 in) diameter. As roots are fragile, handle them carefully.
Propagation From seed, in greenhouse.
Pests and diseases Fairly resistant to parasites. If grown in too dry surroundings, subject to marking of leaf tips, scale insects and red spider.

55   CHAMAEROPS HUMILIS
European fan palm

Family   Palmae.
Origin   Mediterranean region.
Description   Dwarf shrub species which in wild grows from 10 cm (4 in) to 1 m (3 ft), and which in cultivated form may reach more than 2 m (6 ft). The stems are often branched at the base and, as with all palms, bear scars of old fallen leaves. The leaves, straight, stiff and arranged fan-like (palmate), form apical tufts. The stalks are woody and thorny. Each frond, dark gray-green, may measure 60 cm (2 ft) across. Indoors it produces neither flowers nor fruits.

Varieties   *C. humilis* 'Dactylocarpa,' which may grow to 6 m (20 ft); 'Argentea', with silver-gray leaves; 'Elegans,' less bushy; *C. h. robusta*, with bigger leaves.
Care   Does well in direct sunlight. Grows at normal room temperatures, is better outside in summer. Minimum 10°C (50°F) in winter. During dormant period the plant prefers temperatures of 13–16°C (55–61°F). In spring-summer water plentifully and feed every fortnight with liquid fertilizer. When resting, allow soil surface to dry out between waterings. Growing medium consists of organic soil, peat and sand in equal parts. Repot every other year in spring in increasingly big pots, up to 30 cm (12 in); afterwards add fresh soil every year.

Propagation   From seed or basal shoots. In spring remove shoot with its roots and repot in moist growing soil. Keep at room temperature, watering little.
Pests and diseases   Mealy bugs, scale insects, red spider.

---

56   CHLOROPHYTUM COMOSUM 'Vittatum'
Spider plant

Family   Liliaceae.
Origin   South Africa.
Description   Herbaceous plant with tuberous roots. Popular for its graceful lanceolate leaves, light green with a broad creamy-white line down the middle. The curving leaves are 15–30 cm (6–12 in) long. Thin yellow stalks, up to 60 cm (2 ft) long, sprout from the foliage, bearing small white flowers. After flowering, small plants, single or in groups, develop at the tips of the stalks and quickly form roots.

Varieties   *C. comosum* 'Vittatum' is the commonest variety. Cultivars are: 'Variegatum,' with white-bordered green leaves; 'Picturatum,' with a yellow stripe through the leaf; 'Mandaianum,' with shorter leaves, also with a yellow stripe.
Care   Easy to cultivate indoors and good for growing in hanging baskets. The plant adapts to a wide range of conditions. Water sparingly in winter, letting the soil surface dry out between successive applications; water abundantly in spring and summer. Place the plant in bright positions; give a few hours of direct sunlight daily, especially in winter, but protect from very strong sun in summer. The plant does not have a true rest period but its growth slows down in winter. Minimum temperature 8°C (46°F). Feed adult plants every 3 weeks throughout year and grow in equal parts of loam, peat and sand. Repot any time of year.

Propagation   Remove offset plants when leaves are 7–8 cm (about 3 in) and they have roots. Root in water. Then transplant into pots with growing medium.
Pests and diseases   May be attacked by scale insects.

57 CHRYSALIDOCARPUS LUTESCENS
Areca palm, butterfly palm

Family Palmae.
Origin Malagasy Republic (Madagascar).
Description The plant consists of numerous, closely packed, slender stems with highly decorative pinnate fronds borne on long, grooved, yellow or orange stalks. The fronds, frequently growing to a length of more than 1 m (3 ft), are curved and formed of stiff yellow-green leaflets, 60 cm (2 ft) long and 1.5 cm (about ½ in) across. These leaflets or pinnules are arranged in almost opposite pairs. The plant grows slowly.
Care This palm needs exposure to bright light but not to direct sun. It grows regularly, although not more than 15–20 cm (6–8 in) a year, at medium temperatures of 18–22°C (64–71°F) all the year round. It can even stand cooler temperatures but below 13°C (55°F) growth stops. Water abundantly but without flooding. Under 13°C (55°F) merely make sure mixture does not dry out. Give liquid fertilizer fortnightly from March to September. Medium formed of organic soil, peat and sand in equal parts. Repot every other year until in container of required size.
Propagation Easily propagated from seed in April at 18–20°C (64–68°F) but plant growth is extremely slow. A quicker method is, when repotting in spring, to detach basal shoots with some roots and plant them individually in a mixture formed of 1 part organic soil, 1 part peat and 2 parts sand. Wrap in plastic bag and set in medium light.
Pests and diseases Scale insects, mealy bug.

58 CHRYSANTHEMUM FRUTESCENS
White marguerite, Paris daisy

Family Compositae.
Origin Canary Islands.
Description Perennial suffruticose plant with many branches. The stems are woody but soft and the light green leaves are alternate and deeply divided. The numerous flower heads which appear from spring until October are 3–4 cm (1–2 in) in width, with white strap-shaped ray flowers and yellow trumpet-shaped disk flowers. In the wild the plant grows to a height of about 1 m (3 ft) but the pot plant is better with its tips pinched out to confine its size to a maximum of 40 cm (20 in). The plant is generally cultivated as an annual and thrown out after flowering.
Varieties *C. frutescens* 'Etoile d'Or,' with lemon-yellow petals; 'Mary Wooten', with pink petals.
Care Plants can be bought in flower or with partly open buds (if too tightly closed they may not open indoors) and kept in a bright position or in direct sunlight for at least 3–4 hours daily. The best time to buy them is in early spring so that they can flower through the summer. Flowering lasts longer in cool conditions; in any event, the plant should be watered copiously and the pot placed in a holder containing wet gravel. If grown as an annual there is no need to feed it or to repot it as it is thrown away after flowering. The potting medium should be 4 parts organic soil, 2 parts peat and 1 part sand.
Propagation From cuttings or by division, but needs special techniques.
Pests and diseases Prone to animal and plant parasites.

59 CHRYSANTHEMUM MORIFOLIUM
Chrysanthemum

Family Compositae.
Origin China, Japan.
Description They are perennial plants with dark green lobate leaves. Pot plants are 30–40 cm (12–16 in) tall. Flowers are usually double and ball-shaped, very large, up to 10–15 cm (4–5 in), the ligulate (strap-shaped) florets often partly curving inwards to cover the tubulate (tube-shaped) florets. Some varieties have single flower heads. The color of the flowers may be white, yellow, orange, pink or purple.
Varieties 'Claret Glow,' red flowers (August); 'Pinksmoor,' deep pink, double (September); 'Gold plate,' yellow (October); 'Preference,' red (November); 'Marion Stacey' (November), 'Mason's Bronze,' orange-bronze (November).
Care The plant is perennial but is used indoors as an annual, being thrown away after flowering, since the forcing methods to obtain flowers are complicated and best done by experts. As a rule young plants are bought in bud and placed in bright positions, protected from strong sunlight in summer. In winter, however, several hours of daily sunshine help them to grow. To prolong flowering it is best to keep the plants in cool surroundings, at 13–18°C (55–64°F) and to put the pots in bowls of wet gravel. Watering should be very frequent to keep the soil always damp. There is no need to feed. After flowering, in areas where the winters are mild, hybrid chrysanthemums can be planted outdoors and will flower every autumn provided they are not exposed to frost.
Pests and diseases Prone to animal and plant parasites.

60 CISSUS ANTARCTICA
Kangaroo vine, grape ivy

Family Vitaceae.
Origin Australia.
Description This is a climbing, fast-growing plant – up to 60 cm (2 ft) a year – with tendrils for gripping any kind of support, reaching an indoor height of 2–3 m (6–10 ft). The dark green, shiny, ovate leaves have a pointed tip and dentate edges, and measure up to 10 cm (4 in) long. The stalks are red. The flowers, in auxillary clusters, are insignificant. Because the species is not in itself particularly decorative, it is best used in arrangements or as background for other plants.
Varieties *C. antarctica* 'Minima,' bushy and low-growing, is suitable for growing in hanging baskets.
Care Easy to cultivate indoors. Adapts to smoky surroundings and to poor lighting, but prefers bright, indirect illumination. During the short winter rest period it should be kept at around 13°C (55°F). Likes warmth while growing, when it should be watered with moderation. Let the soil surface dry out between waterings. In winter simply avoid letting the soil become dry. Feed every fortnight from April to September. Potting medium is of loam, peat and sand in equal quantities. Repot every spring. To encourage spreading, prune the main stems and branches in March.
Propagation Take 10 cm (4 in) cuttings in June and plant them in mixture of peat and sand, keeping it at 18°C (64°F) in a plastic bag, in bright indirect light. After 6 weeks transplant into final growing medium.
Pests and diseases Subject to red spider.

61 X CITROFORTUNELLA MITIS
Calamondin

Family Rutaceae.
Origin Philippines.
Description Many species of the parent genus *Citrus* (orange, lemon, etc.) can be grown indoors for their decorative glossy leaves and colored fruits. *X Citrofortunella mitis*, a species of a hybrid genus, is the one most often cultivated as a house plant because it is small, not growing to more than 1.50 m (5 ft), and because it produces fruit even when young. It is a miniature tree with dense, short branches bearing bright green, lanceolate, evergreen leaves, 5–10 cm (2–4 in) long. The white flowers, in groups of 3–4, may bloom throughout the year. The fruits, in large numbers, likewise appear all the year round, and sometimes the plant bears flowers and fruits simultaneously. The fruits are orange-yellow, with an acid pulp.
Care Requires plenty of light; in summer can be placed outside in sunny spot, and in winter can go in greenhouse or indoors at 5–10°C (41–50°F). If kept at temperature higher than 10°C (50°F) it will also grow in winter. Water sparingly indoors, but keep the surroundings moist by placing pot in holder filled with damp gravel, and spray the plant. Feed with liquid fertilizer fortnightly in spring–summer. Growing medium formed of loam, peat and sand in equal parts. Repot annually. Prune in spring or pinch out growing tips at virtually any time so as to encourage bushy habit.
Propagation From seed, more difficult from cuttings.
Pests and diseases Mealy bug, red spider (indication that air is too dry).

---

62 CITRUS LIMON 'Meyer'
Meyer's lemon

Family Rutaceae.
Origin India, Southeast Asia.
Description *C. limon* 'Meyer' is a dwarf variety considered to be a hybrid between the lemon and sweet orange, suitable for growing as a house plant. It is a small evergreen tree, up to 1.20 m (4 ft) tall, with glossy, bright green, ovate leaves, up to 10 cm (4 in) long, arranged alternately on thorny branches. The white, scented flowers have 5 petals. The fruit is a small yellow lemon. Flowers and fruits may appear at any time of year and it is not uncommon to find them growing simultaneously on the plants.
Care Requires a lot of light and direct sun. It can be placed outside in the sun during summer, and indoors in winter at room temperature of 18–22°C (64–71°F). It is advisable to give the plant a brief winter rest period at 13–16°C (55–61°F). Water the plants regularly but not copiously; keep the surroundings moist by placing pots on layers of wet gravel and spraying the leaves every now and then. Give liquid fertilizer fortnightly in spring–summer. Highly organic mixture formed of 2 parts leafmold, 1 part peat and 1 part sand. Repot every spring in containers of up to 30 cm (12 in) diameter.
Propagation From seed and subsequently by grafting, or by taking 15–20 cm (6–8 in) cuttings in spring and planting them in mixture of peat and sand. Wrap the pot in plastic bag and put in medium filtered light. Rooting will occur in 2 months.
Pests and diseases Mealy bug, red spider if air is too dry.

63 CLERODENDUM THOMSONAE
Glory bower, bleeding-heart vine

Family Verbenaceae.

Origin West Africa.

Description Climbing evergreen shrub notable for the shape of its flowers. These appear from May to September in loose axillary clusters of a white calyx in the form of a closed bell, from the tip of which emerges a star-like, bright red corolla. The rough, ovate leaves, up to 13 cm (5 in) long and 5 cm, (2 in) wide, are dark green with lighter veining.

Varieties *C. thomsonae* 'Variegatum,' leaves blotched in various shades of green; *C. thomsonae* 'Delectum,' very large violet flowers.

Care For flowering, the plant requires filtered light and in summer can go outdoors in a bright but shaded position. During growth keep the soil wet, place the pot in a holder with moist gravel and spray the foliage daily. Feed fortnightly in growing season. Potting medium of: 1 part loam, 1 part peat and 1 part sand. The plants flower best in small containers. Provide supporting stakes in the pot to help the plant climb. To restrict the height to 1.50 m (5 ft), prune branches of previous year to about half their length in March–April.

Propagation Take 10 cm (4 in) cuttings from April to June. Dip them in root hormone preparation and plant in moist medium of peat and sand. Place pot in plastic bag in indirect light. After 4–6 weeks remove the bag and after about 4 months transplant into proper growing soil.

Pests and diseases Red spider if air dry.

64 CLEYERA JAPONICA 'Tricolor'

Family Theaceae.

Origin China, Japan, Ryukyu Islands.

Description Shrub that grows to an average height of 80 cm (32 in). Elliptic, alternate leaves, 5–10 cm (2–4 in) long, light and dark green with creamy-white borders. The young leaves often have pink edges. The species plant *C. japonica*, with green leaves, sometimes produces small, perfumed white flowers; the variety 'Tricolor' does not normally flower.

Care Likes bright light. Can spend the summer outdoors, in semi-shade. Kept indoors in winter, it needs bright and not overheated surroundings, since it has to spend the resting period at 10–13°C (50–55°F). Water moderately in spring and summer, keeping the soil wet and allowing the surface to dry out between applications. A fortnightly feed is advisable during the same period. While dormant in winter, one-third of the soil should dry out from one watering to the next. If the plant is kept in a warm room, sprinkle the foliage and place the pot in damp gravel. Potting medium is made up of 1 part loam, 1 part peat and 1 part sand. Repot young plants every spring, provide fresh soil for adult plants.

Propagation Take 10 cm (4 in) cuttings in March, dipping them in root hormone preparation, and plant them in equal parts of damp peat and sand. Place in bright, indirect light. Transplant after rooting.

Pests and diseases Subject to red spider if surroundings too dry.

65 CLIVIA MINIATA
Kafir lily

Family Amaryllidaceae.
Origin South Africa.
Description Plant with shiny strap-shaped leaves, up to 60 cm (2 ft) long, curving outwards in a fan, dark green in color. The large flower stalks, up to about 50 cm (20 in) long, grow in March and bear umbels of 10–20 funnel-shaped, orange flowers. These continue blooming until August. The thick, sturdy roots often protrude from the surface of the soil.

Care Needs plenty of light for flowering, including direct sun, provided it is not too strong. Requires a 2-month winter rest at 10°C (50°F). While growing, it does well at room temperature indoors or, in summer, outdoors, but intense heat will shorten the flowering period. Water thoroughly in spring-summer, gradually reducing applications in autumn, and almost suspending them during dormancy. Resume again when flowering commences. Feed every fortnight from March to September. Repot after flowering only every 2–3 years, when roots have filled pot, using a mixture of loam, peat and sand in equal proportions. Cut off flower stalks when they start to wither.

Propagation By dividing the rhizomes of tightly clumped plants or by detaching a lateral shoot with at least 3 leaves in August–September. Plant in mixture of equal parts peat and sand, and place in brightly lit, shaded spot. After rooting, transplant into definitive growing medium.
Pests and diseases Very prone to attack by mealy bug.

---

66 CODIAEUM VARIEGATUM var. PICTUM
Croton

Family Euphorbiaceae.
Origin Southern India to Indonesia.
Description Cultivated for its decorative foliage. It has given rise to a very large number of horticultural varieties with foliage that is extremely variable in form, color and size. The leaves, however, are always smooth, solid and adorned with bright, variegated colors.

Varieties 'Aucubifolium,' elliptical green leaves streaked with yellow; 'Gloriosum superbum,' broad, oval leaves, green with bright yellow veining; 'Fascination,' lanceolate leaves with yellow-orange markings; 'Craigii,' leaves are trilobate with yellow veining.
Care Bright light (but shielded from the sun when it is very hot), failing which the foliage will not take on bright colors. Can be kept at room temperature indoors, and even in winter dormancy the temperature should not drop below 13°C (55°F). To raise the humidity place the pot in a bowl with wet gravel. Spray the foliage and clean it frequently. Water abundantly in spring–summer, but very little while plant is resting. Feed regularly each fortnight from spring to autumn. Very moist potting medium should consist of 3 parts coarse peat, 3 parts leafmold and 2 parts sand. Repot every spring until container is 20 cm (8 in) in diameter.

Propagation From cuttings of tips of side shoots in March–April. Plant each cutting in peat and sand mixture, enclose in plastic bag, or keep in greenhouse at 25°C (77°F). When rooted, uncover it. Transplant after 5–6 months.
Pests and diseases Red spider.

67 COCOS NUCIFERA
Coconut palm

Family Palmae.

Origin Melanesia.

Description In the wild this is a palm up to 30 m (100 ft) high which produces edible, woody, brown fruits, of fibrous appearance, each 20–30 cm (8–12 in) long. It bears large pinnate fronds. When grown indoors, the size is smaller, at most 2–3 m (6–10 ft).

Varieties C. nucifera 'Dwarf Golden Malay' and 'Dwarf Green' are dwarf varieties which produce smaller nuts, colored red, yellow or green, cultivated in tropical zones as fruit trees. C. nucifera 'Nino' is a highly decorative variety of compact habit with elegant pinnate fronds composed of shiny green leaflets.

Care When cultivated indoors it needs a very bright position but not in direct sun. Does well at temperatures of 18–24°C (64–75°F) all year round but cannot stand anything lower than 15°C (59°F). Water regularly, allowing surface of soil to dry out before repeating; if temperature drops to 15°C (59°F) reduce amount of water, making sure mixture does not dry out completely. If the air is too dry place pots in holders filled with moist gravel and peat. Put plants outdoors in semi-shaded position during summer. Give liquid fertilizer once a month from spring to autumn. Growing medium should consist of organic soil, peat and sand in equal proportions. Repot in spring every 2–3 years when the thickened base of the plant emerges above the surface of the soil, but increase the dimensions of the pot gradually because the plant grows better in fairly small containers.

Propagation From seed in February–March at temperature of 20–22°C (68–71°F). The seedlings should be pricked out and, after a year, transplanted into individual pots. Growth, however, is very slow.

Pests and diseases Scale insects and red spider if the surroundings are too dry.

68 COFFEA ARABICA
Arabian coffee

Family Rubiaceae.
Origin Ethiopia.
Description The coffee plant is extremely suitable for growing indoors. In the wild this shrub reaches a height of 5 m (16 ft), but as a pot plant it grows to 1–2 m (3–6 ft). The young plant has a single stem but as it ages it becomes thick and bushy. The dark green, ovate elliptic and pointed, opposite leaves are up to 15 cm (6 in) long and 5 cm (2 in) wide. Adult plants (4–5 years) produce star-shaped white flowers, delicately scented, from August to October. Fruits follow and are initially green, then red and finally brown.
Varieties There is one, *C. arabica* 'Nana,' a dwarf form.
Care Grows well in average light and room temperatures, 18–22°C (64–71°F). During the brief winter rest period, should the temperatures fall below 13°C (55°F), the plant is likely to lose its leaves. It needs a very moist atmosphere; if not, the tips of the leaves wither. Spray the foliage frequently and place the pot in a holder full of wet gravel. Water plentifully in spring and summer, avoiding standing water, and very little in dormant period. Feed fortnightly, except when plant is resting. Grow in equal parts of loam, peat and sand, and repot every spring, lining the bottom of the pot with a good drainage layer.
Propagation Very fresh seeds can be sown in spring and kept (in the greenhouse or in a plastic bag) at 24°C (75°F) in filtered light.
Pests and diseases Scale insects.

---

69 COLEUS HYBRIDUS
Coleus, Painted nettle

Family Labiatae.
Origin Cultivation.
Description The many hybrids in this complex have leaves of different colors and shapes (heart-shaped, ovate with a more or less sharp point, elongated or deeply divided), but all are soft and delicate. The plants produce insignificant blue flowers. They are perennial but are often grown as annuals indoors. They are easily propagated and in a single season may reach a height of 60 cm (2 ft).
Varieties Popular varieties are: 'Brilliancy,' purple leaves with small golden-yellow marks along edges; 'Candidum,' pale green leaves with central white spot; 'Pride of Autumn,' bronze leaves with large purple-red marking.
Care Needs plenty of light and even direct sunlight to keep its colors bright and its habit compact and bushy. Lives happily at average room temperatures but at more than 18°C (64°F) the air should be kept moist by spraying the plant and placing it in a bowl of wet gravel. It soon loses its leaves if the temperature drops below 13°C (55°F) and if it does not get enough water. In fact, the soil should always be kept damp. Feed fortnightly while growing. Growing medium consists of 1 part loam, 1 part peat and 1 part sand; repot up to 2–3 times a season as it grows very fast.
Propagation Tip cuttings, 5–8 cm (2–3 in) long, taken in autumn or at any time during growing season, root easily in water or soil if kept warm in indirect light.
Pests and diseases Red spider if surroundings are too dry.

70 COLUMNEA X BANKSII

Family Gesneriaceae.
Origin In cultivation from Central American parents.
Description The genus comprises a number of evergreen epiphytes, most of them with trailing stems C. x *banksii* is a horticultural hybrid with hanging stems 60–90 cm (2–3 ft) in length. The leaves are opposite, elliptical-lanceolate, slightly fleshy and covered with reddish hairs. The tube-like flowers, 6–8 cm (2–3 in) long, are red with a yellow throat, blooming from November to April, but flowering can continue throughout the year. The flowers are followed sometimes by white, violet-tinged berries.

Varieties 'Splendens' with bright red flowers.
Care Needs bright but indirect light. By varying the duration of light, the plant can then be induced to flower all the year round. It grows well at room temperatures but needs plenty of moisture, so it is necessary to spray it and keep it in a bowl of wet gravel. It does not usually become dormant and should therefore be watered moderately throughout the year, with tepid water, allowing the surface of the soil to dry out between the applications. Feed every fortnight with a fertilizer containing a high measure of phosphate. If plant becomes dormant, suspend feeding. Grow in hanging baskets, using sphagnum or peat and perlite in equal parts. Repotting should be done when the roots have filled the pot.
Propagation In spring–summer, from tip cuttings, 10 cm (4 in) long, which are planted in growing soil at room temperature and in filtered light. Water only a little.
Pests and diseases Subject to attacks by mites and aphids.

---

71 CORDYLINE AUSTRALIS
Grass palm, New Zealand cabbage tree

Family Liliaceae.
Origin Australia, New Zealand.
Description The genus contains various species of shrubs and small trees similar to those of the genus *Dracaena*, with which they are frequently confused. C. *australis* may grow in the wild to 8 m (26 ft), but as a pot plant seldom reaches more than 1 m (3 ft). It has lanceolate green leaves, 60–90 cm (2–3 ft) in length and 5 cm (2 in) in width; they are curved and form compact tufts at the tips of the branches. The lower leaves, as they age, fall and the stem remains bare. Adult plants (8–10 years) grown outdoors in warm climates, often produce large feathery clusters of scented flowers in the spring; indoor plants, however, normally do not flower.
Varieties C. *australis* 'Atropurpurea,' has purple-shaded leaves; 'Doucetii,' with white stripes.
Care The species requires full light, even sunlight, all the year round. Prefers to be in the open provided the winter temperature does not drop below 5°C (41°F). Lives indoors at room temperature. Water plentifully in summer; during winter dormancy simply make sure the soil does not dry out. Feed every 10–15 days from May to September. Growing medium consists of loam, peat and sand in equal amounts. Repot young plants every spring, then only every 2–3 years, or add fresh soil to the same pot.
Propagation Same technique as for *Cordyline terminalis*.
Pests and diseases May be attacked by scale insects.

72 CORDYLINE TERMINALIS
Ti plant, tree of kings

Family Liliaceae.
Origin Southeast Asia.
Description The plant has a short stem with leaves set alternately and very close to one another. The basal leaves fall off with age and the stem gradually gets longer. The leaves are lanceolate, up to 50 cm (20 in) long. The young foliage is crimson-pink and gradually takes on purple, creamy-white and green streaks.

Varieties 'Amabilis,' bronze leaves with pink and cream markings; 'Tricolor,' pale green leaves prominently streaked with red, purple and cream; 'Firebrand,' shiny purple leaves with bronze tints.
Care The species *C. terminalis* is more delicate than *C. australis*. It cannot tolerate direct sunlight or winter temperatures below 10–12°C (50–53°F). Grows normally indoors, same cultivation procedures as for *C. australis*.

Propagation In March–April the future basal or tip shoots are removed and potted in a moist mixture of peat and coarse sand in equal parts. Place at 18°C (64°F) in plastic bags in bright surroundings but not in the sun. When a shoot forms, uncover the pot and begin feeding once a month. After 5–6 months transplant into final growing medium. Cuttings can also be taken from portions of the old stems, 7–8 cm (3 in) long. The plants can be propagated from seeds in spring, keeping the trays at a temperature of 18°C (64°F) or in plastic bags. When the seedlings are 7–8 cm (3 in) high, plant out into growing soil.
Pests and diseases May be attacked by scale insects.

---

73 CRASSULA ARBORESCENS
Silver jade plant, silver dollar, happiness tree

Family Crassulaceae.
Origin South Africa.
Description Sturdy, fleshy, branching plant which does not normally grow, when potted, to more than 1 m (3 ft) high. The small, succulent leaves, 3–5 cm (1–2 in) wide, are obovate and arranged in opposite pairs. They are green with red margins. In spring the species bears numerous small star-shaped flowers, white with pink tinges, but when grown indoors it seldom blooms.

Varieties *C. argentea* 'Variegata' has yellow-streaked leaves and grows more slowly than the species.
Care Needs bright light and direct sun to grow really well. In winter it should be left to rest at temperatures of 7–13°C (44–55°F), but it can stand higher levels. In summer it can go outdoors in the sun. While growing, water moderately, letting much of the soil dry out between applications; when dormant simply make sure the soil does not dry out completely. Feed fortnightly in spring–summer. Must be grown in well-drained medium of 1 part organic soil, 1 part peat and 3 parts coarse sand. Repot every 2 years.

Propagation Very easily done from leaf cuttings, planting latter in above-mentioned mixture and keeping it in a warm, light place. Can also be propagated from stem cuttings.
Pests and diseases Gray mold may appear if drainage is insufficient.

74 CRASSULA FALCATA
Sickle plant, scarlet paintbrush

Family Crassulaceae.
Origin South Africa.
Description Because there is still some confusion over the botanical classification of this plant, *C. falcata* is also known as *Rochea falcata*. A shrub of up to 60 cm (2 ft) in height, with large fleshy stems and dense foliage, each blue-green leaf lanceolate and curving downwards at the tip. The leaves, set opposite, are rough on top and up to 20 cm (8 in) long. House plants often have only one stem. Racemes of many orange-red flowers bloom June to August.
Varieties Hybrid cultivar *C. falcata* x *deceptrix*, more compact than species, has abundant bright red flowers.
Care Needs light and direct sun to grow successfully and to flower. Cultivation requirements and techniques are the same as for *C. arborescens*.
Propagation Can be propagated in many ways. From leaf cuttings in spring–summer; the leaf is detached and the surface of the cut left to dry for 24 hours, after which it is planted in the soil and transplanted after rooting. From stem cuttings in May to July; sections 6–8 cm (2–3 in) long are taken, the surface of the cut left to dry for a few days, and the cutting put into the soil and kept in bright, indirect light. The soil should be slightly dampened. When the cutting is well rooted, after about 3 months, it can be handled like an adult plant. Same method used for propagation of basal shoots.
Pests and diseases If drainage is insufficient, gray mold may appear.

---

75 CROSSANDRA INFUNDIBULIFORMIS
Firecracker flower

Family Acanthaceae.
Origin India.
Description Evergreen shrub which may grow to a height of 50–60 cm (20–24 in). It has wavy, elliptical, shiny dark green leaves which narrow at the juncture to merge with the stalk. The plant produces tubular red flowers terminating in a flat 5-lobed disk. The flowers, in spikes of 2–3, are partially covered by triangular bracts and bloom in April. Flowering may continue throughout the summer.
Varieties *C. infundibuliformis* 'Mona Wallhed,' pink flowers and smaller than the species.
Care From May to September the plant needs to be kept in a brightly lit position, but not in direct sun; during winter dormancy, however, it needs a few hours of sunlight daily. Likes high temperatures; not below 14°C (57°F), average of 18–22°C (64–71°F). The plant requires plenty of moisture, spray the foliage and place pot in a holder of wet gravel. In winter water little and give no food. Water moderately during growing season, letting the top part of the soil dry out between waterings, and feed every fortnight. Grow in equal parts of loam, peat and sand, and repot every spring in pots of up to 16 cm (6 in) diameter.
Propagation From March to June plant semi-woody tip cuttings, 5–8 cm (2–3 in) long, in mixture of peat and sand in equal parts. Keep at 21°C (70°F), in greenhouse or plastic bag, in indirect light. Transplant after 6 weeks.
Pests and diseases Red spider in dry surroundings.

CRYPTANTHUS ACAULIS
Earth star

Family Bromeliaceae.
Origin Brazil.
Description In its native tropical forest environment it grows on tree stumps and in rock clefts, 7–8 cm (3 in) tall and 10–15 cm (4–5 in) across. The leaves are lanceolate, with a pointed or rounded tip and spiny margins; they form rosettes and come in various colors, usually green or with clear longitudinal and transverse stripes, or tinted different colors according to variety. The insignificant whitish flowers may bloom at any time of year but are generally hidden among the foliage.
Varieties C. acaulis 'Argenteus,' leaves covered on both sides with silvery scales; 'Ruber,' pale green, purple-tinted leaves.
Care Easy plant to cultivate, highly suitable for terrariums or can be grown on tree stumps as epiphytes because it needs very little soil. The few roots serve mainly to anchor the plant. It likes bright, even direct, light and high temperatures. Indoors, place the plant in moist gravel to keep atmosphere humid, but water the soil sparingly, letting the top part dry out between waterings. Does not usually rest in winter but it is advisable to feed it only every 3–4 weeks during spring and summer, spraying the foliage with a fertilizer diluted with lime-free water. Grow in peat only, or in a mixture of leafmold and peat. Use small pots, up to 10–15 cm (4–5 in) and repot seldom, only for propagation.
Propagation Detach lateral shoots in April and pot them in wet mixture of peat and sand. Wrap the pot in a plastic bag and place in bright but diffused light. After about 3 months repot in definitive medium.
Pests and diseases Fairly resistant to parasites.

77 CTENANTHE OPPENHEIMIANA 'Tricolor'
Never-never plant

Family Marantaceae.
Origin Brazil.
Description Genus very similar to the genera *Calathea* and *Maranta*, with which it is often confused. As a rule plants of *C. oppenheimiana* have narrower and denser leaves than those of the two other genera. *C. oppenheimiana* 'Tricolor' has elliptical leaves with a pointed tip, up to 30 cm (12 in) long and 10 cm (4 in) wide, on long stalks. The leaves are dark green with large creamy-yellow splotches on the upper side and red markings beneath.
Varieties Only 'Tricolor' is cultivated.
Care Grows well in bright but filtered light and at room temperatures. Minimum temperature 13°C (54°F). Place the pot in a bowl of wet gravel. Water moderately even during growing season; in winter, when the plant is dormant, simply keep the soil from drying out. Feed every fortnight in spring–summer. Growing medium made up of 1 part organic soil, 1 part peat, 1 part sand and 3 parts leafmold. Repot every spring.
Propagation From stem cuttings in spring. Take cuttings with 3–4 leaves, making the cut just below the node, treat the base with a rooting preparation, and pot in mixture of peat and sand in equal parts. Put in greenhouse at temperature of 21°C (70°F) or enclose the pot in a plastic bag and place in bright, screened light in warm surroundings. After rooting (4–6 weeks), transplant into growing medium or remove basal shoots and pot them in same soil.
Pests and diseases Mealy bug, scale insects, red spider.

78 CUPHEA IGNEA OR C. PLATYCENTRA
Cigar plant

Family Lythraceae.
Origin Mexico.
Description Small shrub with oval, lanceolate leaves, pointed at tip, 5 cm (2 in) long and 1.5 cm (½ in) wide. The leathery leaves may have red margins if the plant is well exposed to light. The single, axillary flowers are characteristically cigar-shaped, and are formed of the calyx alone, 2.5 cm (1 in) long, without petals. Color is bright red with a black border and a white and purple throat. Flowering lasts from April to October.
Varieties The variety 'Variegata' has leaves streaked with yellow.
Care Needs a great deal of light and can even stand strong, direct sunshine. Grows successfully in warm indoor surroundings or outside; during winter dormancy it should be kept in cool position if outdoors. Water moderately when growing. When plant is resting, simply ensure that the soil does not dry out. Feed with liquid fertilizer fortnightly in spring–summer. Grow in equal quantities of loam, peat and sand, repotting every spring. The plant becomes less decorative as it ages, and therefore it should not be kept for more than 2 years.
Propagation In September take tip cuttings, 5–7 cm (2–3 in) long, and plant them in damp mixture of peat and coarse sand in equal parts. Enclose in plastic bag and place in bright, screened light. After rooting, repot in growing medium and treat like adult plants.
Pests and diseases Resists parasites fairly well.

79 CYCAS REVOLUTA
Sago palm

Family Cycadaceae.
Origin Eastern and southeastern Asia.
Description The family Cycadaceae comprises plants resembling palms. They have an upright stem with a tuft of feathery evergreen leaves at the tip. *C. revoluta*, cultivated as a house plant, has a pineapple-shaped stem which only just projects from the surface and bears erect, outward-curving leaves in a rosette, up to 1 m (3 ft) in length. Each leaf is stiff and formed of narrow, needle-like leaflets, 7–15 cm (3–6 in) long, embedded in a central vein 1 cm (½ in) across. The stalk is spiny. The plant is dioecious and very slow-growing (1 leaf a year).
Varieties *C. revoluta* 'Mako,' with a twisted stem and outward-curving leaves about 50 cm (18 in) long.
Care It does well either in direct sun or in strong, filtered light. It is fairly resistant to cold, provided this is not prolonged. Indoors it should be kept at room temperatures all year round since it does not have a rest period. It is easy to cultivate as a house plant because it needs neither specially moist conditions nor particular attention. Water moderately all year round, wetting the mixture well but letting it dry out between waterings. A liquid fertilizer should be given monthly from March to September. Growing medium consists of organic soil, peat and sand in equal amounts. Repot every 2–3 years.
Propagation In spring from seed or by potting basal shoots in growing medium. Lengthy and difficult procedures.
Pests and diseases Red spider, scale insects.

---

80 CYCLAMEN PERSICUM
Cyclamen

Family Primulaceae.
Origin Eastern Mediterranean.
Description It has an underground tuber from which the small leaves and flower stalks stem directly. The leaves are round or ovate, green with silvery markings. The flowers, on stems 20 cm (8 in) long, are large and of various colors: white, pink, salmon or dark red, according to variety.
Varieties There are a large number of cultivars.
Care Difficult to get to flower indoors over a period of years, so is usually discarded after first flowering. Needs well-lighted surroundings (even direct sun in winter) and likes to be kept cool, at 13–18°C (55–64°F). Above 18°C (64°F) the flowers will last a shorter time unless there is a supplement of high humidity. Watering can be done by immersing the pot for 10 minutes in a bowl of water without letting the water come over the top, then letting it dry off. Avoid getting the tubers wet, as these easily rot. Give liquid fertilizer fortnightly during flowering and growth. When cultivated for several years, place out in the open in June, in a shady spot, reducing and eventually suspending watering. Place the pot with tubers in a cool position until October. During this period change the soil (loam, peat and sand in equal amounts) completely, and repot in same container. Then keep the plant cool and in good light until the leaves sprout. When buds appear, bring indoors.
Propagation From seed, but not possible indoors.
Pests and diseases Gray mold, mildew, fusarium wilt, root rot, etc.

81 CYMBIDIUM HYBRIDS

Family Orchidaceae.
Origin Southeast Asia.
Description The *Cymbidium* plants cultivated indoors are horticultural hybrids of epiphytic species. Most suitable as house plants are the dwarf hybrids with up to 30 flowers per plant every year, each with a diameter of 6–8 cm (2–3 in). There are very many varieties with flowers that are erect or drooping, scented, and red, pink, yellow, white or green. They bloom from February to June and last several weeks. The leaves are leathery and strap-shaped.
Varieties Hybrid cultivars have largely replaced the original species. 'Balkis,' white flowers; 'Baltic,' green flowers; 'Cariga,' yellow flowers; 'Prince Charles,' pink flowers; 'Rosanna Pinkie,' pink flowers.
Care These are some of the easiest orchids to cultivate indoors. They do well in bright, screened light and at room temperature. In winter give a short rest period at 15°C (59°F). The soil should be watered with moderation, being left to dry between applications. If temperature exceeds 18°C (64°F) place pots in bowls with wet gravel and spray leaves. Liquid fertilize fortnightly during growth. Potting mixture should be 1 part organic soil, 2 parts osmunda fiber and 1 part sphagnum moss; plus a pinch of bonemeal and charcoal. Repot in alternate years after flowering.
Propagation After flowering uproot the rhizome, clean it in running water and cut it into pieces, each with two pseudobulbs and some roots. Pot in orchid mixture and for about a month water the plant very little and spray daily.
Pests and diseases Scale insects and mealy bug.

82 CYPERUS PAPYRUS

Papyrus plant, Egyptian paper plant

Family Cyperaceae.
Origin Mediterranean region.
Description A plant known in ancient times when it was used for making paper. It grows to 2–3 m (6–10 ft), and thus needs plenty of space. Each of the smooth stems, up to 2–3 cm (1 in) thick, terminates in a dense, pendulous, thread-like inflorescense, about 20 cm (8 in) long, surrounded by a few bracts and bearing small flowers. The variety *C. papyrus* 'Nanus' grows to a height of 60 cm (2 ft).
Care In the wild the plant grows in swamps and along river banks. It is a difficult species to raise indoors as it needs plenty of moisture and cannot stand winter temperatures below 15–18°C (59–64°F). If cultivated indoors, it must be kept in very well-lighted positions in pots of about 20 cm (8 in), filled with a mixture of organic soil, peat and sand in equal quantities, the pot being placed in a shallow bowl of water. The potting medium and the roots must, in fact, always be kept moist, otherwise the tips of the bracts turn brown. When growing conditions are right, the plant develops large clusters of long stalks; if there is insufficient light, however, no new stems will grow. Feed liquid fertilizer every 4 weeks. Repot in spring when vegetation resumes.
Propagation Easily done in spring by division of clumps. Uproot the plant and break it into sections, cutting the root mass from top to bottom and then separating with the fingers. Each portion is separately planted in the growing medium.
Pests and diseases Reasonably resistant to parasites.

83 CYRTOMIUM FALCATUM
Japanese holly fern

Family Aspidiaceae.
Origin China, Japan.
Description A species of fern, it is composed of a rhizome just beneath the soil surface and covered with a silvery crust. From the rhizome come the stalks, 10–15 cm (4–5 in) long, which bear dark green, stiff fronds, up to 60 m (2 ft) in length; these are formed of pairs of pinnate leaflets slightly resembling those of holly. They are, in fact, thick, oval in shape with a sharp tip and dentate edges, about 10 cm (4 in) long. The spore-cases develop on the lower surface of the adult leaves.
Varieties C. faleatum 'Rochfordianum,' robust, the fronds broader and fuller, up to 30 cm (12 in) long.
Care Prefers living in bright, screened light, but can also be kept in dimmer conditions provided it is put in bright light every 2–3 days. Does well at room temperatures, but if above 21°C (70°F) the pot should be placed in a holder of wet gravel. Minimum winter temperature 10°C (50°F). When kept indoors it does not rest in winter. Water moderately, therefore, all year, allowing the soil surface to dry out between successive waterings and feeding every 15–20 days with a standard liquid fertilizer. Medium formed of 1 part loam, 1 part sand and 3 parts leafmold. Repot in spring.
Propagation In spring divide the rhizomes, each cut section having 3–4 leaves and a few roots. Cover the rhizome lightly with soil and place in bright, filtered light, watering little.
Pests and diseases Aphids, scale insects.

84 DATURA SUAVEOLENS
Angel's trumpet

Family Solanaceae.
Origin Brazil.
Description Species cultivated for its magnificent flowers. In the wild it is a small tree or shrub growing to 4–5 m (13–17 ft); grown indoors it is of smaller size. The leaves are oval-elliptical and the large pendulous flowers, trumpet-shaped, have a highly fragrant corolla. The flowering period is end of summer to autumn.
Varieties There is a cultivar with double flowers.
Care The species needs bright light and several hours of direct sunshine daily. It does well at medium room temperatures of 18–22°C (64–71°F) and likes to be put outside in summer, in a sunny position but sheltered from the wind. Water plentifully from spring to autumn, letting the soil surface dry out before repeating. Reduce amount of water in winter. Give fertilizer with high content of potassium every 3–4 weeks from spring to autumn. Growing medium should consist of organic soil, peat and sand in equal parts. Repot in early spring when plant is still small; in the case of large specimens it is enough to change the top layer of the soil every year.
Propagation Usually from cuttings in spring. Plant these in mixture of equal parts peat and sand, and wrap in plastic bag.
Pests and diseases Scale insects.

85 DAVALLIA CANARIENSIS
Deersfoot fern

Family Davalliaceae.
Origin S.W. Europe, Canary Islands, Madeira.
Description The plant belongs to the group of ferns. It has a rhizome, covered in pale brown scales, which creeps along the surface. Height 30–40 cm (12–16 in). The fronds are leathery, triangular, divided into 3–4 pinnules which in turn are formed of very slender leaflets. It is very suitable for growing in bowls or hanging baskets.
Care This is a hardy species, easy to keep indoors because it requires less humidity than many other ferns. It likes bright light but not direct sun. Does well at room temperatures but also at lower levels provided not below 13°C (55°F). Water moderately, letting the top part of the soil dry out between applications. If the temperature dips below 13°C (55°F) at any time, merely keep the soil from drying out completely. Feed with liquid fertilizer fortnightly in spring–summer. Growing medium formed of 3 parts coarse peat, 3 parts leafmold and 2 parts coarse sand. Repot young plants every spring and change the soil of adult plants.
Propagation In spring divide the rhizomes into 7–8 cm (3 in) sections, each with 1–2 fronds. Plant each portion in a moist mixture of peat and sand in equal parts, wrap in plastic bag and place in bright, shielded light at room temperature. After 3–4 weeks, when rooted, uncover the seedling gradually for increasingly long periods. After 3–4 months transplant into growing medium.
Pests and diseases Aphids, scale insects.

---

86 DIEFFENBACHIA MACULATA
Spotted dumb-cane

Family Araceae.
Origin Brazil.
Description This plant, cultivated indoors for its ornamental foliage, may reach a height of 1 m (3 ft) in a pot. Its ovate, elongated leaves, measuring more than 30 cm (12 in) in length, are dark green, and in the original species have large creamy-white patches. There are, however, varieties which have silvery or pale yellow markings. As the sap is poisonous and an irritant, avoid contact with eyes and mouth. If you handle the leaves, wash hands thoroughly.
Care The plant should be placed in average light; in summer it can go outdoors but only in completely shaded spots. It can be kept at room temperature, away from drafts, but needs plenty of surrounding moisture, so the pot should be set in a holder filled with wet gravel or damp peat. It cannot stand temperatures below 15°C (59°F). During the growth period it should be watered sparingly, and in winter the amount must be further reduced. It is best to place the pot in water for a short time, and then let it drain off. Make sure, however, not to allow the water to touch the sole and, even more, the stem, for this easily succumbs to rot. When grown indoors it may not even become dormant. Give liquid fertilizer fortnightly in spring–summer. Growing medium 1 part organic soil, 1 part peat and 1 part sand; repot small plants into containers up to 20 cm (8 in) every spring.
Propagation By method as described for *D. amoena* (overleaf).
Pests and diseases Bacterial mold of stem base.

87 DIEFFENBACHIA AMOENA
Dumb-cane, mother-in-law plant

Family Araceae.
Origin Tropical America.
Description The genus *Dieffenbachia* comprises various species of perennial evergreen plants cultivated for their ornamental foliage. *D. amoena* is one of the most vigorous species and can grow to more than 1 m (3 ft) in height. The leaves are elliptic-oblong, green with white marbling along the veins. The sap is poisonous and irritating, so avoid any contact with eyes and mouth. If you have to handle leaves, wash hands thoroughly.

Varieties *D.* 'Exotica,' opaque green, with creamy-white markings; *D.* 'Exotica Alba,' almost completely white leaves and green borders.
Care Same as for *D. maculata.*

Propagation From April to June tip cuttings, 10–15 cm (4–5 in) long, are taken, each cut being made just below a node. Remove the lower leaves and after treating the base with a rooting preparation bury the cuttings in pots full of a damp mixture of peat and coarse sand, or perlite, in equal parts. Place at 21–24°C (70–75°F) in greenhouse or wrap pots in plastic bags, putting them in bright, filtered light. After rooting, remove the bags, water moderately and feed every fortnight. After two months transplant into final growing medium and treat as adult plant. The plant can also be propagated by cutting the stem into 7–8 cm (3 in) sections and burying each one horizontally in the rooting medium of the cuttings. Treat in the same way as the tip cuttings.

Pests and diseases Subject to bacterial stem rot.

---

88 DIONAEA MUSCIPULA
Venus fly trap

Family Droseraceae.
Origin Eastern United States.
Description Carnivorous, perennial, rhizomatous plant with leaves arranged in a basal rosette. Each leaf is on a broad petiole and the lamina is divided into 2 lobes with a central contractile vein; the leaf margin is scattered with bristles and the top part of each lobe has 3 hairs. When an insect brushes against these hairs, the lobes fold and close, entrapping it; then the leaves produce enzymes which digest the insect. The plant may grow to a height of 20–30 cm (8–12 in) and sometimes bears groups of 5–10 white flowers in June.

Care Difficult to cultivate as a house plant. It needs partially shaded positions but can stand direct sun or shade equally well. During winter dormancy it should be kept in cool places, but not below 4–5°C (39–41°F); while growing it needs normal room temperatures. The potting medium should consist of acid leafmold and sphagnum moss in equal proportions, plus a little powdered charcoal. Pots of 30 cm (12 in) should be used. Water with rain water in spring and summer, in winter just enough to prevent drying out. Feed fortnightly, except when dormant.

Propagation From seed, in autumn, in mixture of equal parts sand and sphagnum moss; place pane of glass or sheet of polyethylene over the container. The rhizome can also be divided in spring, potting each piece separately. Wrap container in a polyethylene bag.
Pests and diseases Only if conditions are suitable.

89 DIPLADENIA SANDERI (MANDEVILLA SANDERI)

Family Apocynaceae.
Origin Brazil.
Description Woody climbing plant which, given suitable support, reaches a height of 4 m (13 ft). The shiny, opposite, elliptic leaves, are up to 5 cm (2 in) long. The trumpet-shaped flowers, pink with orange throat, form showy terminal clusters and bloom from June to September. With regular pruning it can be raised as a shrub. Often, but not always, the plant dies after flowering. *Dipladenia sanderi* now belongs to the genus *Mandevilla*. Although its correct name is *Mandevilla sanderi*, it is still commonly referred to as *Dipladenia sanderi*.

Varieties *M. sanderi* 'Rosea,' pink flowers; the hybrid cultivar *M.* x *amabilis* 'Alice du Pont,' dark red flowers.

Care Likes bright but filtered light. During growth period keep at average room temperatures, and during winter dormancy at 12–14°C (53–57°F). Water normally in spring-summer, allowing surface of soil to dry out between applications, and keeping pot in a bowl of wet gravel, spraying foliage daily. Water very little in winter. Feed fortnightly from spring to autumn. Grow in medium of loam, peat and sand in equal parts, and repot every March. Prune drastically in autumn because the plant flowers only on current year's branches.
Propagation Take young stem tip cuttings in spring, potting them in mixture of peat and sand in equal amounts. Keep at 24–27°C (75–80°F) or put in plastic bag, in well-lit position, but not in the sun.
Pests and diseases Red spider if air is too dry.

90 DIZYGOTHECA ELEGANTISSIMA
False aralia, finger aralia

Family Araliaceae.
Origin New Hebrides.
Description Formerly classified under the genus *Aralia*, this shrub is still often known as *Aralia elegantissima*. It reaches a height of 1.20 m (4 ft) and is a slow grower, cultivated for its ornamental foliage. The palmate, finger-like leaves are composed of 7–10 leaflets with dentate margins and are 8 cm (3 in) long and 1 cm (about ½ in) wide. The young leaves are reddish, the leaves of the adult plant are dark green.

Varieties *D. elegantissima* 'Castor' is a cultivar with broader leaflets, purple tinged with a white central vein.
Care The plant must be placed in bright light but not in the sun. It grows at room temperatures and during winter dormancy requires a temperature of around 15°C (59°F). The surrounding humidity must be high, so spray the foliage frequently and set the pot in a bowl of wet gravel. Water moderately, however, throughout the year, allowing the top part of the soil to dry out between applications. Feed liquid fertilizer every fortnight in growing season. Potting medium made up of 1 part organic soil, 1 part peat and 1 part coarse sand. Repot in early spring alternate years. House plants often form a single stem without branching; to obtain a shrubby plant it is best to put several plants in one pot.

Propagation From seed, in spring, but it is difficult to get good results from this method indoors.
Pests and diseases Not much prone to ailments.

91 DRACAENA DEREMENSIS
Striped dracaena

Family Agavaceae.
Origin Tropical Africa.
Description Shrubby plant cultivated for its ornamental foliage. Indoors it may reach a height of 1.20 m (4 ft). The green leaves are sword-shaped, with parallel veins, up to 45 cm (18 in) long and 5 cm (2 in) wide.

Varieties More common for indoor use than the species proper are two varieties: D deremensis 'Bausei,' with a white band running down the middle of the leaf; and 'Warneckii,' with white bands and a central green vein.
Care Needs to be kept in bright but filtered light. Does well at room temperatures of 18–24°C (64–75°F); minimum winter temperature 12°C (53°F). Since it requires plenty of humidity it should be placed in a bowl full of damp gravel and the foliage sprayed periodically. Water plentifully during growth, but do not allow the pot to stand in water. Apply very little in dormancy period and let the medium half dry out between successive waterings. Give liquid fertilizer every fortnight from June to September. Grow in medium of organic soil, peat and sand in equal amounts. Repot the plant in April every year, in pots up to a diameter of about 30 cm (12 in).

Propagation Same method as used for *D. fragrans*.
Pests and diseases Subject to scale insects and a fungal parasite which causes leaf spots.

---

92 DRACAENA FRAGRANS
Corn plant

Family Agavaceae.
Origin Tropical Africa.
Description Similar to *D. deremensis* but may grow bigger, up to 1.50 m (5 ft) in height. The leaves are 40–90 cm (16–36 in) long and 10 cm (4 in) wide, curved and rather limp.

Varieties In addition to the pure species with green leaves, there are horticultural varieties with multicolored leaves; 'Massangeana' (Cornstalk plant), with a broad yellow central stripe; 'Lindenii,' with broad yellow margins. The older, lower leaves tend to fall, leaving a bare stem with a tuft of leaves at the tip. In the wild the plant produces scented flowers, but these appear only rarely in house plants.
Care Environmental needs and cultivation techniques as for *D. deremensis*.

Propagation Can be done March–April or September from basal shoots, tip cuttings or stem cuttings. The basal shoots and tip cuttings should be young and 10 cm (4 in) in length. Old stems can be cut into 5 cm (2 in) sections, each with a bud, leaves being removed. Plant each portion in an 8 cm (3 in) pot, in a barely damp medium of peat and coarse sand in equal parts, and kept at 20–24°C (68–78°F) or enclosed in a plastic bag in indirect light until rooting occurs. Remove the bag, water moderately, letting the top of the soil dry out between waterings. Feed every fortnight with a liquid fertilizer. When the roots appear on the surface, transplant into growing soil and handle the plant as an adult.

Pests and diseases Scale insects, leaf spotting.

93 DRACAENA MARGINATA
Malagasy dragon tree

Family Agavaceae.
Origin Unknown.
Description May grow to a height of 2 m (6 ft). When young, the plant is bushy. Eventually it loses its basal leaves, so that the adult plant consists of an erect, bare stem with a tuft of curving leaves, about 40 cm (16 in) long and 1.5 cm (½ in) wide, at the tip. The stem bears triangular scars of the fallen leaves. The foliage of the species plant is green with delicate dark red markings.

Varieties There is a variety with much more colorful and decorative foliage; 'Tricolor', which has leaves striped in green, creamy-white and pink.
Care This is the easiest *Dracaena* species to grow indoors because it tolerates a greater range of humidity. It does well in diffused light and average room temperatures, and in warmer climates can go outside in sheltered positions. Water generously and spray foliage periodically during growth season. When dormant, simply avoid letting the soil dry out completely. Feed fortnightly with standard liquid fertilizer from June to September. Growing medium formed of organic soil, peat and sand in equal parts. Repot every April, in pots with a diameter of up to 30 cm (12 in). In subsequent years merely supply fresh soil every spring.
Propagation As for *D. fragrans*.
Pests and diseases Scale insects, fungal leaf spotting.

94 DRACAENA SANDERANA
Ribbon plant

Family Agavaceae.
Origin Cameroons, Zaire.
Description It is a shrub 60 cm (2 ft) in height. The thin, sturdy stems form dense branches; the elliptic leaves, 8 cm (3 in) long and 4 cm (about 2 in) wide, are in groups of 2–3, dark green with cream markings.
Care Must stand in bright but filtered light and at temperatures of 18–24°C (64–75°F). Minimum winter temperature 10°C (50°F). Fairly easy to cultivate because it is not too particular about humidity, but it is advisable to place the pot in a bowl of moist peat or gravel and to spray the foliage from time to time. During the growing season water plentifully and feed with a standard liquid preparation. While dormant, simply prevent the compost from drying out completely. Growing medium should consist of 1 part organic soil, 1 part peat and 1 part coarse sand or perlite. Repot in April. The maximum diameter of the pot should be 15–20 cm (6–8 in).
Propagation As for *D. fragrans*.
Pests and diseases Scale insects, fungal leaf spotting.

95 ECHEVERIA HARMSII
Red echeveria

Family Crassulaceae.
Origin Mexico.
Description Succulent formed of a main stem that terminates in a rosette of leaves; it also bears sparse leaves, from the axils of which sprout stalks ending in a smaller rosette. The leaves are lanceolate, covered with soft, short hairs. Color is green with reddish-brown edges. Flowering stems, 15 cm (6 in) long, appear in June, bearing flowers singly or in small clusters at tip. These flowers are 2–3 cm (about 1 in) in length, bell-shaped, red with yellow borders.
Care Easy to grow indoors, in bright, sunny positions. Lives at room temperatures but prefers a winter resting period at 13–16°C (55–61°F). Water moderately while plant is growing, letting half of the soil dry out between applications; avoid wetting the leaves, which easily rot. During dormancy do not let soil dry out completely. Give liquid fertilizer fortnightly in growing season. Medium formed of 1 part loam, 1 part peat and 2 parts coarse sand. Repot every spring, putting a drainage layer of gravel in bottom of pot; mulch surface of soil with sand.
Propagation In spring, detach a side rosette with stem from parent plant, shorten stem to 2 cm (1 in) and plant it in growing soil. Can also be propagated from stem and leaf cuttings.
Pests and diseases Scale insects, rust.

---

96 ECHEVERIA DERENBERGII
Baby echeveria, painted lady

Family Crassulaceae.
Origin Mexico.
Description Succulent 5–8 cm (2–3 in) tall. It consists of a short stem which bears one or more almost round rosettes, each with a diameter of up to 8 cm (3 in). Other rosettes form continuously on short lateral stalks from the leaf axils of the parent plant. The numerous, inward-curving leaves, 2–4 cm (1–2 in) long, are blue-green with red margins and are covered with a waxy sheen; they form dense cushions of rosettes. The flower stalks, 8 cm (3 in) long, bearing racemes of red or yellow flowers, appear in June.
Care Easy to cultivate, the plant likes sunny positions. During the growing period it lives happily at room temperatures or in the open; while resting it needs a temperature of 13–16°C (55–61°F). Water moderately in spring-summer, letting half the soil dry out between applications. In winter merely make sure the soil does not dry out completely. The best way to water is to immerse the pot. Give liquid fertilizer fortnightly during growth. Medium formed of 1 part loam, 1 part peat and 2 parts coarse sand. Place a drainage layer at bottom of pot and cover surface of soil with sand to prevent water settling and causing leaves to rot. Repot every spring in pots of 8–10 cm (3–4 in) diameter.
Propagation From rosettes, as described, for *E. harmsii*, or from leaf cuttings. Detach leaves in spring and plant them in slightly damp sand.
Pests and diseases Scale insects. Rust may cause yellow blotches on leaves.

97 EPIPHYLLUM X ACKERMANNII (X HELIOCHIA VIOLACEA)
Orchid cactus

Family Cactaceae.
Origin Tropical America.
Description This plant is an intergeneric hybrid derived from crossing *Neliocereus speciosus* and *Nopalxochia phyllanthoides*. These hybrids have succulent, flattened, dark green stems with toothed edges equipped with small spines. The stems hang down and are branched at the base to form large tufts. The funnel-shaped flowers, up to 10–15 cm (4–6 in) wide, bloom in May–June. Red-flowered hybrids bloom only by day and the flowers grow from the top part of the stem. Many white and yellow hybrids, on the other hand, flower at night from the base of the stem, often giving out a strong perfume.
Care Easy to cultivate, it does well in warm, humid surroundings, in good light but not direct sun; in summer it can go outside in a shady position. Spray the plants daily but water abundantly only in spring–summer. During the brief rest period that follows flowering and during the rest of the growth cycle, water with moderation. Apply a liquid potassium-rich fertilizer when the buds start to appear. Suspend feeding as soon as the flowers are to a large extent open. Growing medium should consist of 1 part coarse sand and 3 parts peat or leafmold. Repot annually, after flowering.
Propagation Hybrids from cuttings May–July. Detach side shoots, dry off for a day, then plant in mixture, keeping moist. Results from seed are unpredictable.
Pests and diseases Scale insects; nematode worms cause root galls.

---

98 EPIPREMNUM AUREUM
Ivy-arum, Devil's ivy

Family Araceae.
Origin Solomon Islands.
Description Climbing plant similar to *Philodendron* and better known as *Scindapsus*, this being the name until quite recently. In its natural environment it climbs tree trunks to considerable heights. The stems are yellowish-green and the green leaves have yellow streaks and spots. The heart-shaped leaves, pointed at the tip, are 6–10 cm (2–4 in) long in young plants; those of adult plants, grown in large tubs, may be very big, 20–60 cm (8–24 in) long and 20–50 cm (8–20 in) wide.
Varieties *E. a.* 'Golden Queen,' almost entirely golden-yellow leaves; 'Marble Queen,' creamy buds and marbled green and white leaves.
Care Easy to grow indoors, can be used in hanging baskets or as a climber. Needs diffused but bright light, especially for the more colorfully marked varieties. Average temperature 18–24°C (64–75°F) throughout year, never beneath 15°C (59°F). Water regularly, allowing soil surface to dry out between waterings in spring–summer; water sparingly in winter. If room is warm, spray with lime-tree water. Give liquid fertilizer fortnightly from April to October. Medium formed of loam, peat and sand in equal amounts. Unnecessary to repot every year.
Propagation From tip cuttings, 10 cm (4 in) long, in spring, getting them to root in water.
Pests and diseases Hardly subject to ailments.

99 EPISCIA CUPREATA
Carpet plant, flame violet

Family Gesneriaceae.
Origin Colombia, Venezuela.
Description Cultivated for its foliage and attractive flowers, this species has a short stem which produces stolons or runners which, when they make contact with the soil, originate new plants; in this way, provided the pot is large, a thick carpet is formed. The leaves are ovate with toothed margins, and their rather rough surface is covered with dense down. The dimensions of the leaves vary from 5–12 cm (2–5 in) long and 3–8 cm (1–3 in) across; their color is copper with pale green or silver markings along the principal veins. The runners are red or green. In the spring, flowers (usually single) appear; the tubular yellow corolla opens into 5 scarlet lobes. Flowering continues until the autumn. There are numerous hybrids which vary in color.

Varieties 'Acajou,' dark brown leaves with silver-green veining and central area; 'Emerald Queen,' emerald-green leaves turning to bronze; 'Frosty,' emerald-green leaves with bronze margins and silver-white central area.

Care Thrives on bright light. Prefers temperatures of 21–23°C (70–73°F). Should be kept away from drafts and requires plenty of humidity, so place pot in bowl of wet gravel. Water plentifully but little when dormant in winter, especially if temperature below 16°C (61°F). Give liquid fertilizer fortnightly. Potting mixture formed of sphagnum moss, peat and perlite in equal parts. Repot in spring.

Propagation Cut off a stolon and pot it separately.
Pests and diseases Aphids.

---

100 ERICA GRACILIS
Rose heath

Family Ericaceae.
Origin South Africa.
Description The genus *Erica* comprises a large number of species, only a few of which are suitable as house plants. *E. gracilis* is a woody shrub which grows up to 45 cm (18 in) tall in a pot, and up to 30 cm (12 in) across. The needle-like, green leaves, in whorls, are 3–6 mm (about ¼ in) long. Each of the many side shoots produces racemes of 3–4 bell-shaped flowers, pink, purple or white, according to the variety, from September to December.

Care Likes bright light but not direct sunlight. Not easy to keep indoors because it prefers low temperatures, ideally 8–10°C (46–50°F); for that reason it is often treated as an annual, being kept in a cool position while flowering and afterwards thrown out. Water plentifully all year round with lime-free water, keeping the soil always damp; also spray the foliage frequently and put the pot in a bowl full of wet gravel. A liquid fertilizer every fortnight from May to September is useful but not obligatory. Grow in clay pots of 15 cm (6 in) filled with lime-free soil made up of 2 parts peat and 1 part fine sand. Repot in March. When flowering is over it is helpful to remove flower heads.

Propagation As for *E. hyemalis*.
Pests and diseases Scale insects, gray mold, mildew, rust.

101 ERICA HYEMALIS
French heather

Family Ericaceae.

Origin Unknown; perhaps a horticultural hybrid.

Description Upright shrub, up to 60 cm (2 ft) tall, with a diameter of up to 30–40 cm (12–16 in). Needle-like leaves in whorls; tubular flowers, 5 mm (about ½ in) long, white with pink tinge, in long terminal racemes. Flowering period November to January. There are many cultivated hybrids with variously colored flowers.

Varieties *E. h.* 'Prof. Diels' is a winter-flowering cultivar with an abundance of blue-tinged scarlet flowers. Other hybrid varieties are: *E.* 'Osterglocken,' dark pink flowers in March–April (in Europe); *E.* 'Ostergruss,' pink-purple flowers in April–May; *E.* 'President Carnot,' pink, white-spotted flowers.

Care Like all ericas, it needs bright but diffused light and prefers cool temperatures. It detests lime so must be grown in an acid medium and watered with rain water. For growing techniques, see *E. gracilis.*

Propagation Ericas are difficult to propagate indoors. Cuttings can be taken in March, 2.5 cm (1 in) long, and buried in a bowl filled with a mixture of one-third each peat and sand and two-thirds crocks. Cover with polyethylene (if mist-spraying is not possible) and place at 16°C (61°F) in closed surroundings, applying lime-free water. Transplant after rooting occurs.

Pests and diseases Scale insects, mildew, gray mold, rust.

102 EUONYMUS JAPONICUS
Japanese spindle tree

Family Celastraceae.

Origin Japan

Description The genus comprises many species of woody shrubs, evergreen or deciduous, but only *Euonymus japonicus* is cultivated as a house plant. It is a many-branched evergreen with leathery, obovate, finely dentate leaves, 3–6 cm (1–2 in) long. It does not flower indoors.

Varieties There are many varieties: *E. japonicus* 'Albomarginatus,' green leaves with white margins; *E. j.* 'Aureopictus,' golden-yellow spot in center of leaf; *E. j.* 'Microphillus Variegatus,' small, white-edged leaves, which grows only to 45 cm (18 in).

Care Fairly difficult to grow indoors. Needs bright but filtered light when growing. In winter it requires 3–4 hours of daily sunshine. During winter dormancy it prefers surroundings at temperature of 10–13°C (50–55°F) but does well throughout year at 13–16°F). Can stand up to 18°C (64°F) indoors if placed in a bowl full of wet gravel. Water normally in growing season, letting the upper part of the soil dry out between successive waterings; in winter dormancy simply make sure that the medium does not dry completely. Give liquid food fortnightly from April to September. Potting medium formed of organic soil, peat and sand in equal parts. Repot in spring.

Propagation Take tip cuttings 8 cm (3 in) long in spring; treat with hormones and put in mixture of peat and sand in equal parts, keeping at 21–24°C (70–75°F) in filtered light.

Pests and diseases Mildew, aphids, scale insects.

103 EUPHORBIA BALSAMIFERA

Family Euphorbiaceae.
Origin Canary Islands.
Description Succulent species with large, light gray, branching stem up to 2 m (6 ft) tall. The leaves grow in rosettes from the top of the branches; they are thick and fleshy, lanceolate or ovate-oblong, blue-gray, 18–24 cm (7–10 in) long.

Care Easy to grow, the plant needs no special attention and often does better if neglected. It likes sunny positions. It can be kept throughout the year at average temperatures of 18–22°C (64–71°F), minimum 10°C (50°F). Water with moderation in growing season from September to April, and during summer dormancy merely ensure that soil does not dry out entirely. Feeding should also be moderate, once every 1–2 months while growing. Mixture should consist of 1 part organic soil, 1 part peat and 2 parts sand. Put a good drainage layer in the pot. Repot in September, increasing diameter of container to 20 cm (8 in).

Propagation Easily multiplied from seed; also by cuttings, but this is more difficult. In September take a tip cutting and dip it in water to stem flow of latex. Leave the cutting to dry for a few days, then plant in equal parts peat and sand.

Pests and diseases Prone to rotting if overwatered. Scale insects and mealy bug.

104 EUPHORBIA MILII
Crown of thorns

Family Euphorbiaceae.
Origin Malagasy Republic (Madagascar).
Description The genus *Euphorbia* contains a large number of plants. All contain latex, a milky sap, which in some is merely an irritant, in others poisonous. *E. milii*, also known as *E. splendens*, is a semi-prostrate succulent shrub, up to 1 m (3 ft) in height, with thorny stems. Groups of ovate-elliptic leaves, 5–6 cm (2 in) long, sprout from the tip of the stems; they last a few months and then drop off. The new leaves develop only on young shoots. The inflorescences are formed of heart-shaped, yellow or red bracts which surround the small flowers and which grow on long stalks from the upper part of the stem. The flowering period is from March to September, but may continue all year round.

Varieties *E. milii lutea*, silver-gray leaves and yellow bracts; *E. milii prostrata*, pendulous branches up to 1 m (3 ft) long and salmon-pink leaf bracts.

Care Likes direct sunlight; the more light, the longer the flowers last. Does well in warm, dry surroundings. Water moderately throughout the year, letting the top part of the soil dry out between applications. After flowering, give less water; this applies also if temperature falls below 16°C (61°F). Feed with liquid fertilizer fortnightly from June to September; if the plant continues flowering, feed once a month in winter. Medium formed of 1 part loam, 1 part peat and 2 parts sand. Repot every other year.

Propagation Same technique as for *E. pulcherrima*.
Pests and diseases Not much subject to parasitic ailments.

105 EUPHORBIA PSEUDOCACTUS
Yellow cactus

Family Euphorbiaceae.
Origin South Africa.
Description Succulent plant which can grow up to a height of 1.5 m (5 ft). It has upright stems and branches, without leaves, and with 3–5 ribs; pairs of thorns are 1 cm (½ in). It exhibits characteristic yellow fan-like marks on the stems, which are 3–5 cm (1–2 in) broad, narrowing at intervals along their entire length.
Care Likes positions in full sunlight or at any rate very brightly-lit spots. Keep at room temperature, 18–22°C (64–71°F) when plant is growing, and at 8–12°C (46–53°F) during winter dormancy. Water moderately from spring to autumn, letting two-thirds of the soil dry out before rewatering. In mid-autumn reduce watering and while plant is dormant simply make sure the soil does not become unduly moist. Feed every fortnight during growth. The potting medium should be 1 part organic soil, 1 part peat and 2 parts sand. Put a drainage layer in bottom of pot. Repot in spring in pots of up to 20 cm (8 in).
Propagation From seed or tip cuttings in June. Immerse cutting in water to prevent latex from flowing out (parent plant needs spraying for the same reason). Let the cutting dry out for a few days and plant in mixture of peat and sand in equal parts. Cover the surface of the soil with sand. Leave at room temperature and in diffused light, watering little.
Pests and diseases Not much subject to parasitic ailments.

106 EUPHORBIA PULCHERRIMA
Poinsettia, Christmas plant

Family Euphorbiaceae.
Origin Mexico.
Description A deciduous-leaved shrub which in its native environment reaches a height of 2 m (6 ft); a number of horticultural varieties, growing to 30–40 cm (12–16 in), suitable as house plants, have been obtained. The ovate, lobate leaves, 10–15 cm (4–6 in) long, are green with lighter veining. The inflorescence consists of insignificant yellow flowers surrounded by 10–20 dark red bracts, up to 15–20 cm (6–8 in) in length. The plants flower November to February.
Varieties 'Annette Hegg', 'Annette Hegg Supreme,' crimson; 'Rosea,' 'Ecke's White,' white bracts.
Care Once it has lost its colored bracts, the poinsettia will seldom produce new flowers when raised indoors. Keep the plant indoors at room temperature in a well-lit spot, even a sunny position in autumn-winter, away from drafts. Water the soil thoroughly but let it partially dry out before repeating. Feed fortnightly from April to September. When the bracts drop off prune the plant 5 cm (2 in) from the base and let it rest in a bright place at around 15°C (59°F). Mixture should consist of organic soil, peat and sand in equal parts. Repot in April.
Propagation Take cuttings in April and after keeping them in water for a day plant in mixture of equal parts peat and coarse sand. Place in greenhouse at 16–18°C (61–64°F) or in polyethylene in filtered light.
Pests and diseases Prone to various ailments.

EUPHORBIA TIRUCALLI

Pencil tree, milkbush, Indian tree spurge

Family Euphorbiaceae.
Origin Central Africa.
Description In its natural habitat the plant may grow to a height of 8–10 m (26–33 ft), but as a house plant it seldom reaches more than 1.50 m (4 ft). It is a shrub of characteristic appearance, with circular, many-branched stems bearing tiny leaves, 1 cm (½ in) in length, which soon fall, leaving the twigs bare. The pencil-like twigs, 6–10 mm (under ½ in) thick, are bright green.
Care Likes sunlight and well-lit positions in general. Keep the plant at room temperature, 18–22°C (64–71°F), during growth period; while dormant in winter keep the plant at 8–12°C (46–53°F). Water moderately from spring to autumn, allowing two-thirds of soil to dry out before rewatering. In mid-autumn reduce amount of water and during rest period decrease even further, just enough to keep soil damp. While plant is growing feed a liquid fertilizer every fortnight. Growing medium consists of 1 part loam, 1 part peat and 2 parts sand, with a drainage layer at bottom of pot. Repot in spring.
Propagation At the end of spring take tip cuttings and immerse in water to arrest flow of latex; the parent plant should also be sprayed for the same reason. After leaving the cutting to dry for a few days, plant in a barely damp mixture of peat and sand in equal parts. Leave at room temperature and in filtered light, watering little
Pests and diseases Not greatly subject to parasites.

108 EXACUM AFFINE
Persian violet, Mexican violet

Family Gentianaceae.

Origin Island of Socotra (Indian Ocean).

Description Herbaceous, perennial plant cultivated for its beautiful flowers. It is usually grown as an annual, bought at the start of summer and discarded after flowering. It is 10–30 cm (4–12 in) tall and has numerous branches which bear groups of glossy, ovate leaves, 2–3 cm (1 in) long. The flowers are bright blue with yellow stamens, 1.5 cm (½ in) across, and fragrant. Flowering is from spring to autumn.

Varieties *E. affine* 'Atrocaeruleum,' dark lilac flowers; 'Blithe Spirit,' white flowers; 'Midget,' dwarf variety with bright blue flowers.

Care Ideally placed in bright positions, but not sunlight, and at average temperatures of 18–22°C (64–71°F). It needs a good deal of humidity, so it is best to place the pot in a holder full of moist gravel and to spray foliage frequently. Water plentifully, always keeping the soil damp. Feed with a liquid preparation fortnightly while flowering. Medium formed of 1 part organic soil, 1 part peat and 1 part sand. Pots of 10–12 cm (4–5 in). It is a good idea to cut the flowers when they fade so as to prevent them from forming seeds: this prolongs flowering.

Propagation From seed at beginning of spring. Growers also do sowing in October and keep the seedlings under glass in winter, repotting them in early summer.

Pests and diseases Aphids; red spider if surroundings are too dry.

109 X FATSHEDERA LIZEI
Ivy tree, Miracle plant, Botanical wonder

Family Araliaceae.

Origin Hybrid of horticultural origin.

Description Hybrid obtained from crossing *Fatsia japonica* 'Moseri' with *Hedera helix* var. *hibernica*, and combining the characteristics of both parents. It is an evergreen shrub of erect habit, growing to a height of about 1 m (3 ft). When it gets taller it tends to droop and so needs supporting. The leaves are up to 20 cm (8 in) broad, smaller than those of *Fatsia*, palmate with 5 lobes.

Varieties 'Variegata' has white-edged leaves.

Care It adapts successfully to different environmental conditions but prefers bright light, though not direct sun. During growth it does better at high temperatures. In winter keep below 10°C (50°F) but will tolerate quite high temperatures provided the pot is placed in a holder filled with gravel or damp peat. 'Variegata' enjoys warm surroundings and a temperature of not less than 16°C (61°F), even during winter dormancy. Water normally and when plant is resting, in a cool position, make sure soil does not dry out completely. Apply liquid fertilizer every fortnight during growth period. Medium: 1 part loam, 2 parts peat and 1 part sand. Repot every spring.

Propagation In spring take 10 cm (4 in) tip cuttings. Plant in damp mixture of peat and sand in equal parts. Cover with polyethylene, keep at 18–21°C (64–70°F) in filtered light.

Pests and diseases Aphids.

110 FATSIA JAPONICA
Japanese aralia

Family Araliaceae.
Origin Japan, S. Korea, Ryukyu Islands.
Description Also known as *Aralia japonica* and *Fatsia sieboldii*. It is a rapid-growing shrub, up to 1.5 m (5 ft) tall, with woody stems which indoors develop few branches. The glossy leaves are fan-shaped with 7–9 lobes, 15–45 cm (6–18 in) wide and borne on long stalks of 40 cm (16 in). On plants grown in the open, umbels of white flowers, 2–4 cm (1–2 in) across, on racemes 20–40 cm (8–16 in) in length, appear in October; house plants seldom flower.
Varieties *F. japonica.* 'Moseri,' slower-growing, with bigger leaves; 'Variegata,' creamy-white blotches on leaves.
Care Very hard to grow indoors, but in areas with mild winters it can be cultivated outdoors at a minimum temperature of 2°C (35°F). It does well in sun or shade, provided surroundings are bright. Prefers a temperature of around 16°C (61°F). Above 18°C (64°F) the leaves tend to fade; increase humidity. During winter dormancy keep at 7–8°C (44–46°F). Water generously; when plant is dormant water moderately, let surface of soil dry out before repeating. Give liquid fertilizer every fortnight while growing. Potting medium: loam, peat and sand in equal amounts. Repot every year in containers of up to 25 cm (10 in).
Propagation From cuttings of basal shoots, planted in mixture of peat and sand, kept in the greenhouse at 15°C (59°F) in filtered light, or in a plastic bag.
Pests and diseases Aphids.

111 FICUS BENJAMINA
Weeping fig

Family Moraceae.
Origin India to the Philippines.
Description The genus *Ficus* comprises many species of trees and shrubs, evergreen or deciduous, and of erect, climbing or trailing habit. It is a shrub which can reach a height, in a tub, of 2 m (6 ft), with thin, slightly pendulous twigs and elliptic leaves, pointed at the tip, 6–10 cm (2–4 in) long. Pale green when young, the foliage becomes darker with age. The plant has a very graceful appearance overall. In warm climates it can live in the open.
Varieties *F. benjamina* 'Exotica' (called 'Java fig'), is a very elegant, handsome variety with long, curving branches bearing oval, leathery, pendulous leaves, about 10 cm (4 in) long. *F. b.* 'Variegata' (or 'Variegated mini-rubber') is a smaller cultivar of the original species, its leaves blotched creamy-white on surface and margins.
Care Can be kept in bright but filtered light and can also take a few hours of sunlight daily. Does well at room temperatures; in winter prefers to spend a period at 13–15°C (55–59°F). During growth water normally but allow soil to dry out between applications. Give liquid fertilizer every fortnight in spring–summer. Medium made up of organic soil, peat and sand in equal parts. Repot every other year, in spring, in containers of up to 30 cm (12 in). It tends to lose leaves at the end of winter, but others develop in spring.
Propagation As for *F. deltoidea.*
Pests and diseases Scale insects; red spider if air dry.

112 FICUS DELTOIDEA
Mistletoe fig

Family Moraceae.
Origin India, Malaya, Indonesia.
Description Also known as *F. diversifolia* because of the size of its leaves, ranging from 2.5 cm (1 in) to 8 cm (3 in). These are obovate, rounded and leathery, dark green above and pale green to reddish underneath. In the wild takes the form of a small tree or large shrub, and because it grows as an epiphyte it is commonly called the mistletoe fig. Indoors it reaches a height of 30–60 cm (1–2 ft). It is the only indoor species of *Ficus* to produce fruits; these are small, inedible, red or yellow, and grow in the axils of the upper leaves all the year round.
Care Needs a bright position but not direct sun. Does well at room temperature but in winter prefers dormant period at 7–10°C (46–50°F). Water moderately, letting part of the soil dry out between applications. Too much water causes the lower leaves to fall. Give liquid fertilizer fortnightly from May to September. Growing medium formed of 1 part organic soil, 1 part peat and 1 part sand. Repot every 2 years.
Propagation From April to June take 10 cm (4 in) cuttings of side shoots, set them in a moist mixture of peat and sand in equal parts, then wrap in a plastic bag and keep in filtered light or place in the greenhouse at 16–18°C (61–64°F). When shoots appear, remove bag and water sparingly. After 4 months repot in growing medium.
Pests and diseases Scale insects; red spider if atmosphere too warm and dry.

113 FICUS ELASTICA
Rubber Plant

Family Moraceae.
Origin Tropical Asia.
Description The plant's common name is derived from its latex, from which rubber is extracted. It is one of the most popular house plants, growing to 2.5 m (8 ft), whereas in the wild it is a tree up to 30 m (100 ft) in height. The indoor form has an unbranched stem. The variety 'Decora' is cultivated more often than the original species, but both have dark green, glossy, leathery, oval leaves with a prominent central vein; those of the species are slightly pendulous, up to 30 cm (12 in) long, and those of the variety curve upwards, up to 40 cm (16 in) long. The young leaves are wrapped in a reddish sheath or stipule; and the principal vein on the underside is also red. Pinching the terminal shoots causes the plant to branch.
Varieties Other varieties are: 'Robusta,' larger, rounder leaves; 'Black Prince,' similar to 'Robusta' but with very dark green leaves; 'Tricolor,' leaves streaked pink and cream; 'Doescheri,' pink central veining and gray and cream patches on leaves; 'Schryvereana,' creamy rectangular marks on leaves; 'Variegata,' narrower, more pendulous leaves than other varieties, and spotted yellow.
Care As for *F. lyrata.*
Propagation From cutting of shoot with leaf, but because such large leaves are subject to strong dehydration it is not easy to get successful results indoors. Can also be propagated by air-layering but this is a lengthy procedure.
Pests and diseases Red spider, mealy bug, scale insects.

114 FICUS LYRATA
Fiddle-leaved fig

Family Moraceae.
Origin West Africa.
Description Also called *Ficus pandurata*. Reaches a height of 1.5 m (5 ft); the unbranched stem bears very big, ovate leaves, 40 cm (16 in) long and up to 22 cm (9 in) wide, broader at the tip than the base. The leaves are glossy, leathery, dark green and with wavy margins. Pinching the terminal shoots causes the plant to branch.
Varieties *F. lyrata*. 'Phyllis Craig' is a cultivar smaller than original species.
Care Needs same surroundings and cultivation as *F. elastica*. Both like bright but indirect light; the varieties of *F. elastica* with variegated foliage need more illumination than others, and if possible several hours of sunshine daily. All are happy at normal room temperature but are adaptable. During winter they prefer to be kept at 15–18°C (59–64°F). Water moderately all year round, allowing half the soil to dry out between applications; too much water causes lower leaves to fall. Feed liquid fertilizer each fortnight in spring-summer. Growing medium formed of 1 part organic soil, 1 part peat and 1 part sand. Repot alternate years, in spring, only when roots have filled pot. Do not use pots that are too big because the roots are better kept fairly constricted. The leaves should be cleaned of dust from time to time with a damp sponge.
Propagation From cuttings or by air-layering, but it is not easy to get good results indoors.
Pests and diseases Red spider if atmosphere too dry; scale insects.

---

115 FICUS PUMILA
Creeping Fig

Family Moraceae.
Origin Indochina to Japan.
Description Creeping plant which can grow to over 1.5 m (5 ft) in height. Can also be grown in hanging baskets, letting the stems trail. The stem is many-branched and the heart-shaped leaves are thin and slightly crinkled, 2 cm (1 in) long. When the plant is trained to climb up a moss-encased pole it emits aerial roots.
Varieties *F. pumila*. 'Variegata' has leaves marbled with cream.
Care Likes medium indirect lighting or shady positions. Of all fig species this can best stand the cold, and it can be grown in the open provided it is put in a sheltered spot protected from frost. Indoors keep at room temperature but in winter it likes a rest period at 7–10°C (44–50°F). Watering must be done very carefully; moderate amounts, letting the surface of the mixture dry out between successive applications, but never allowing it to become completely dry, even in winter, as this will cause leaves to drop. Feed every 2 weeks from May to September with a liquid preparation. Growing medium made up of 3 parts leafmold, 3 parts peat and 2 parts sand. Repot every other year, in April.
Propagation In April take 15 cm (6 in) tip cuttings and pot in a moist mixture of peat and sand in equal parts, removing the lower leaves. Put the pot in a plastic bag in filtered light. Remove bag when new shoots appear. Repot after 4 months.
Pests and diseases Scale insects, red spider.

116 FITTONIA VERSCHAFFELTII
Mosaic plant

Family Acanthaceae.
Origin Peru.
Description Small perennial plant with ornamental foliage. Reaches a height of 5–10 cm (2–4 in) and bears ovate, more or less pointed leaves, 5–10 cm (2–4 in) long, arranged in pairs. These are green and crisscrossed by a dense network of purple veins.
Varieties *F. v.* 'Pearcei'; *F. v.* 'Argironeura' (nerve plant), netted with white veins.
Care This is a difficult house plant because it needs medium to low temperatures and high humidity, conditions hard to obtain indoors. Exposure to medium light, well screened, in winter, and shade in summer. Ideal temperature is 18°C (64°F) throughout the year, but the species will tolerate both lower – though not under 13°C (55°F) – and higher levels. Does well in a terrarium where it can benefit from a constant temperature and high humidity. Place the pot in a bowl full of wet gravel and spray foliage every day. Do not over-water. Feed with a liquid fertilizer fortnightly in spring and summer. A growing medium of 3 parts leafmold, 3 parts peat and 2 parts coarse sand provides the roots with constant moisture. Repot in spring, using shallow bowls.
Propagation From tip cuttings with leaves, rooting them in mixture of peat and sand in equal parts and keeping in filtered light. Alternatively by layering, placing a pot with the above mixture close to the parent plant and rooting a branch of the latter in the new pot.
Pests and diseases Stem root rot.

---

117 FORTUNELLA JAPONICA
Marumi kumquat

Family Rutaceae.
Origin Japan.
Description Small tree or thorny shrub, botanically related to the genus *Citrus*. It is like an orange tree but smaller, up to 3–3.5 m (10–12 ft). The leaves, elliptical and persistent, are 8 cm (3 in) long and 2 cm (1 in) wide, with a slightly winged leaf stalk. The white flowers, single or in groups of 2–4, bloom in April and are highly perfumed. The fruits resemble oranges but are much smaller, with a thick orange rind, 3 cm (1 in) in diameter.
Varieties *F. japonica.* 'Variegata' has leaves that are streaked in white.
Care Should be kept in sunniest possible positions, either indoors at room temperature, or in the open while growing. In winter it needs a rest period at 13–16°C (55–61°F), with a minimum temperature of 10°C (50°F). Water normally during growth without letting water collect in pot, and place pot in a bowl filled with wet gravel. Give a liquid fertilizer fortnightly in spring–summer; while flowering, however, the plant benefits from a fertilizer with a high potassium content. Growing medium should be highly organic, made up of 2 parts leafmold, 1 part peat and 1 part sand. Repot every spring in containers of up to 30 cm (12 in). At end of winter prune, if need be, to keep foliage in shape.
Propagation From seed.
Pests and diseases Mealy bug and red spider.

118 FUCHSIA X HYBRIDA

Fuchsia, Lady's eardrops

Family Onagraceae.

Origin Horticultural hybrids from species in Central America and New Zealand.

Description Small trees or shrubs, height 1–2 m (3–6 ft), with an erect or prostrate habit; some dwarf species. The deciduous leaves are in pairs or groups of 3–5, ovate with pointed tip and dentate margins, 3–6 cm (about 1–2 in) long. The flowers are highly ornamental, developing at the tip of pendulous stalks; they are bell-shaped, consisting of a tubular calyx, terminating in 4 lobes, and of a corolla with 4 overlapping petals. Basic colors are white, pink, red, crimson and purple. Calyx and corolla are often of different colors. Flowering season as house plants March to November.

Varieties There are many cultivars, mostly derived from hybridization of different species and varieties. Among those of erect habit are: 'Jack French,' bright red calyx and purple corolla; 'Citation,' pink calyx and white corolla; 'Checkerboard,' red calyx with white lobes and dark red corolla; 'Constellation,' double ivory flowers; 'Snowcap,' red calyx and white corolla. The following cultivars are of trailing habit and ideal for growing in hanging baskets: 'Cascade,' white calyx tinged with violet and dark red corolla; 'Golden Marinka,' golden leaves and red flowers; 'Swingtime,' bright red calyx and white corolla.

Care May be planted outside in mild climates not subject to winter freezes; in colder climates they should preferably be kept outdoors in summer (in bright positions but not in direct sun). Not easy to cultivate indoors because they need a good deal of light for flowering and a humid environment. The best way to succeed with fuchsias is to buy small plants of 10–15 cm (4–6 in) in spring and allow them to acclimatize indoors by placing the pots in holders filled with wet gravel and spraying the foliage several times a day. The optimal temperature for cultivation is 15°C (59°F); during rest period it is 8–10°C (46–50°F), still in the light, although the plants are often thrown away after flowering. Water plentifully while plants are growing, but very little during dormancy. Feed once a week when flowering, fortnightly for rest of growing period. Mixture made up of loam, peat and sand in equal parts. Hanging baskets are best for trailing varieties. In spring shorten the branches by two-thirds and keep plants at room temperature. As soon as shoots appear, repot.

Propagation In spring or autumn by tip cuttings set to root in greenhouse.

Pests and diseases Aphids, whiteflies.

119 GARDENIA JASMINOIDES
Gardenia, Cape jasmine

Family Rubiaceae.
Origin China.
Description The genus *Gardenia* comprises many species of flowering shrubs, of which the only one cultivated as a house plant is *G. jasminoides*. It is an evergreen which, when pot grown, does not usually exceed 50 cm (20 in) in height. The leaves are elliptical, dark green, glossy and leathery, in pairs or in whorls of 3. The single flowers are white and highly scented, with a semi-double or double corolla, and bloom from June to September; diameter 5–10 cm (2–4 in).
Varieties There are many, including. 'Belmont,' 'Florida,' and 'Veitchii' (or Jasmine rose').
Care Needs bright light but not direct sun and a temperature of 16–18°C (61–64°F) while buds are forming. When flowers appear, it will stand up to 24°C (75°F). During bud development keep surroundings moist by spraying the plant (but not the open flowers) daily and placing the pot in a bowl with wet gravel. Water normally in spring–summer (with lime-free water), wetting the soil completely, but allowing the surface to dry between successive waterings. Growing medium: leafmold and peat in equal parts. Feed with preparations for acid-loving plants every fortnight from March to September. Repot every year in spring. Winter flowering induced by cutting the shoots formed in summer–autumn ('Veitchii' variety). Prune after flowering.
Propagation Root tip cuttings in greenhouse at 18°C (64°F).
Pests and diseases Aphids, scale insects, red spider.

120 GASTERIA MACULATA

Family Liliaceae.
Origin South Africa.
Description Small succulent cultivated for its ornamental leaves arranged in two rows, one above the other; they are pointed, 15 cm (6 in) long and almost 5 cm (2 in) wide, the upper surface being concave and the underside rounded, and covered with tiny gray-white warts. The plant is 20 cm (8 in) tall. Leaves of young plants are in a flat double row and this is sometimes permanent.
Care It can stand both shade and dry air, but prefers bright though filtered light. Growth, in spring and summer, is slow, and during this period the plant should be kept at average room temperatures or outdoors in the shade. In winter it requires a rest period at 10°C (50°F). Water normally, wetting the soil thoroughly but allowing the surface to dry out before watering again. Reduce amount of water in winter. There is no need to feed the plant as this results in excessive growth. The very porous potting mixture should be made up of 1 part loam, 1 part peat and 2 parts coarse sand. Repot every year in June, using large containers to encourage the sprouting of side shoots. When the pot is maximum 20 cm (8 in) in diameter, simply change the mixture.
Propagation In summer remove side shoots with roots and plant them in growing medium. If they have no roots, let them dry for a few days and then plant them; they will root in a couple of weeks. Treat them immediately as adult plants.
Pests and diseases Mealy bug.

121 GLORIOSA ROTHSCHILDIANA
Glory lily, climbing lily

Family Liliaceae.
Origin Tropical Africa.
Description Climbing species which may reach height of 2 m (6 ft), with tuberous roots. The glossy leaves are lanceolate, the upper ones ending in tendrils. The flowers, similar to those of the Turk's-cap lily, have 6 recurved petals with wavy edges. They bloom from June to August and are single, crimson with yellow borders. Raised in a greenhouse, the plant can be induced to flower from February onward.
Care The plant needs a lot of light and direct sunshine. The optimal temperature for growing is 15–18°C (59–64°F). Water abundantly (but do not let water collect) during growth and set the pot in a bowl full of wet gravel. Feed with a low-concentration liquid fertilizer every fortnight. In winter the epigeal (above ground) part of the plant dies, and the tubers should be kept at 10–12°C (50–53°F). In early spring these can be repotted in a mixture of 1 part loam, 1 part peat or leafmold and 1 part sand. Each tuber produces 2–3 stems, which have to be supported.
Propagation In February or March detach the small tubers which have formed among the roots of the parent plant; these can be planted and left to germinate at a temperature of 15–18°C (59–64°F), and then handled as adult plants. Can also be propagated from seed, but only in a greenhouse.
Pests and diseases Uneven temperatures and humidity levels may cause dark spots to appear on leaves.

122 GREVILLEA ROBUSTA
Silk oak, silky oak

Family Proteaceae.
Origin Queensland and New South Wales.
Description Small tree or shrub cultivated for ornamental foliage. As a pot plant it can reach a height of 2 m (6 ft) in 2–3 years, but in its native surroundings it grows to 15–20 m (50–65 ft). The bipinnate leaves, 30–45 cm (12–18 in) long, resemble those of ferns and are hairy underneath; when they appear they are pale brown but later turn bright green. Plants grown indoors do not usually flower.
Care In mild climates the plant can live all year round outdoors; minimum winter temperature 4–6°C (39–43°F). In any case it prefers being outside in spring and summer because it can do with direct sunlight, even if it tolerates average lighting. Does well at room temperature indoors but if over 18°C (64°F) the pot should be placed in a bowl full of wet gravel or peat. Water normally when the plant is growing most vigorously (May–September), allowing surface of mixture to dry out before watering again; at the same time give a liquid fertilizer every fortnight. In winter merely make sure the soil does not dry out completely. The growing medium should be neutral or slightly acid, formed of 1 part lime-free soil, 1 part peat and 1 part sand. Repot every spring, in containers up to 30 cm (12 in) in diameter.
Propagation From seed, in spring, at temperature of 13–16°C (55–61°F).
Pests and diseases Reasonably resistant to parasites.

123 GUZMANIA LINGULATA
Scarlet star, orange star

Family Bromeliaceae.
Origin Tropical America.
Description Epiphytic form with bright green, glossy, curving leaves, up to 45 cm (18 in) long, arranged in a rosette. The flower stalk, up to 30 cm (12 in) in length, grows from the center of the rosette and bears creamy, triangular bracts, 6 cm (2 in) long, at the tip, enfolding the yellow flowers. The latter do not bloom long (usually appearing in late winter), but the colored bracts persist for several weeks.
Varieties 'Cardinalis,' slightly bigger than the species with brighter red bracts; 'Minor' has 10 cm (4 in) leaves and a central funnel-like inflorescence on a very short, thick stalk.
Care Has to be kept in bright but filtered light and in warm, moist surroundings; minimum temperature 18°C (64°F). Spray the plant daily with lime-free water and place pot in bowl containing wet gravel. Water abundantly in spring–summer, less in winter, allowing upper part of mixture to dry out between applications. Keep the central funnel filled with fresh water, except during actual flowering. Feed with diluted liquid fertilizer every fortnight (soil and rosette), spraying the foliage. Porous, lime-free potting medium consisting of leafmold and peat in equal parts, or leafmold, sand and chopped fern roots in equal quantities. Repot every spring in containers of maximum 10 cm (4 in) diameter.
Propagation In April detach the rooted shoots, at least 8 cm (3 in) long, produced by the parent plant and pot them individually.
Pests and diseases Reasonably resistant to parasites.

---

124 GYNURA PROCUMBENS
Purple passion vine

Family Compositae.
Origin Cultivation.
Description Perennial herbaceous plant with trailing stem, or a climber if given suitable support; height 1.5 m (5 ft). It is grown for its triangular, irregularly incised leaves, 7–10 cm (3–4 in) long; they are soft and covered with very ornamental, violet down. In spring and summer it produces orange flowers with a rather disagreeable smell, so it is best to cut them off before they open.
Care Because the plant looks best when young, it is advisable to replace it every couple of years. To keep the foliage well colored, it is necessary to give the plant several hours of daily sunlight, especially in winter. It lives at normal room temperature but in the winter prefers a position at 12–14°C (53–57°F), minimum 10°C (50°F). If above 18°C (64°F), keep the surroundings humid by placing the pot in a bowl of wet gravel. Do not spray the foliage, however, as the leaves may become stained. Water normally, allowing the surface of the mixture to dry between successive waterings. Under 15°C (59°F), reduce amount of water. Give liquid fertilizer once a month all year round. Medium formed of organic soil, peat and sand in equal parts. Repot in spring.
Propagation In spring take 10 cm (4 in) tip cuttings and pot in equal parts peat and sand, keeping pot in bright but shaded position at about 20°C (68°F). Keep the mixture moist. When the plantlets are 15 cm (6 in) tall, at around 1–2 months, repot them in groups in proper growing medium.
Pests and diseases Species subject to aphid attacks.

125 HAEMANTHUS MULTIFLORUS
Blood Lily

Family Amaryllidaceae.
Origin Tropical Africa.
Description Bulbous plant with leaves on short, speckled stalks. The leathery, fleshy leaves are strap-shaped, about 30 cm (12 in) long. The flower stalk bears a rounded inflorescence, 8–12 cm (3–5 in) across, wrapped inside a spathe with outward-furling valves. The inflorescence consists of large numbers (up to 100) of coral-pink or red flowers. The base of the petals is purple and the stamens are yellow. The plant may live for many years and will flower annually indoors.
Care During the growing season the plant needs bright light, if possible with 1–2 hours of direct sunshine daily, at average temperatures of 18–22°C (64–71°F). During winter dormancy, light is unimportant but temperature should not drop below 13°C (55°F). Water with moderation, letting surface of mixture dry out prior to repeating. Reduce amount of water as the rest period approaches, and in winter simply make sure the soil does not get dry. Give a fertilizer with high potassium content fortnightly during period of growth. Potting medium should consist of 1 part organic soil, 1 part peat and 1 part sand. Repot in spring only when bulb and roots and have filled pot.
Propagation Separate the secondary bulblets formed by the main bulb and plant them individually, burying them half-way in soil.
Pests and diseases Bulb rot.

126 HAWORTHIA MARGARITIFERA
Wart plant

Family Liliaceae.
Origin South Africa.
Description The genus *Haworthia* comprises many species of small succulents cultivated for their ornamental foliage. In their native environment they live almost buried in the sand, receiving light only through the tip protruding from the surface. For this reason they do not like direct sun. All the species described here sprout lateral shoots which in the course of 1–2 years become groups of plantlets. *H. margaritifera* reaches a height of 8 cm (3 in) and has a diameter of 15 cm (6 in). The lanceolate leaves are 7–8 cm (about 3 in) long and 3 cm (1 in) broad at the base, forming a rosette around a very short stem. The upper surface of the leaf is flat, the lower has a keel-like ridge near the tip. The leaves are dotted with clusters of pearly white warts; the outer ones are erect, the inner ones curved towards the center of the rosette. From June onward the plant emits thin, hard flower stalks, which bear whitish flowers. These stalks should be cut off when they appear as the flowers are not decorative and, when grown indoors, the plant will either not bear ripe fruits or will produce seeds that fail to germinate.
Varieties *H. 'Margaritifera'* (not to be confused with the species of the same name) with pearly white warts.
Care Same as for *H. reinwardtii*.
Propagation As for *H. tessellata*.
Pests and diseases All *Haworthia* species are subject to fungal rot in young plants if overwatered. Scale insects easily nest among densely packed leaves.

127 HAWORTHIA REINWARDTII

Family Liliaceae.
Origin South Africa.
Description Succulent with stems 15 cm (6 in) long, covered by dense, fleshy, triangular leaves which curve inward. Each leaf is 3–4 cm (1–2 in) long, 1.5 cm (½ in) broad and equally thick, dark green to reddish, covered in tiny warts. The flowering stalks, which appear in June, bear whitish blooms, which should be removed as they form because they are not ornamental and, when cultivated indoors, will either not give fruits or will produce nongerminating seeds.

Varieties *H. reinwardtii* var. *chalwinii* forms a rosette 20 cm (8 in) high with spirally arranged leaves and white warts; *H. r. kaffirdriftens* has larger white warts.
Care All *Haworthia* species dislike direct sun and prefer moderate lighting. They live at room temperatures of 18–22°C (64–71°F) but below 15°C (59°F) during dormancy, from December to March. During spring–summer water moderately, completely wetting the mixture but allowing the surface to dry out before a further application. In rest period avoid soil becoming wholly dry. Do not feed. Potting medium: 1 part organic soil, 1 part peat and 2 parts sand. Grow in bowls or shallow containers and repot in spring when vegetation recommences. Increase the pot diameter only if the plant covers the whole surface. Leave space of a few centimeters between the plant and the rim of the pot.

Propagation As for *H. tessellata.*
Pests and diseases See *H. margaritifera.*

128 HAWORTHIA TESSELLATA

Family Liliaceae.
Origin South and Southwest Africa.
Description The leaves are clustered in rosettes about 5 cm (2 in) tall and 7 cm (3 in) wide, around amost nonexistent stems. Each fleshy leaf is 3 cm (1 in) long and 2 cm (almost 1 in) wide at the base, triangular in shape, incised at the margins and curved outward. The color is dark green to reddish, with crisscrossing white bands that form rectangular patterns on the upper surface. The lower surface is covered with whitish spots. The flower stalks appear in June and should be removed. The species produces runners which bear other rosettes.

Varieties Two natural varieties are *H. tessellata* var. *parva*, with small leaves, and *inflexa*, with blunt leaves, the edges curving inwards.
Care As for *H. reinwardtii.*

Propagation All *Haworthia* species described here sprout lateral shoots freely; these develop into new rosettes. They are easily multiplied by detaching the young rosettes in June and, if they have roots, potting them immediately in growing mixture, treating them as adult plants. If the shoot has no roots, let it dry out for 2–3 days after cutting, then pot it in growing mixture and treat as adult plant. The plants are also easily propagated from seed. Sow seed in spring at temperature of 20°C (68°F). Growth is rapid. The different species also hybridize easily with one another.

Pests and diseases As for *H. margaritifera.*

129 HEBE X ANDERSONII
Veronica

Family Scrophulariaceae.
Origin Hybrid of horticultural origin (H. salicifolia x H. speciosa).
Description Evergreen flowering shrubs which as house plants grow to a height of 1 m (3 ft). The leaves are oblong elliptic with a wavy surface, green with faint creamy streaks. The pale violet flowers are in compact spikes, blooming from July to October.
Varieties 'Variegata' is a cultivar with leaves that have broad margins of creamy-white.
Care The plant enjoys filtered light and not excessively bright positions. In summer it is better put outdoors in the shade. Bring indoors in winter but in cool places at around 10–12°C (50–53°F). Water abundantly in spring–summer, wetting the mixture thoroughly but not letting any water collect in the pan. Reduce watering in winter. Give liquid fertilizer fortnightly from spring to late summer. Growing medium formed of organic soil, peat and coarse sand in equal proportions. Repot in spring (May) only if container has become too small.
Propagation From cuttings in spring–summer. Plant cuttings in mixture of equal parts peat and sand, wrap in plastic bag and place in filtered light.
Pests and diseases Aphids may attack flowers, young leaves and tips of young branches.

---

130 HEDERA HELIX
English Ivy

Family Araliaceae.
Origin Europe.
Description Climbing evergreen plant with woody stem. It has two types of branch: the young ones have leaves with 3 or 5 lobes and aerial roots that attach themselves to any surface, and adult ones, without aerial roots, produce flowers and black fruits and entire leaves.
Varieties Most suitable for pot plants: 'Aureovariegata,' yellow-streaked leaves; 'Discolor,' small leaves with red and cream markings; 'Glacier,' small leaves, 3 cm (1 in) long and 2 cm (almost 1 in) wide, with silver-gray marks and pinky-white margins; 'Sagittaefolia,' dark green leaves with 5 lobes, the central one is long and triangular.
Care The varieties with streaked leaves need bright light and direct sun for several hours a day; those with green leaves prefer indirect light. The above-mentioned varieties grow easily at room temperature, but in winter it is advisable to keep them for a short period at 10°C (50°F). If the temperature is above 18°C (64°F), spray the plants daily. Water normally but reduce in resting period. Feed with liquid fertilizer fortnightly in spring–summer. Growing medium formed of loam, peat and sand in equal parts. Repot every year, in March. Prune to encourage bushy habit.
Propagation Take tip cuttings in spring and root them in water. Then plant 2–3 rooted cuttings in a single pot.
Pests and diseases Red spider if air is dry.

131 HEDYCHIUM GARDNERIANUM
Kahili ginger-lily

Family Zingiberaceae.
Origin Northern India.
Description Herbaceous perennial of considerable size; when grown as a house plant it may reach to well over 1 m (3 ft). The sturdy stems develop from an underground rhizome and bear sheathed leaves arranged in 2 rows. The leaves are lanceolate, 25 cm (10 in) long. The terminal spikes of flowers resemble orchids; they are yellow with red stamens, 5 cm (2 in) long. The flowering season is from July to September.

Care Will thrive in filtered light or partly sunny positions. During the growing period (March–October) it should be kept at room temperature, 18–22°C (64–71°F); in winter only the rhizome survives and this must be kept at 7–10°C (44–50°F), planted in a barely damp mixture that should not be allowed to dry out. When growth resumes in March, increase watering and continue to step up as the plant grows. During this time apply a liquid fertilizer every fortnight. Repot annually in March, changing the mixture. In autumn prune flower stems to within a few centimeters of base.
Propagation By division of rhizomes in March–April.
Pests and diseases Scale insects.

132 HELXINE SOLEIROLII (SOLEIROLIA)
Corsican carpet plant, Mind-Your-Own-Business, baby's tears, Irish moss, Corsican curse, Japanese moss

Family Urticaceae.
Origin Corsica, Sardinia.
Description Small perennial herbaceous plant with prostrate habit. It grows to a height of 10–30 cm (4–12 in), with a diameter of 1 m (3 ft) and more. The thin pink branches sprout roots as they grow, and clusters of pale green leaflets.
Varieties 'Argentea,' leaves with silvery streaks; 'Aurea,' leaves with golden-yellow streaks.

Care Very suitable for growing in hanging baskets. It does well both in shady and sunny (several hours a day) positions. Can be kept at room temperature, 18–22°C (64–71°F) all year round, and will live in open where not likely to suffer frost in winter. Water normally throughout the year if the plant does not become dormant; if it does, reduce amount of water. Avoid any standing water. Feed fortnightly with liquid fertilizer from May to August. Be careful not to wet the leaves with fertilizer or they may scorch; should this happen, spray foliage with water. Potting medium formed of organic soil, peat and sand in equal amounts. Repot every year in March–April. It is often treated as an annual, propagating it anew. It can be pruned, to check growth, at any time of year.

Propagation By dividing the clumps in April–May and transplanting the sections into standard growing mixture; or from cuttings.
Pests and diseases Fairly resistant to parasites.

133 HEMIGRAPHUS ALTERNATA
Red ivy

Family Acanthaceae.
Origin Possibly Indonesia.
Description Plant with fleshy stems up to 30 cm (12 in) long which droop downward and form roots as they touch the soil. They are bright red and bear rough, heart-shaped or ovate, opposite leaves on bright red stalks. The upper surface of the leaf is metallic purple-gray with prominent veins, the underside is dark red. The leaf margins are toothed. In September the species produces insignificant white flowers.
Varieties Apart from the original species there is the variety 'Exotica' with rougher leaves of darker purple.
Care Suitable for cultivation in hanging baskets, the plant needs bright light but not direct sun. Does well at high room temperatures all year round, but should this exceed 21°C (70°F) place the pot in a bowl with wet gravel and spray plant daily. Water plentifully during growth, but in winter period of dormancy (about 2 months) apply just enough to prevent mixture from drying out. In spring–summer give liquid fertilizer fortnightly. Medium formed of leafmold and peat in equal parts. Repot every 2 months while growing, in containers of up to 14 cm (6 in). Replace the plant every year.
Propagation The plant is easily propagated by taking tip cuttings, 5–8 cm (2–3 in) long, at any time of year, rooting them in water in bright, filtered light. When rooted, transplant 3–4 cuttings into pot full of standard growing mixture.
Pests and diseases Not very prone to attacks by parasites.

---

134 HIBISCUS ROSA-SINENSIS
Rose mallow, Chinese rose, Chinese hibiscus

Family Malvaceae.
Origin Origin unknown but probably Tropical Asia.
Description Evergreen shrub which in native surroundings grows to a height of 10 m (33 ft); as a house plant it reaches 1.5 m (5 ft). The leaves are ovate or ovate-acuminate, with toothed margins, 5–7 cm (2–3 in) long and 2–3 cm (about 1 in) wide. The flowers bloom from June to September in the upper leaf axils and are short-lived; they are 10–15 cm (4–6 in) across, dark crimson, with 5 petals.
Varieties *H. rosa-sinensis.* 'Cooperi,' crimson flowers and variegated ivory and crimson leaves; 'Aurantiacus,' single flowers with crinkled edges, salmon with purple center.
Care Indoors in sunny position several hours a day at room temperature, 18–22°C (64–71°F) from spring to autumn. In summer outdoors; winter resting period (from December to February) at 13°C (55°F). Water the plant normally. During winter prevent soil becoming too dry. Give liquid fertilizers. Growing mixture: loam, peat and sand in equal parts. Repot every spring. In March prune plants that are too big.
Propagation From April to July take tip or stem cuttings 10 cm (4 in) long and plant in moist mixture of peat and sand in equal parts. Place in greenhouse at 16°C (61°F). Enclose in plastic bag and keep pot in filtered light. After rooting, remove plastic, begin watering and feed every fortnight. After 3 months repot in standard growing medium.
Pests and diseases Aphids.

135　HIPPEASTRUM HYBRIDS
Amaryllis

Family Amaryllidaceae.
Origin Horicultural.
Description Genus similar to *Amaryllis,* with which it is often confused. It is a bulbous plant with ribbon-like leaves, up to 45 cm (18 in) long, turning outward. The flowering stem, about 45 cm (18 in) tall, appears on one side of the bulb in late winter, usually before the leaves, and bears 2–4 large, funnel-shaped flowers, 15 cm (6 in) across, each lasting several weeks. Each bulb may produce 2 flowering stems. The original species are no longer sold commercially but many hybrids have been produced with flowers of various colors. In winter only the bulb survives.
Varieties H. 'Bouquet,' H. 'Prima Donna,' H. 'Candy Cane,' H. 'Nivalis.'
Care Plant the bulbs in September, half-burying them in the potting medium, and keep indoors at 10–14°C (50–57°F). When growth commences, the plants need sunlight to flower. During flowering period, keep in indirect light not above 18°C (64°F). Water sparingly during dormancy; when growth begins, gradually increase amounts sufficiently to keep soil moist during the growing season. Then reduce watering again and interrupt it in autumn. In winter the bulb should remain dry. Feed from August to October with a preparation containing a high measure of potassium. Growing medium formed of highly organic soil, peat and sand in equal parts. Repot only every 3–4 years.
Propagation When repotting, remove the bulbils that form around the parent bulb and repot them separately.
Pests and diseases Not much subject to ailments.

136　HOWEA FORSTERIANA
Kentia palm, paradise palm

Family Palmae.
Origin Lord Howe Island (Oceania).
Description Formerly known as *Kentia forsteriana* and still often called by that name, it is a palm up to 3 m (10 ft) in height and with a spread of up to 2 m (6 ft) when grown indoors. The leaves are dark green, pinnate, 50 cm (20 in) long and 30 cm (12 in) wide, formed of narrow leaflets 50–60 cm (20–24 in) long and 2–3 cm (about 1 in) wide. It is single-stemmed and the leaves curve outward. Plants grown indoors produce neither flowers nor fruits.
Care It is easy to grow indoors because it is not particular about surroundings. It likes bright, preferably diffused, light and can be kept at normal room temperatures, even tolerating a fairly dry atmosphere. Minimum winter temperature 7°C (44°F). Water plentifully during spring–summer, without letting water settle in pot; in winter, when the plant is resting, water as necessary to prevent the mixture drying out. Give liquid fertilizer every fortnight during growing season. Potting medium made up of 1 part organic soil, 1 part peat and 1 part sand. Repot every other year, in April, up to 30 cm (12 in) containers. Dust off the leaves from time to time, placing them under a light jet of warm water.
Propagation From seed; germinate at 27°C (80°F) in February (in hotbed). When first leaves appear, prick out seedlings. Growth is very slow and propagation is usually difficult indoors.
Pests and diseases Scale insects and red spider.

137 HOYA BELLA
Miniature wax plant

Family Asclepiadaceae.
Origin India.
Description The genus *Hoya* comprises diverse species of evergreen plants with climbing or trailing stems, cultivated for their foliage and highly ornamental flowers. The species *H. bella* is a many-branched plant whose slender stems grow erect up to 30 cm (12 in) and then droop downward. The fleshy leaves are opposite, ovate, pointed, 2–3 cm (1 in) long and 1.5 cm (½ in) wide, gray-green with a thin chestnut band down the center. The waxy, scented flowers, star-shaped, are grouped in umbels of 5–10; they are white with a purple center and bloom from May to September.
Care Ideal for growing in hanging baskets, it requires bright light and direct sun. Average room temperature, 18–22°C (64–71°F) is best for growth; minimum winter temperature 10°C (50°F). During spring–summer water the mixture normally, allowing the surface to dry out before repeating; in dormant period simply keep the soil from drying out entirely. Feed fortnightly with liquid preparation containing plenty of potassium. Growing medium made up of organic soil, peat and coarse sand in equal parts. Repot in alternate years in April. Pinch tips of plants to encourage branching and cut off dead flowers but not flowering stalks.
Propagation In spring take 7–10 cm (3–4 in) stem cuttings and root them in mixture of equal parts sand and peat at 16–18°C (61–64°F) in greenhouse or enclosed in plastic bag. Rooting occurs in about 2 months. At this point uncover plant and feed it. After another month transplant into standard soil mixture.
Pests and diseases Scale insects.

138 HOYA CARNOSA
Wax flower, wax plant

Family Asclepiadaceae.
Origin Queensland (Australia) to China.
Description Sturdy climbing plant which clings to supports by aerial roots. It grows rapidly and may reach a height of 4–5 m (13–16 ft). The fleshy leaves are opposite, elliptic, 7 cm (3 in) long and 2–3 cm (about 1 in) wide. The flowers are waxy, grouped in umbels of 10–30, and scented. They bloom from May to September and are white or pale pink. The same stem can produce a second set of flowers.
Varieties There are two varieties with multicolored foliage: 'Exotica,' and 'Variegata.'
Care Bright light and direct sun for several hours daily. Can live at room temperature, 18–22°C (64–71°F) throughout year; minimum temperature while growing is 16°C (61°F), during dormancy 7°C (44°F). Water normally in spring–summer, letting soil surface dry out between applications. During winter simply avoid surface drying out completely. Feed liquid fertilizer with high potassium content fortnightly while growing. Potting medium: organic soil, peat and sand in equal amounts. Repot every spring.
Propagation From stem cuttings, 7–10 cm (3–4 in) long, taken in spring. Dip the base of the cutting in a root hormone and plant in mixture of peat and sand, rooting at 16–18°C (61–64°F) or placing in plastic bag in medium light. After rooting (in about 2 months), uncover the plant and begin watering and feeding moderately. After another month repot in proper growing medium.
Pests and diseases Scale insects.

Hyacinth

Family Liliaceae

Origin Developed in cultivation from an Eastern Mediterranean species.

Description The hyacinths grown as house plants are all derived from the species *H. orientalis*; the original species, however, is not very common, and it is the large-flowered varieties that are mostly cultivated. They are bulbous, very fragrant plants with strap-shaped leaves; they bloom in spring, each bulb producing a single flower stalk. The raceme, 10–15 in (4– in) long, bears bell-shaped flowers with curved petals in various colors: white, yellow, pink, red and blue. There is also a spontaneous variety, *H. orientalis* 'Albulus,' which produces 2–3 slender scapes bearing white, pink or blue racemes with fewer flowers. The bulb is big, on average 17–18 cm (7 in), and can be forced to induce winter flowering.

Varieties 'Blue Packet,' dark blue flowers, excellent cultivar for spring forcing; 'City of Harlem,' flowers of an unusual yellow; Edelweiss,' white flowers; 'Pink Pearl,' deep pink flowers.

Care In autumn pot the bulbs in a moist mixture of loam, peat and sand in equal amounts, burying them only partially. Keep the pots at a temperature of under 10°C (50°F) and in complete darkness for 8–10 weeks (6 weeks for forced bulbs) to stimulate rooting. After this period gradually give them more light, still keeping them in cool place, and water with moderation, letting the surface of the mixture dry out before repeating. When the buds begin to sprout, bring them into normal light. The flowers may need staking. Plant at intervals during autumn to ensure a winter-spring flowering period of 2–3 months. Having flowered, the bulb will not flower indoors the following year and should therefore be planted in the garden. This plant is suitable, too, for cultivating in water. Select containers just big enough to allow the bulb to rest against the neck so that only the base is in water; keep in darkness and in cool spot until the roots have formed (these must always remain submerged in water) as well as a few shoots, then bring them into the light at room temperature.

Propagation From offsets produced by the main bulb, but in order to get good flowers these must be enlarged by special methods not practicable indoors.

Pests and diseases Bulb rot, various bacteria and viruses.

140 HYDRANGEA MACROPHYLLA
Hydrangea, Hortensia

Family Saxifragaceae.
Origin Japan.
Description Also known by name *H. hortensis*. It is a sturdy deciduous plant which in a pot grows to a height of 60 cm (2 ft). The leaves are ovate with toothed edges, 10–15 cm (4–6 in) long and 5–10 cm (2–4 in) wide, set opposite on stems. The plant produces large, spherical flower clusters from July to September. In acid or neutral soil the flowers become blue, in alkaline soil they range from pink to red, the color deepening as the pH value of the soil rises.
Varieties There is a natural variety, *H. macrophylla* var. *serrata* which is more suitable than the original species for growing indoors because of its smaller size and more compact habit.
Care Usually flowers only once indoors. When it has finished it should be planted outside or thrown away. It should be placed in a bright position but not in direct sun. Cool temperatures of 14–16°C (57–61°F) prolong flowering for about 2 months; if the temperature is higher, the flowers fade much sooner. Water should be plentiful and the soil always moist. Feed the plant fortnightly with a liquid fertilizer. To deepen the color of blue flowers, apply aluminum sulfate to soil during bud formation; to keep the pink color, add lime. Growing mixture formed of organic soil (lime-free for blue-flowered varieties), peat and sand in equal parts. After flowering, place outdoors in organic soil, and in shady positions.
Propagation By stem tip cuttings, but difficult indoors.
Pests and diseases Aphids, red spider, thrips.

---

141 HYPOCRITA RADICANS (NEMATANTHUS GREGARIUS)
Goldfish plant

Family Gesneriaceae.
Origin Brazil.
Description The plant is cultivated for its ornamental foliage, but above all for its highly decorative flowers. The stems are initially erect and then curve, bearing smooth, fleshy, dark green leaves, 2–5 cm (1–2 in) long. In June–July, red flowers with orange borders bloom.
Care The plant needs a lot of light, even direct sun if not too strong. It can be kept indoors at room temperature, but preferably not too high, 18°C (64°F), all year round. In summer it can be put outside in a spot sheltered from the heat and from too much sunshine. Water normally in spring–summer; wet the soil completely without flooding it, but let the surface dry out before watering again. Reduce amount of water in winter. Give liquid fertilizer every fortnight from April to September. The growing medium must be highly organic and porous; leafmold, peat and sphagnum moss in equal proportions, plus a few pieces of charcoal. The plant does not like to be repotted, so it is necessary only to replace with fresh soil or to make a change when the plant grows too big for the pot. The best time is March–April.
Propagation Take 5 cm (2 in) tip cuttings and plant in damp mixture of equal parts peat and sand. Cover with plastic and set in bright, indirect light at 20°C (68°F). After rooting, uncover the young plants and water with moderation. A couple of months later transplant into definitive medium.
Pests and diseases Stem rot due to overwatering.

142 HYPOESTES PHYLLOSTACHYA

Freckle face, measles plant, polka dot plant

Family Acanthaceae.
Origin Malagasy Republic (Madagascar).
Description Also wrongly known by the name *H. san-guinolenta*, it is a shrub with extremely decorative foliage. It can grow very tall, but it is best to pinch out the tips so as to restrict the height to 40–50 cm (16–20 in), which at the same time encourages the densely bushy habit. The ovate leaves, 6 cm (2 in) long and 3 cm (1 in) wide, are green with pink patches and bright red veining. The main and secondary branches are also red. In March–April rather insignificant small purple-red flowers appear.
Care The plant needs bright light to keep its color, and also direct sun, except at the hottest time of day. Does well at room temperature of 18–22°C (64–71°F) but will not stand temperatures below 15°C (59°F). In summer it can go outdoors, though not in full sun. Water normally during spring–summer, letting the top part of the soil dry out before repeating; water very little during the brief winter rest period and allow the soil to become dry before giving any more. Feed with liquid fertilizer every fortnight during growth. Mixture made up of organic soil, peat and sand in equal parts. Repot in spring in bowls or baskets.
Propagation Tip cuttings may be taken from spring to autumn. These, about 10 cm (4 in) long, are rooted in water after removing the lower leaves; when the roots are 5 cm (2 in) long, pot them in normal soil in 8 cm (3 in) containers. Cuttings can also be rooted in peat and sand at 18–21°C (64–70°F) in diffused light. The plant can also be propagated from seed in spring.
Pests and diseases Aphids, scale insects.

143 IMPATIENS WALLERIANA

Busy Lizzie, patience plant, patient Lucy

Family Balsaminaceae.
Origin East Africa
Description A perennial species with succulent stems, it grows as a pot plant to a height of 30–40 cm (12–16 in). The leaves are elliptic, sometimes heart-shaped at the base, green or bronze-tinged, with red or brown patches on the lower side. Flowering season from June to October.
Varieties Cultivars are mostly obtained by crossing 2 species of *Impatiens,* and include: 'Scarlet Baby,' scarlet flowers, 15 cm (6 in) tall; 'Orange Baby,' orange flowers, same height.
Care Keep in bright but filtered light. Do well at room temperatures but at more than 24°C (75°F) need to be kept moist by daily spraying, the pots being placed in bowls of wet gravel. If during winter light or temperature is reduced – the latter to below 13°C (55°F) – the plant becomes dormant and should be watered very little, without allowing the mixture to dry out completely. If this does not happen, water normally all year round, letting the top of the soil dry out between applications. Liquid fertilizer fortnightly in spring–summer. Growing medium 1 part organic soil, 1 part peat and 1 part sand. Repot every other year, in April.
Propagation Tip cuttings 5–7 cm (2–3 in) in length are taken in summer and rooted in water. When the roots are 2 cm (1 in) long, plant them in growing mixture. Many varieties can also be propagated from seed in spring, at 18–21°C (64–70°F), the pots being placed in filtered light.
Pests and diseases Red spiders, aphids, whitefly.

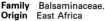

144 IPOMOEA BATATAS
Sweet potato vine, yam

Family Convolvulaceae.
Origin Central America.
Description A perennial plant normally grown for the sake of its large, tuberous, edible roots. It can be cultivated indoors as an annual. It produces large numbers of very long, twining, reddish-purple stems which bear soft, narrow, trilobate, pale green leaves, 4–6 cm (2 in) in length.
Care It is very simple to grow. The plant should be set in a hanging basket and the mass of greenery which it produces then left to hang down; alternatively, the stems can be trained to climb trellises or other supports. The plant adapts to a wide range of lighting conditions: sun, bright filtered light or medium light; but it does not respond to positions that are too dark. It should be kept at room temperature throughout the winter. In autumn a tuberous root (preferably one that has been dug directly from the garden, or one that has already started to sprout) is placed in a transparent pot full of water, not touching the bottom; the water level should reach about halfway up the tuber. After a few days germination should commence and production of stems and leaves in large quantities will continue throughout the winter and ensuing spring; after this the plant should be discarded. No special attention is required; it is enough to maintain the water level, adding more as it is used up, and always keeping it at room temperature.
Propagation By means of the tuberous roots which should be bought every year.
Pests and diseases Fairly resistant to parasites.

---

145 IRESINE HERBSTII
Blood leaf, beafsteak plant

Family Amaranthaceae.
Origin Brazil.
Origin Perennial, bushy herbaceous plant cultivated for its deep red foliage and stems; the latter are fleshy, up to 60 cm (2 ft) in length, and bear ovate, heart-shaped leaves, up to 8 cm (3 in) long and 5 cm (2 in) wide. The leaf veining is a lighter red than the blade itself. Plants grown indoors do not usually produce flowers, which are in any event insignificant.
Description In addition to the species, there is a variety, 'Aureoreticulata,' its red leaves tinged with green and with yellow veining.
Varieties The plant requires bright light and several hours of daily direct sunshine to maintain its vivid coloration. It does well at room temperatures throughout the year, but the surrounding air should be kept humid by placing the pot in a bowl filled with damp gravel. Water plentifully during growth season to keep mixture wet but do not allow water to collect. Reduce watering in winter, but do not let mixture dry out. Give liquid fertilizer fortnightly from spring to autumn. Potting medium made up of organic soil, peat and sand in equal parts. The plant is fast-growing and needs repotting once or twice a year in containers of up to 15 cm (6 in).
Care In spring take 5–7 cm (2–3 in) tip cuttings and root them in water in filtered light (using an opaque glass container). When the roots are 2 cm (1 in) long, plant the cuttings in growing medium, putting 2–3 in each pot.
Propagation Aphids, red spider.

146 JACARANDA MIMOSIFOLIA

Family Bignoniaceae.
Origin Tropical America.
Description Also known under the names *J. acutifolia* or *J. ovalifolia*. A shrub or small tree which in its native zones grows to a height of 15 m (50 ft); in a pot it is 1–2 m (3–6 ft). The plant has a single stem which, when it reaches about 60 cm (2 ft), branches out freely to form fine, spreading foliage. The leaves are bipinnate and persistent, similar to those of mimosa or certain ferns, the leaflets having entire or toothed margins. Each leaf may be 30 cm (12 in) long and 10 cm (4 in) wide. The tubular blue flowers, in axillary clusters, do not appear in indoor plants.
Care The species needs bright light and at least 3–4 hours of daily sunshine. During the growth season it does well at room temperatures but requires a winter rest period at about 16°C (61°F). In mild climates it can go outside so long as the winter temperature does not fall below 8°C (46°F). During growth water normally, wetting the soil completely but allowing the surface to dry out before repeating. While the plant is dormant merely prevent the soil from drying out entirely. Give liquid fertilizer every fortnight from spring to autumn. Growing medium made up of 1 part loam, 1 part peat and 1 part sand. Repot every spring in bigger containers, up to a maximum of 24 cm (10 in).
Propagation From seed. Immerse the seeds in water for 24 hours, then plant each one in a small 6 cm (2 in) pot and set in bright, indirect light at 20–25°C (68–77°F). Keep the mixture barely damp. When the seedling is 20 cm (8 in) tall, prick out and handle as adult plant.
Pests and diseases Reasonably resistant to parasites.

147 JACOBINEA CARNEA (JUSTICIA CARNEA)
Brazilian plume, flamingo plant, king's crown

Family Acanthaceae.
Origin Brazil.
Description Evergreen, rapidly growing, many-branched shrub which as a house plant may grow to a height of 1.20 m (4 ft). The rough, ovate and pointed leaves, set opposite in pairs, are 15 cm (6 in) long and 6 cm (2 in) wide, with prominent veining. Flowers are pink, tubular, two-lipped at the tip; they bloom in August–September.
Care Not easy to cultivate indoors. It requires at least 3–4 hours of sunlight daily, and bright light at all times. During growth it lives at normal room temperature, but needs plenty of humidity and must be sprayed daily, the pot being set in wet gravel. Winter rest at 13°C (55°F). While growing, water just enough to keep the soil moist, without letting water settle; during dormancy, prevent soil from drying out completely. Liquid plant food fortnightly during growth. Potting medium: loam, peat and sand in equal parts; repot several times, if necessary, while plant is growing.
Propagation From tip or stem cuttings in spring. Cut 5–10 cm (2–4 in) portions from just below a node, remove basal leaves and dip each cutting in hormone rooting preparation; then plant in mixture of equal parts peat and sand. Wrap in plastic bag and place in bright, filtered light, or in greenhouse at 20°C (68°F). After rooting, in 2–3 weeks, uncover and water sparingly, starting to feed fortnightly. After about 2 months from beginning of propagation transplant into growing soil and treat as adult.
Pests and diseases Red spider if atmosphere too dry.

148 JASMINUM OFFICINALE

Jasmine, white jasmine, poet's jasmine, jessamine

Family Oleaceae.
Origin China, India.
Description Two species can be cultivated indoors: *J. officinale* and *J. polyanthum*. The former is a sturdy climber with opposite, pinnate leaves formed of 5–7 leaflets. The latter has white scented flowers in plumes and is winter-flowering. From June to October *J. officinale* produces loose clusters of highly scented flowers; the corolla is tubular, with 5 white petals.

Varieties (of *J. officinale*) 'Affine,' large pink-flushed flowers; 'Aureum,' yellow-streaked leaves.

Care Well-lighted positions with several hours of direct sunlight every day, provided this is not too strong. They prefer a temperature of around 15°C (59°F) and need a winter rest at 6–10°C (43–50°F). Water plentifully in spring–summer to keep the mixture moist; reduce watering during dormancy, letting the surface of the soil dry out before repeating. Liquid fertilizer fortnightly during growth. Mixture formed of loam, peat and sand in equal quantities. Repot every spring, then provide with fresh soil annually.

Propagation In August–September take tip cuttings just beneath a node, or branch cuttings with a small portion of attached twig. Plant in moist mixture of equal parts peat and sand, in pots of 8 cm (3 in) diameter. Wrap the pots in plastic bags and place in bright light but not direct sun. When a new shoot forms, this is confirmation of rooting. Uncover and allow to gain strength, then plant in standard growing medium.

Pests and diseases Aphids may attack young shoots; scale insects attack stems and leaves.

149 JATROPHA PODAGRICA

Tartogo, gout plant

Family Euphorbiaceae.
Origin Central America, West Indies, Colombia.
Description Succulent shrub up to 2 m (6 ft) high, formed of densely packed branches, warty at the base. The leaves are shield-shaped, made up of 3–5 lobes, measuring about 25 cm (10 in) across; they are dark green and leathery, the stalk inserted almost in the center. The scarlet or coral flowers are fleshy and set in showy clusters.

Care The plant needs very bright and preferably direct light. During the growing season it should be kept at normal room temperatures of 18–22°C (64–71°F); in winter a period of dormancy at around 12°C (53°F) is advisable. Water with moderation during spring–summer, allowing about two-thirds of the soil to dry out before watering again. During dormant period simply make sure the soil does not become completely dry. Give liquid fertilizer fortnightly from April to September. Growing medium made up of 1 part organic soil, 1 part peat and 2 parts sand. See that bottom of pot is well drained. Repot every spring, increasing the diameter of the container to maximum 2 cm (8 in).

Propagation From tip cuttings in May–June. After taking the cutting, dip it in water to halt flow of latex. Let the cutting dry for a couple of days, then plant in mixture of equal parts peat and sand.

Pests and diseases Prone to rot if overwatered; scale insects and mealy bug.

150 KALANCHOE BLOSSFELDIANA
Flaming Katy

Family Crassulaceae.
Origin Malagasy Republic (Madagascar).
Description Herbaceous, perennial shrub with erect habit, growing to a height of 30 cm (12 in) and cultivated for its attractive winter flowers which last 2–3 months. The fleshy, ovate or elliptic leaves, set opposite, have toothed edges and are up to 7 cm (3 in) long; they are green, often bordered red. The flowers, red in the species plant, are tubular and carried in large clusters at the tip of leafless stems.
Varieties 'Orange Triumph,' orange flowers; 'Goldrand,' yellow flowers. Miniature varieties, 14–20 cm (6–8 in) tall, are: 'Vulcan,' 'Tom Thumb' and 'Norisfener,' all with red flowers. Varieties with orange or yellow flowers are rarer.
Care The plant is usually bought in flower and is normally discarded when this is over because it is difficult to make it flower repeatedly indoors. It likes light and direct sun. Can be kept at room temperature and should be watered moderately while flowering, with about half of the mixture allowed to dry out before watering again. Give liquid fertilizer every 3 weeks while in flower. If kept over the winter, reduce watering and give it a temperature of 10–13°C (50–55°F). Very porous potting mixture should be made up of 1 part organic soil, 1 part peat and 2 parts coarse sand or perlite; put a drainage layer of crocks at the bottom of the pot, maximum 12 cm (5 in) diameter. Repot in spring.
Propagation Take 7–10 cm (3–4 in) tip cuttings in spring, let them dry for a couple of days and plant in mixture of equal parts peat and sand, keeping them in warm, well-lit surroundings and watering moderately.
Pests and diseases Easily attacked by scale insects.

151 X LAELIOCATTLEYA HYBRIDS

Family Orchidaceae.
Origin Horticultural hybrids.
Description Group of hybrid orchids derived from crossing of the genera *Laelia* and *Cattleya*. Flowering generally occurs between October and March.
Varieties Among the many varieties, the following can be recommended: 'Anna Ingham,' groups of 3–5 dark purple-red or dark lilac flowers; 'Derna,' yellow and purple flowers, 1–2 to each flowering stem; 'Dorset Gold,' flowering stalks bearing up to 6 yellow or purple-red flowers.
Care A relatively easy type of orchid for cultivating indoors. Needs bright but not direct light. Does well at room temperature but will not tolerate fluctuations or temperatures below 13°C (55°F). If temperature exceeds 21°C (70°F) the plant should be sprayed every day and the pot placed in a bowl of wet gravel. Water the plant normally during growth but allow the mixture to dry out almost completely before watering again. After flowering, the plant needs a 6-week rest period during which watering should be greatly reduced. Give liquid fertilizer for orchids with every 3–4 waterings during growth. Mixture formed of equal parts osmunda fiber and sphagnum moss. Repot when the plant has filled the pot, at the end of the dormant period.
Propagation Divide the rhizome into 2 parts in spring, getting rid of dry portions, and pot each separately. Keep in medium light for 1–2 months, watering very little; then handle as for adult plants.
Pests and diseases Scale insects, red spider.

152 LANTANA CAMARA
Yellow sage, shrub verbena

Family Verbenaceae.
Origin West Indies.
Description Shrub up to 2 m (6 ft) high. Only a dwarf hybrid variety is cultivated indoors, since it alone flowers as a pot plant. It grows to a height of 1.20 m (4 ft) but if kept pruned can be restricted to about 40 cm (16 in). The elliptic leaves have a rough surface and toothed margins. The tubular flowers are in rounded corymbs which sprout from the leaf axils between May and October.
Varieties There are many cultivars with white, yellow or pink flowers, but the only horticultural variety that will flower indoors is *Lantana x hybrida* 'Nana.'
Care Likes full sunlight and needs 3–4 hours of it daily all year in order to flower. Adapts well to room temperatures from spring to autumn. Rest period in winter at 10°C (50°F). Water abundantly while growing but in winter simply make sure the mixture does not dry out entirely. Liquid fertilizer every fortnight during growth. Potting medium: 1 part organic soil, 1 part peat and 1 part sand. Repot annually in March. Discard after 3–4 years.
Propagation Take 10 cm (4 in) cuttings from a nonflowering branch in August. Cut below a node, strip off the leaves and, after dipping the cuttings in rooting hormone preparation, plant them in a mixture of equal parts peat and wet sand. Place in greenhouse at 18°C (64°F) or in a plastic bag, exposing them to bright but filtered light. Leave the rooted cuttings over the winter; in February–March stop the tips to encourage a bushy habit and then, in March, repot in standard growing soil, treating as adult plants.
Pests and diseases Very prone to attacks by whitefly.

153 LAURUS NOBILIS
Bay tree, sweet bay

Family Lauraceae.
Origin Mediterranean region.
Description Evergreen shrub which in its native surroundings, in the open, grows to a height of 6 m (20 ft). Its leaves are leathery, lanceolate-elliptic, with wavy edges, and strongly aromatic. The plant is dioecious. Inconspicuous yellow-green flowers appear in April. Pollinated female plants then produce berry-like fruits.
Care It can flourish either in sunny or in shaded positions, provided there is adequate light. From spring to autumn it can also be kept indoors at room temperature, although it is better outdoors in a sheltered spot, as a tub plant. It needs a winter rest period at 5°C (41°F). The plant should be watered plentifully in spring–summer, with no water left to stand. In winter merely prevent the mixture from drying out entirely. Liquid fertilizer every 3 weeks from spring to autumn. Growing medium: loam, peat and sand in equal parts. Repot every other year, in spring. Prune summer–autumn.
Propagation Tip cuttings of 10 cm (4 in) can be taken in August–September or in April. They are planted in a wet mixture of peat and sand or perlite in equal proportions and put in an unheated greenhouse. Rooting occurs in about a month, at a temperature of 18°C (64°F). Transplant them the following spring into growing soil. Growth is slow and some 2 years are needed before the new plant reaches reasonable dimensions.
Pests and diseases Subject to attacks by scale insects.

154 LILIUM LONGIFLORUM
Eastex lily, white trumpet lily

Family Liliaceae.
Origin Japan.
Description The genus *Lilium* comprises an extremely large number of bulbous plant species which produce beautiful flowers. There are also many hybrids. The species *L. longiflorum* and its hybrids is one of the few that can be cultivated indoors. It has a yellow bulb from which develops a straight stem that bears 20–40 glossy leaves, 10–12 cm (4–5 in) long. The stem may give out aerial roots. The flower, white with golden anthers and outward-turning petals, is very fragrant. Flowering normally occurs in June–July but florists have flowering plants, forced under glass, as early as February.
Varieties 'Arai 5,' 'Georgia Belle,' 'Hiromoto.'
Care For indoor cultivation plants are bought in bud and kept until they finish flowering, when they are thrown away as they will not flower again under these conditions. It is possible to obtain flowering but only by special methods, impracticable indoors. The plants need exposure to the sun for several hours daily, but protection from fierce heat. They are adaptable as regards temperature, doing well at ordinary room temperature, 18–22°C (64–71°F), but flowers last longer in cool positions. Water abundantly during flowering season; avoid water collecting. Feeding is not necessary for the brief time in which the plants are indoors. Mixture formed of 1 part organic soil, 1 part peat and 1 part sand.
Propagation The pure species from seed or bulb, the hybrids from offset bulbs produced by parent plant.
Pests and diseases Bulb rot, induced by plant parasite; aphids.

155 LITHOPS FULLERI
Living stones, pebble plants

Family Aizoaceae.
Origin South Africa.
Description A succulent which looks exactly like a stone. Each plant, furnished with roots but virtually without any visible stem, is formed of 2 thick, fleshy, semicircular leaves that are fused together, with a groove along the upper side. On sunny September afternoons single daisy-like flowers, white with a yellow center, grow from these splits of the leaf. The leaves shrivel after flowering and 2 new ones then form, appearing the following spring. *L. fulleri* may form small clumps comprising 2–3 pairs of leaves, but growth is extremely slow.
Care This plant needs several hours of direct sun daily throughout the year. When growing it can be kept at normal room temperature; during winter dormancy the temperature should be 5–10°C (41–50°F). Water sparingly from spring to autumn, letting about three-quarters of the soil dry out before repeating; during rest period give no water at all. Does not need to be fed. Very porous mixture formed of 1 part loam, 1 part peat and 2 parts sand; place a layer of crocks at bottom of pot to assist drainage. Repot every 3–4 years.
Propagation From seed, in April, at temperature of 21°C (70°F), but growth is slow. Alternatively by clump division, in June. Cut up the clumps, letting the pieces dry for a couple of days, then pot in normal mixture, watering very little and setting in filtered light. Give no water in winter and expose the plant normally to the sun the following spring.
Pests and diseases Scale insects; mold if compost too wet.

156 LIVISTONA CHINENSIS
Chinese fan palm, fountain palm

Family Palmae.
Origin China.
Description In its native surroundings this palm with decorative fan-shaped leaves takes the form of a tree, while as a house plant it assumes the likeness of a shrub. The glossy pale green leaves are borne on stalks 30–40 cm (12–16 in) long, which are thorny for about half their length. Each leaf measures 60 cm (2 ft) long and is equally broad, being deeply incised into segments which are pointed at the tip.
Care The plant needs bright light but not direct sun. It grows well at normal room temperatures of 18–22°C (64–71°F) all year round, for it does not need a resting period, but if the winter temperature drops below 14°C (57°F) growth is impaired. Water normally in growing season, allowing the surface of the soil to dry out between successive applications; if the plant is permitted to become dormant simply make sure that the soil does not get completely dry. Give liquid fertilizer fortnightly from spring to autumn. Growing medium made up of organic soil, peat and sand in equal parts. Repot every spring in containers of up to 30 cm (12 in); in subsequent years just replace with fresh soil.
Propagation From seed; but because each seed is covered with a hard integument, these should be kept in water for some days and then sown at a temperature of 25°C (77°F). It is a very lengthy procedure.
Pests and diseases Scale insects, red spider.

157 MANETTIA INFLATA
Firecracker vine

Family Rubiaceae.
Origin Uruguay, Paraguay.
Description Climbing plant cultivated for its beautiful flowers which appear end-March and continue until October. Its ovate-lanceolate leaves are 5 cm (2 in) long; the tubular flowers, covered in thick down and carried on long stalks, sprout from the leaf axils. Each flower has a green calyx with 5 outward-curving sepals and a yellow corolla with red hairs at the base.
Care The plant needs supports, or it may be trailed from hanging baskets. It likes bright positions but not direct sunlight. During growth it should be kept at ordinary room temperatures; in winter it requires a cooler 13–15°C (55–59°F). Water plentifully in growing season so as to keep the mixture damp but without allowing water to collect; during dormancy merely avoid letting the soil dry out completely. Feed with liquid fertilizer fortnightly from spring to autumn. Potting mixture made up of 1 part organic soil, 1 part peat and 1 part sand.
Propagation Take tip cuttings in spring–summer from nonflowering stems. Each 10 cm (4 in) cutting should be taken beneath a node and planted together with a couple of others in a pot filled with peat and sand in equal parts. Dampen the mixture slightly, enclose in plastic bag and place in bright, filtered light. When rooted, uncover, water sparingly and feed every fortnight. As soon as roots appear transplant into standard mixture.
Pests and diseases Aphids.

158　MARANTA LEUCONEURA
Prayer plant.

Family Marantaceae.
Origin Brazil.
Description Herbaceous evergreen plant. The ovate leaves, up to 12 cm (5 in) long, are emerald green with reddish-brown patches or with yellow and dark green patches, according to variety. Older leaves become darker. The plant grows to about 20 cm (8 in) and the leaves close at night.

Varieties Best known is *M. leuconeura* 'Massangeana,' with smaller leaves than those of the species; 'Erythro-neura,' green leaves, with dark red main and lateral veining, and a central yellow stripe, the underside is purple-red; 'Kerchoviana,' bright green leaves with lighter veining, and a double row of squarish dark brown or dark green patches down the sides of the principal vein, the underside is pale blue-gray.

Care The plant requires bright light but detests direct sun. It does well at average temperatures of 18–21°C (64–70°F) all the year round but has a rest period in winter when growth ceases. It needs high humidity and therefore the pots should be placed in bowls filled with moist gravel, and the foliage sprayed daily with lime-free water to avoid the formation of white spots. The plant is also suitable for growing in terrariums. During the growing period the mixture must always be kept moist; during dormancy allow the surface to dry out between successive waterings. Liquid fertilizer fortnightly from spring to autumn. Growing medium of loam, peat and sand in equal proportions. Repot every spring.

Propagation In April divide the clumps by cutting the rhizome and plant each portion separately.
Pests and diseases Red spider.

159　MEDINILLA MAGNIFICA
Rose grape

Family Melastomataceae.
Origin Philippines.
Description A bushy plant which in its native environment grows to a height of 2.50 m (8 ft) and as a pot plant to more than 1 m (3 ft). The stem is quadrangular, woody and many-branched. The stalkless, folding leaves are ovate and leathery, with wavy edges, each measuring up to 30 cm (12 in) long and 12 cm (5 in) wide. The magnificent flowers bloom from March to June.

Care The plant is very difficult to cultivate indoors because it requires controlled levels of temperature and humidity. The best position for it is between two windows. In spring and summer it needs bright but indirect light; in winter it can take direct sunlight. Give it average to high temperatures, 18–27°C (64–80°F), but in winter keep it at 15–18°C (59–64°F) when resting, this being essential for flowering. Water moderately, letting the upper part of the soil dry out before repeating. In winter simply avoid letting the soil dry out. Humidity, however, should be high; place the pots in bowls filled with moist gravel and spray the foliage daily if temperature goes above 18°C (64°F) during dormant period. Give liquid fertilizer fortnightly from time buds open until September. Growing medium formed of leafmold, peat and sand in equal parts. Repot every spring. Prune after flowering.

Propagation By means of tip cuttings, but not possible indoors.
Pests and diseases Very prone to red spider.

160 MICROCOELUM WEDDELLIANUM
Dwarf coconut palm

Family Palmae.

Origin Indonesia.

Description Formerly called *Cocos weddellianum*, this is a slow-growing palm which as a pot plant can grow to a height of 1–1.20 m (3–4 ft). The pinnate leaves, which in the adult plant may measure 1 m (3 ft) long and 25 cm (10 in) wide, are formed of narrow, dark green leaflets arranged along a central axis and covered with blackish scales. Better than adult plants are young ones, 20–30 cm (8–12 in) tall, with smaller leaves. Indoor plants do not produce flowers, nor do they normally have a stem.

Care Easy to cultivate, it likes bright light but not direct sun. Does well at room temperatures of 16–27°C (61–80°F) for whole year, but temperature must not fall below 15°C (58°F). Requires high measure of humidity and should therefore be kept all year round in bowl filled with gravel and moist peat. Water moderately, letting surface of mixture dry out before repeating. If temperature falls to 15°C (58°F) reduce watering but avoid allowing soil to dry out. Feed with liquid fertilizer once a month from spring to autumn. Potting medium formed of organic soil, peat and sand in equal proportions. Repot every 2–3 years in spring when the swollen base of the plant appears above the surface of the soil, but do not greatly increase size of pot because the plant grows best in fairly small containers.

Propagation From seed, but very slow growing.

Pests and diseases Red spider, scale insects.

---

161 MIMOSA PUDICA
Sensitive plant

Family Leguminosae.

Origin Brazil.

Description A small shrub often confused with plants of the genus *Acacia* which include the yellow-flowered mimosa commonly sold by florists. *M. pudica* has pale green pinnate leaves which retract when touched, the stalks bending at the same time; after half an hour, if not further disturbed, the leaves resume their normal position. The globular flower heads are pink and feathery, blooming from July to September in the leaf axils.

Care The species is short-lived and loses its beauty as it ages, for which reason it is usually cultivated as an annual and discarded after flowering. It needs bright light and direct sun, though not when at hottest, for 3–4 hours daily. It does well all year round at normal room temperatures of 18–22°C (64–71°F) and needs plenty of humidity, so place pots in bowls filled with damp gravel. The plant will not tolerate foul air or fumes. Watering should be sufficient to wet the mixture entirely but the surface must dry out before repeating. Give liquid fertilizer fortnightly from June to September. Growing medium formed of 1 part organic soil, 1 part peat and 1 part sand. Repot several times a season if roots fill pot.

Propagation Sow seed in February–March, using seed soil, setting 2–3 per 8 cm (3 in) pot and keeping it in bright, filtered light at a temperature of 18–20°C (64–68°F). Water the mixture sparingly. When the seedlings are 4–5 cm (2 in) high, prick out the sturdiest in standard growing mixture.

Pests and diseases Reasonably resistant to parasites.

162 MONSTERA DELICIOSA
Ceriman, Swiss cheese plant, Mexican breadfruit

Family Araceae.
Origin Mexico, Guatemala.
Description Large species also known as *Philodendron pertusum*. The stems are furnished with aerial roots by which means the plants, in their native surroundings, cling to the bark of trees. As house plants they need moss-covered poles as supports. The glossy leaves are extremely decorative, up to 1 m (3 ft) long and 60 cm (2 ft) wide, those of adult plants being deeply incised and perforated. The mature plant produces spiky flowers enclosed in a cream-colored spathe, followed by an edible fruit which smells like a pineapple. Both may appear simultaneously at any time of year but very rarely in house plants.
Varieties *M. deliciosa* 'Variegata,' leaves speckled creamy-white; 'Borsigiana,' very slow grower, smaller leaves.
Care Requires bright but filtered light, and can take sunlight in winter. Does well at room temperatures of 18–22°C (64–71°F) all year round; increase humidity by placing pot in layer of moist peat, spraying the foliage often and keeping the moss pole damp. Water normally, allowing surface of soil to dry out before repeating. Give liquid fertilizer fortnightly from April to September. Mixture formed of 2 parts leafmold, 1 part peat and 1 part sand. Repot every spring.
Propagation From stem cuttings, each with a leaf. Take these in June and plant them in mixture of peat and sand in equal parts, at temperature of 24–27°C (75–82°F). Rooting is hard to achieve indoors. Propagation by air-layering is slower but more reliable.
Pests and diseases Red spider attack if air too dry.

---

163 MUSA ALUMINATA 'DWARF CAVENDISH'
Dwarf banana, Cavendish banana, Canary Islands banana, Chinese banana, governor banana, dwarf Jamaica

Family Musaceae.
Origin Southeast Asia.
Description Belongs to the same family as the plant which produces the edible banana and is similar in appearance, although much smaller. In the wild it bears fruits that are edible. As a house plant it grows to little over 1 m (3 ft) in height. It is formed of an upright stem which bears large elliptic leaves 60–90 cm (2–3 ft) long and 30 cm (1 ft) across. The whitish flowers, enveloped in purple bracts, are in pendulous whorls.
Care The plant thrives on bright light, if possible with a few hours of sunshine each day provided this is not too strong. It can be kept at room temperature, 18–22°C (64–71°F) throughout the year but during winter growth slows down. Water copiously while plant is growing but reduce amounts in winter. Give liquid fertilizer fortnightly from April to September. Growing medium formed of 1 part organic soil, 1 part peat and 1 part sand. Repot every spring, increasing containers to maximum 25–30 cm (10–12 in) diameter.
Propagation The plant produces offshoots which are detached in March–April and planted individually in normal growing mixture.
Pests and diseases Scale insects, mealy bug.

164 MYRTUS COMMUNIS
Myrtle

Family Myrtaceae.
Origin Mediterranean regions.
Description Evergreen shrub with many branches, a typical species of Mediterranean shrubland. As a house plant it does not normally grow taller than 1 m (3 ft). The small, lanceolate leaves have a pointed tip; they are bright green and when rubbed give out a characteristic scent. The single, fragrant flowers are 2 cm (1 in) wide and bloom from June to August.

Varieties *M. communis* 'Microphylla,' most frequently cultivated indoors. Its leaves are 2 cm (1 in) long, it does not grow taller than 60 cm (2 ft). 'Variegata,' leaves of up to 5 cm (2 in), with white edges.
Care It needs a great deal of direct light, and its happiest position is in a south-facing window. During winter it can do with a rest period at 8–10°C (46–50°F); the rest of the year it can be kept at 18–20°C (64–68°F), but if it is too hot or if the air is too dry the plant loses its leaves. In summer it can go outside in the sun. Water generously during the growing season with lime-free water, and at regular intervals but in smaller amounts during dormancy. Feed once a month in spring–summer only. The slightly acid or neutral growing medium should consist of 1 part organic soil, 2 parts peat and 1 part sand. Repot in spring.

Propagation Take cuttings, together with portion of branch to which attached, in spring. Plant in mixture of peat and sand and wrap pot in plastic bag. Rooting takes about 2 months.
Pests and diseases Scale insects.

---

165 NEOREGELIA CAROLINAE

Family Bromeliaceae.
Origin Brazil.
Description Plant with hard, glossy leaves in bright, metallic colors, green, copper and crimson, arranged in a flat basal rosette. The color of the foliage, especially in the center of the rosette, changes while plant is in flower.

Varieties *N. carolinae* 'Marechalii,' (Blushing Bromeliad), compact, with smaller leaves than in species plant, during flowering the center of the plant turns crimson; 'Meyendorfii,' green leaves tinged with copper; 'Tricolor,' leaves streaked in pinky-white and dark green.
Care Easy to cultivate plant, it likes exposure to bright, but preferably filtered, light, and can also stand direct sun. Does well throughout year at average room temperatures of 18–24°C (64–75°F) and needs no rest period. Will not tolerate temperatures below 10°C (50°F). Water the mixture sparingly but spray the plants daily with rain water, keeping the central cup full of water and renewing it every couple of months. Set the pots in bowls filled with moist gravel. Feed low-concentrate liquid fertilizer every 2–3 weeks throughout year, filling the central cup and wetting the foliage. Growing mixture formed of leafmold, peat and sand in equal parts.

Propagation The plant produces offset rosettes which can be detached with their roots from the parent plant in spring. Plant in moist mixture of peat and sand, enclosing pot in plastic bag, and keep in moderate, filtered light. After about 2 months repot in standard growing medium.

Pests and diseases Fairly resistant to parasites.

166 NARCISSUS TAZETTA

Narcissus

Family Amaryllidaceae.

Origin Canary Islands, Mediterranean region, China, Japan.

Description The genus *Narcissus* comprises a very large number of bulbous plants grown for their highly decorative, fragrant flowers, single or in clusters, which bloom in early spring. *N. tazetta*, together with its hybrids, is the most suitable species for indoor cultivation: the clustered flowers are white or yellow or a combination of both colors, depending on the variety. Each flower is formed of 5 lobes and a short central corona frequently in a contrasting color. The bulbs are suitable for forcing in order to induce winter flowering. Each bulb produces a flower stalk 30–40 cm (12–16 in) tall and strap-shaped leaves.

Varieties Many horticultural varieties are derived from the crossing of *N. tazetta* with *N. poeticus.* Among the commonest cultivars are: *N. tazetta* var. *papyracens* ('Paper White'), totally white flowers; 'Geranium,' white lobes and deep orange corona; 'Cheerfulness,' creamy yellow flowers and orange lobes in the center; 'Cragford,' white lobes and orange corona.

Care The bulbs, when grown indoors, flower only once and are then discarded. Whether for forcing or not, they should be planted in autumn and kept at temperatures of 6–8°C (43–46°F) for 8–10 weeks; the unforced bulbs must remain in darkness, the forced ones either in light or darkness. After planting them in a mixture of organic soil, peat and sand in equal parts in such a way that about half the bulb projects above the surface, wrap the pot in black plastic bag. The mixture must be kept slightly damp. When the shoots are 8 cm (3 in) long and the buds start to appear, bring the pots into a warm place and expose them gradually to light, eventually giving them some sun. This acclimatization takes a couple of weeks. There is no need to feed. To prolong flowering season, keep the plants at 16–18°C (61–64°F). The bulbs can also be cultivated in shallow containers filled with gravel and water in such a manner that the water covers the base of the bulbs. Keep these at 8–9°C (46–48°F) and in the dark for 8–10 weeks, and when the shoots are 8 cm (3 in) long, with buds, expose them gradually to warmth and light.

Pests and diseases Bulb rot.

167 NEPHROLEPIS EXALTATA
Ladder fern, sword fern

Family Davalliaceae.
Origin Tropical America.
Description Species of fern commonly grown indoors. It has an upright rhizome, the tip of which projects above ground, and its curving, pinnate, divided or feathery leaves are up to 1.50 m (5 ft) long. More often cultivated than the species proper are varieties with smaller and more delicately divided fronds. Stolons from the rhizome produce new plants. The spore-cases appear on the underside of the fronds.

Care This plant has to be in a bright position but cannot stand direct sun; for brief periods it can be kept in moderate light. Does well throughout year at room temperature and has no rest period. It dislikes temperatures of under 10°C (50°F) and if they go above 21°C (70°F) the plant should be set in a bowl with moist gravel and the foliage sprayed every day. Water plentifully and frequently so that the mixture is always damp. Give liquid fertilizer fortnightly during spring–summer to plants potted in peat (less fertile) and monthly to those in soil. Suitable mixtures are peat, sand and vermiculite in equal parts or 2 parts leafmold, 1 part organic soil, 1 part peat and 1 part sand. Repot in spring only if roots have filled container, gradually increasing its size; otherwise replace only a part of the mixture.

Propagation A new rooted plant can be obtained at any time by cutting off the stolon or runner. Plant it in growing soil and treat as adult plant. The species plant can also be propagated from spores, but not the varieties.
Pests and diseases Aphids, scale insects.

---

168 NERIUM OLEANDER
Oleander, rose bay

Family Apocynaceae.
Origin Mediterranean region.
Description Evergreen, many-branched shrub with, leathery, lanceolate leaves. House plants only flower July–August. The flowers consist of a tubular corolla which opens into 5 flattened lobes. The whole plant is very poisonous.
Varieties There are many varieties with single or double corolla and with flowers of different colors: white, pink, red or purplish-red. *N. oleander* 'Variegata,' leaves streaked with creamy-white at the edges.

Care The species needs direct sun the whole year round and is better placed outdoors in summer. Indoors it lives at room temperature and has a winter rest period at 12–14°C (53–57°F). If not protected it can stand temperatures down to 8°C (46°F). In spring–summer water normally and let the surface of the soil mixture dry out before a further application; do not allow the roots to become dry or the flower buds will wither and not open. Give liquid fertilizer fortnightly from May to September. Potting medium made up of organic soil, peat and sand in equal parts. Repot every spring and then simply provide fresh soil annually. Prune the plant after it has finished flowering.

Propagation In June take 10–15 cm (4–6 in) tip cuttings from non-flowering shoots and root them in water, transplanting them into potting medium when they are 3 cm (about 1 in) long. The cutting can also be rooted in a mixture of peat and sand in equal proportions.
Pests and diseases Very prone to attacks by scale insects.

169 NERTERA GRANADENSIS
Bead plant, coral-bead plant

Family Rubiaceae.
Origin Andes (to Cape Horn), New Zealand, Tasmania.
Description Creeping, perennial evergreen plant, the close-ly interlaced stems forming a cushion 7–8 cm (about 3 in) high. The stems bear fleshy, stalkless green leaves, set opposite and rounded in shape, 5 mm (about ¼ in) wide. Roots develop from the leaf nodes of the stems. Insignificant flowers are produced in June, followed by orange-red berries which fall after a number of months.
Care Coming from high mountain zones at some 2,000 m (6,500 ft) above sea-level, the plant needs direct sunlight for 3–4 hours a day and surroundings that are not too warm, 14–17°C (57–62°F). If cultivated in rooms that are too warm or insufficiently bright, the plant becomes straggly, produ-cing many leaves but few fruits. Water so as to wet the mixture completely, but let the surface dry out before repeating; spray the foliage daily and place the pot in a bowl filled with wet gravel. In winter the plant has a brief rest period during which watering must be reduced, but not allowing roots to become dry. Feed moderately in order not to encourage excessive leaf growth at the expense of flowers and fruits; apply liquid fertilizer once a month from the end of flowering until berries ripen. Potting mixture formed of organic soil, peat and sand in equal parts. Repot in spring, using 8–10 cm (3–4 in) bowls.
Propagation In spring divide clumps of old plants into 5–6 small portions, planting them individually in bowls of fresh soil.
Pests and diseases Not subject to many disorders.

170 NIDULARIUM FULGENS
Blushing cup

Family Bromeliaceae.
Origin Brazil.
Description Epiphytic plant up to 30 cm (12 in) tall with strap-shaped leaves in rosettes. The glossy leaves have spiny, toothed edges; they are pale green with darker green patches. The central leaves of the rosette turn red when the plant is about to flower. Flowers may appear at any time of year. After flowering, the rosette dies and is replaced by offset shoots which develop into new rosettes.
Care The species likes bright light but not direct sun. It does well at normal room temperatures of 18–24°C (64–75°F) throughout the year and can stand a minimum of 13°C (55°F). Because the plant needs plenty of humidity it should be sprayed frequently with rain water and the pot set in a bowl of wet gravel or packed with moist peat. From spring to autumn water normally, letting the surface of the mixture dry out before watering again. Keep the central cup full of water, changing it monthly. In winter prevent the mixture from drying out entirely. Feed with liquid fertilizer fortnightly from April to September. The potting medium, with little lime, should be formed of leafmold, peat and sand in equal parts. Repot in spring only if the roots have filled the pot.
Propagation In spring–summer cut off a lateral rosette and plant it in a pot with a moist mixture of sand and perlite in equal proportions. Place inside plastic bag in bright, filtered light. After rooting, remove bag and 2–3 months later transplant into standard growing medium.
Pests and diseases Not very prone to attacks by parasites.

171 ODONTOGLOSSUM HYBRIDS

Family Orchidaceae.
Origin Tropical America.
Description The genus *Odontoglossum* comprises many species of epiphytic orchids which by virtue of crosses among themselves and with related orchid genera have produced a large number of hybrids. From the tip of each pseudobulb sprout 1–3 strap-shaped leaves folded longitudinally in a V. The stems, each bearing numerous flowers, grow from the base of the pseudobulb. Flowers may appear at any time of year and are long-lasting.
Varieties O. 'Elise,' magnificent orange-yellow flowers; O. 'Alispum,' flowers with crinkled edges.
Care Needs bright but indirect light; during winter it can do with several hours of sunshine daily. Ideal temperature for cultivation is around 15°C (59°F) throughout the year. The plant requires plenty of moisture for which reason it should be sprayed, even twice a day, if the temperature rises above 15°C (59°F), and pots should be placed in bowls filled with wet gravel or enveloped with damp peat. Water the soil moderately and let the surface dry out between applications. In winter the plant benefits from a brief rest period during which very little water is given, simply making sure that the soil does not dry out completely. Give liquid orchid fertilizer with every 3– 4 waterings. Potting medium formed of 2 parts osmunda fiber, 1 part sphagnum moss and a little sand. Repot every year, putting a layer of crocks in the bottom.
Propagation By dividing the rhizome into sections, each bearing at least 4 pseudobulbs. Pot each portion in recommended mixture.
Pests and diseases Scale insects, red spider.

172 ONCIDIUM HYBRIDS

Family Orchidaceae.
Origin Tropical America.
Description The genus *Oncidium* contains many species of epiphytic orchids which have been crossed among themselves to create numerous cultivated hybrids. The types most frequently grown indoors have ovoid pseudobulbs with 1–2 large leaves at the tip. The branched stems are curved and bear large numbers of flowers. Some hybrids flower in summer, others in winter.
Varieties 'Doctor Schragen,' large, nut-colored flowers; 'Helen Brown,' a dwarf variety.
Care The plant needs plenty of direct sunlight except at hottest times of day. While growing it lives at a temperature of around 18°C (64°F), and if it rises above this level the pots should be set in a layer of moist gravel and the plant sprayed every day. In winter or after flowering in the case of hybrids that bloom in winter, the plants need a rest period of 4 weeks at 13°C (55°F), when the mixture should be watered very little. During growth watering should be in moderation, allowing about half of the soil to dry out between successive applications, and feeding with a liquid fertilizer for orchids with every 3–4 waterings. The growing medium should consist of 2 parts osmunda fiber, 1 part sphagnum moss and a little sand. Repot every spring or alternate years.
Propagation In spring divide the rhizome into portions, each bearing 2–3 pseudobulbs and pot them individually, exposing them to filtered light for the first 6 weeks.
Pests and diseases Red spider, thrips.

173 OPHIOPOGON JABURAN
White lily-turf

Family Liliaceae.
Origin Japan.
Description Herbaceous perennial which forms large clumps. The green strap-shaped leaves, up to 60 cm (2 ft) long and 1 cm (½ in) wide, grow directly from the roots. In late summer the plant produces flower stems that bear drooping inflorescences of tubular, white flowers. After flowering, dark blue berries appear.
Varieties O. jaburan 'Argenteovittatus,' leaves striped lengthwise in white; 'Aureovariegatus,' leaves with golden-yellow stripes; 'Variegatus,' creamy-striped leaves; 'Caeruleus,' dark green leaves and blue-violet flowers.
Care The plant requires bright light in order to flower but cannot stand direct sun. It prefers to be kept cool at temperatures of 13–18°C (55–64°F) but will adapt to higher levels. Minimum winter temperature 10°C (50°F). Water normally during growth period, wetting the soil mixture thoroughly but allowing its surface to dry out before watering again. During the winter rest period simply make sure the soil does not dry out completely. Give liquid fertilizer fortnightly while growing. Growing medium formed of 1 part organic soil, 1 part peat and 2 parts sand. Repot in spring only if the clumps have filled the container.
Propagation In spring divide clumps that are too crowded, cutting them into portions each possessing roots and about 10 leaves. Plant each section individually in standard soil and treat as adult specimens.
Pests and diseases Aphids.

174 OSMANTHUS FRAGRANS
Sweet olive

Family Oleaceae.
Origin Himalayas to China, Japan.
Description Evergreen shrub with spherical, compact habit. The leaves are ovate, leathery, glossy light green. As a house plant it may grow to 1.5 m (5 ft) and more. It flowers twice, in spring and autumn. The small creamy-white flowers are highly scented.
Varieties O. fragrans aurantiacus has orange as well as white flowers.
Care Does well at average temperatures of 18–22°C (64–71°F), but in summer, climate permitting, it likes to be put outside in the sun or half-shade, protected from the wind. Water regularly, allowing the surface of the soil to dry slightly before repeating. Give standard liquid fertilizer fortnightly from April to October. Growing medium should consist of organic soil, peat and coarse sand in equal proportions. Drain the bottom of the pot with gravel because the plant must not be left in standing water. Repot in spring in containers of up to 25 cm (10 in).
Propagation Layering is the best method for indoor plants although it is a lengthy procedure. In September place a pot filled with growing mixture alongside the parent plant. Attach a branch from the latter to the soil of the adjoining pot, allowing the tip to protrude. Rooting takes 1–2 years.
Pests and diseases Subject to attacks by mealy bug and scale insects.

175 OXALIS DEPPEI
Lucky clover

Family Oxalidaceae.
Origin Mexico.
Description The genus comprises many plant species, some of them weeds, others ornamental garden forms. *O. deppei* is a small herbaceous plant, 10 cm (4 in) tall, consisting of an underground rhizome from which sprout long stalks bearing groups of 4 heart-shaped leaflets; each of these is 2–4 cm (1–2 in) long, green with a light purple band above, gray-green beneath. The flowers, with 5 bright red petals, are in loose clusters.
Care These plants can be forced for winter flowering. They need light, sunny positions at average temperatures, 18–22°C (64–71°F), but also do well in cooler surroundings, down to a minimum of 10°C (50°F). During growing season water normally, letting the surface of the soil dry out slightly before repeating; during rest period (March–April) give no water. Feed moderately; 2–3 times during entire growth period is sufficient. Potting mixture formed of organic soil, peat and sand in equal parts. The tubers can be potted up to the end of April or, so as to have winter flowers, in September, when pots should be kept in a bright but cool position, at 15°C (59°F) and watered sparingly.
Propagation By division of rhizome in April. Each portion should be planted separately.
Pests and diseases Reasonably resistant to parasites, but is sometimes attacked by aphids.

176 PANDANUS VEITCHII
Screw pine

Family Pandanaceae.
Origin Polynesia.
Description Evergreen shrub with woody stem terminating in a tuft of sword-shaped, stalkless leaves about 1 m (3 ft) in length. The plant likewise grows to a height of more than 1 m (3 ft). The leaves, green with lengthwise white striping, have sharply spiny edges. Adult plants develop thick aerial roots which bury themselves in the soil, raising the base of the plant out of the pot.
Varieties *P. veitchii.* 'Compactus' has smaller leaves, 40–60 cm (16–24 in) long and 4 cm (2 in) wide.
Care The species needs several hours of direct sunlight daily throughout the year. It lives at room temperature, 18–22°C (64–71°F), but because it dislikes dry air it should be placed in a bowl filled with damp gravel or packed in moist peat. Water plentifully during growth, keeping the soil constantly damp but draining off water; in winter dormancy simply avoid letting the soil dry out completely. Feed with liquid fertilizer fortnightly in spring–summer. Potting medium formed of 1 part organic soil, 1 part peat and 1 part coarse sand. Repot every spring and if necessary provide fresh soil in autumn.
Propagation In March–April take basal shoot cuttings and pot them in moist mixture of equal parts peat and sand. Root in unheated greenhouse or enclose in plastic bag and keep in bright, filtered light. After rooting, in 4–6 weeks, gradually uncover plant.
Pests and diseases Red spider.

177 PAPHIOPEDILUM HYBRIDS
Venus's slipper, slipper orchid

Family Orchidaceae.
Origin Tropical Asia.
Description The genus *Paphiopedilum* comprises various species of ground orchids without pseudobulbs. The strap-shaped leaves develop in separate clumps on a rhizome and have a deep groove along the central vein. The flower stalk, bears a single flower with a slipper-shaped lip. The flowers are shiny and waxy in appearance. The two lower petals and the lip are joined together. Flowers bloom from autumn to spring, according to variety. There are numerous hybrids derived from interspecific crosses.
Varieties *P. x h. superbum*, dark red tepals spotted with green; *P. x h.* 'C. S. Bali,' dark red tepals, with a white and yellow stripe.
Care These plants must be provided with bright but filtered light. In autumn and winter it may be helpful to add fluorescent lighting in order to bring on flowers. Average room temperatures are suitable throughout the year. If temperature rises above 21°C (70°F) spray the plants every day and place pots on layers of damp gravel. After flowering, the plant is dormant for some 6 weeks during which time it is only necessary to prevent the soil from drying out altogether. Apply liquid orchid fertilizer with every 3–4 waterings, except during dormancy. Growing medium formed of 2 parts osmunda fiber, 1 part sphagnum moss and a little sand. Repot when flowering is over.
Propagation After flowering, cut the rhizome into pieces, trying not to break the roots, and pot each individually.
Pests and diseases Red spider; root rot if overwatered.

---

178 PASSIFLORA CAERULEA
Passion flower

Family Passifloraceae.
Origin Brazil.
Description Very vigorous climbing plant formed of slender stems which cling to supports with spiral tendrils. The palmate leaves, divided into 5–9 lobes, are about 8 cm (3 in) long and up to 12 cm (5 in) wide, dark green with a glossy surface. Flowering is in summer and early autumn. The flower consists of 5 sepals and 5 white petals of equal length, within which is a corona of colored filaments. Also in the center are 5 golden anthers and the brown stigmas.
Care The plant likes bright light with at least 3 hours of direct sun every day. It grows at medium temperatures of 18–22°C (64–71°F) but in winter needs a period of rest at around 10°C (50°F). Water abundantly but without letting any collect during growth period, and in dormancy simply avoid letting the soil become dry. Give liquid fertilizer fortnightly from March to October. Mixture formed of organic soil, peat and sand in equal parts. Repot every spring in container of maximum 20 cm (8 in) since plant flowers more generously in small pots.
Propagation In June take 10 cm (4 in) tip cuttings, dip in root hormone preparation and pot in moist mixture of peat and sand. Keep in unheated greenhouse or in plastic bag in filtered light. Uncover after rooting, in about 1 month, water moderately and feed every fortnight. Repot in growing medium the following spring. In early spring prune drastically and repeat procedure every year.
Pests and diseases Aphids, cucumber mosaic virus.

179 PELARGONIUM X DOMESTICUM

Geranium, Lady Washington pelargonium

Family Geraniaceae.
Origin Cultivation.
Description A hybrid complex with several S. African species in its parentage. Subshrubs 30–40 cm (12–16 in) high, with slender, many-branched stems, slightly woody at base. The rough leaves are rounded with lobed or wavy, toothed margins, 5–8 cm (2–3 in) long and wide. When rubbed, the leaves give out a characteristic smell. The flowers grow in umbels of about 10 stalks; each flower, 5–7 cm (2–3 in) across, consists of a funnel-shaped corolla with 5 petals, 2 of which are bigger than the others. The color is variable but the petals are darker underneath and the corolla has a dark eye.
Varieties The following are recommended as having particularly decorative flowers: 'Grand Slam,' bright red with dark patches; 'Mino Lorenzen,' pink with red patches; 'Grossmama Fischer,' orange; 'Lavender Grand Slam,' lavender with dark markings; 'Letha,' deep pink.
Care See *P. peltatum*.
Propagation From June to August take 10 cm (4 in) tip cuttings from below a node. Remove lower leaves and budding flowers, dip the base of the cutting in a rooting hormone preparation, plant in small pots filled with peat and sand in equal parts, and place in bright, indirect light. Water moderately until a new shoot appears, and then increase amount of water. After a month the plant can be put in the sun. Transplant into standard growing mixture when roots fill the pot. Cuttings can also be rooted in water.
Pests and diseases Basal rot and mildew if overwatered.

180 PELARGONIUM PELTATUM

Ivy-leaved geranium, trailing geranium

Family Geraniaceae.
Origin South Africa.
Description A species from which many hybrid forms have been derived. The long, trailing stems are slender and very delicate. The leaves vary in appearance according to the cultivar; some are rounded, with a diameter of 5–7 cm (2–3 in), others are lobate, like those of ivy. The leaf surface may be either hairy or smooth and glossy. The flower stalks are 20 cm (8 in) long and bear small flower heads; each flower has 5 petals but there are also varieties with double flowers. They bloom from May to October. It is an ideal plant for balconies and patios, grown in hanging baskets.
Varieties Double flowers: 'S. Cristina,' white; 'Rigi Sport,' bright pink; 'Galilee,' pale pink; 'Moulin Rouge,' bright red. Single flowers: 'Balcon Imperial,' bright red; 'Balcon Lilla,' lilac-pink.
Care All types of geranium need bright light and direct sun for at least 4 hours daily while they are growing. They can be kept at room temperature and require a period of winter rest; *P. peltatum* varieties should be kept at about 10–13°C (50–55°F), but *P. x domesticum* varieties prefer higher temperatures, 15–18°C (59–64°F). Water regularly but not to excess during growth, letting the soil surface dry out before repeating. Reduce watering during dormancy, especially if the plants are kept cool. While plants are growing, feed fortnightly with a potassium-rich fertilizer. Potting medium formed of loam, peat and sand in equal proportions.
Pests and diseases See *P. x domesticum*.

181 PELLAEA ROTUNDIFOLIA
Button fern

Family Adiantaceae.
Origin New Zealand.
Description This is a distinctive plant that differs markedly from other ferns. The short, thin, blackish stems grow directly from an underground rhizome and bear the fronds, each consisting of a strong central filament to which the stiff, rounded pinnules or leaflets, about 1 cm (½ in) long, are attached alternately. Each frond terminates in a pinnule. The pinnules of the sterile fronds have slightly toothed borders, whereas those of the fertile fronds have the lower edges rounded to conceal the spore-cases. The plant is of trailing habit.
Care Very suitable for growing in hanging baskets or bowls, the fern needs bright light but dislikes direct sun. It can be kept throughout the year at average temperatures without becoming dormant; if the temperature rises above 21°C (70°F) it is a good idea to spray the foliage daily. The plant cannot stand variations in humidity so the soil should always be kept moist, neither too wet for fear of rotting the roots, nor too dry. Apply a low-concentrate liquid fertilizer once a month. Growing medium should consist of peat, sand and vermiculite in equal parts or of 2 parts leafmold, 1 part loam, 1 part peat and 1 part sand. Repot in spring only if roots have filled container.
Propagation By dividing the rhizome in spring.
Pests and diseases Aphids, scale insects, mealy bug.

182 PEPEROMIA CAPERATA
Peperomia, emerald ripple

Family Piperaceae.
Origin Tropical America.
Description Small, bushy, herbaceous plant. The fleshy, heart-shaped leaves are dark green with pink stalks. The spikes of white flowers bloom from early summer to late autumn.
Varieties These include *P. caperata* 'Emerald Ripple,' 'Little Fantasy,' and 'Variegata.'
Care Needs bright, filtered light and does well all year round at normal room temperatures. If the air is too dry and the temperature very high the plants tend to lose their leaves, so they should be sprayed often and the pots placed on damp gravel. Minimum temperature 12°C (53°F). The soil should be watered very little and left to dry out almost entirely before a further application. Feed with a low-concentrate liquid fertilizer once a month from May to September. Potting medium: 3 parts leafmold, 3 parts peat and 2 parts coarse sand. Repot young plants only in spring.
Propagation Easily propagated from tip and leaf cuttings. In the former case take 5–8 cm (2–3 in) cuttings in spring–summer and plant them together in a pot filled with a mixture of equal parts peat and sand, setting it in bright, filtered light. In the second case remove young but mature leaves with stalks and plant latter up to the joint with the leaf blade in the same mixture.
Pests and diseases Scale insects; red spider.

183 PEPEROMIA OBTUSIFOLIA
Pepper face

Family Piperaceae.
Origin Mexico to northern South America.
Description Herbaceous shrub. The fleshy, rounded obovate leaves are dark green with purple shading, 10–15 cm (4–6 in) long. The stems are reddish-purple. Spikes of white flowers bloom from end-spring to late autumn.
Varieties *P. obtusifolia* 'Variegata,' gray-green leaves streaked creamy-white; 'Albomarginata,' gray-green, silver-edged leaves; 'Greengold,' golden markings; 'Minima,' dwarf form not exceeding 15 cm (6 in) in height.
Care Needs indirect but bright light; varieties with colored foliage also benefit from a few hours of daily sun during winter. The plants do well throughout year at average room temperatures of 18–22°C (64–71°F), but if the temperature is too high and the air too dry the plants need frequent spraying and the pots should be placed in moist gravel. The soil, on the other hand, needs very little watering, and should be left to dry out almost completely before any more is given; in winter even less water should be provided. Feed with low-concentrate liquid fertilizer once a month from May to September. Growing medium formed of 3 parts leafmold, 3 parts peat and 2 parts sand. Repot only young plants every year.
Propagation From April to June take 7–8 cm (3 in) tip cuttings and plant in groups in 6–8 cm (3 in) pots filled with slightly damp mixture of peat and sand in equal parts. Place pots in bright, filtered light at around 18°C (64°F) and water very sparingly. Rooting occurs in 4–6 weeks; when roots fill pot, transplant into growing medium.
Pests and diseases Scale insects, red spider.

184 PERSEA AMERICANA
Avocado, alligator pear

Family Lauraceae.
Origin Mexico, Central America, West Indies.
Description In its areas of origin and in many other tropical zones with high temperatures, the Avocado is cultivated for its edible fruits, which are pear-shaped drupes 10–20 cm (4–8 in) long and 7–10 cm (3–4 in) across. It is also grown as an ornamental house plant. A small evergreen tree, it has twisted branches and rough, longitudinally streaked bark. The dense foliage is made up of leathery leaves, arranged alternately and mainly towards the tip of the branches. The leaf blade is elongate-ovate or elliptic, dark green above and bluish-green below. The leaves, downy when young, subsequently become smooth. The inflorescences are axillary panicles composed of greenish flowers. Indoors, of course, the plant gives no fruit.
Varieties These are all varieties based on fruit differences, and are not ornamental.
Care It enjoys well-lit positions, including sun. It thrives at average room temperatures, 18–24°C (64–75°F) all year round, but in summer it is best to take it outside. Water plentifully during spring–summer; reduce in autumn–winter. Give liquid fertilizer every fortnight from April to September. Medium formed of organic soil, peat and sand in equal proportions. Repot in spring.
Propagation Easily propagated from seed, getting it to germinate in sand or water and then pricking out in growing mixture; but the procedure is slow.
Pests and diseases Scale insects, mealy bug.

185 PHILODENDRON BIPINNATIFIDUM
Upright philodendron

Family Araceae.
Origin Brazil.
Description Non-climbing species which may grow to a height of 1 m (3 ft) and more. The leaves, on stalks 50 cm (20 in) long, are arranged around a central corona. Adult plants develop a short stem. The leaves are dark green, measuring about 40 cm (16 in) long and wide, arrow-shaped and deeply incised, though not as far as the central vein. The leaves of the young plants are heart-shaped and only slightly notched. The adult leaves develop after 2 years.
Care An easy plant to grow, it requires bright, indirect light and can be kept at average room temperatures of 18–22°C (64–71°F) throughout the year. In winter, however, its growth slows down. From spring to autumn water so as to wet the mixture well, but allow the surface to dry out before repeating. In winter reduce amount of water but do not let the soil dry out. Give liquid fertilizer every fortnight from April to October. Potting medium formed of 1 part organic soil, 2 parts peat and 1 part sand. Repot in spring only when roots have filled pot, in tubs of up to 40 cm (16 in); the latter have a bigger base than ordinary pots and are therefore better balanced.
Propagation From tip cuttings, following the method used for *P. scandens,* but results are more uncertain. In fact, large plants tend to transpire a lot, so that cuttings often dry out. The plant can also be propagated from seed, sowing in spring and keeping the seedbed at a temperature of 26–27°C (79–80°F). When the seedlings are 5 cm (2 in) high, prick them out and treat them as adults.
Pests and diseases Aphids; root rot.

186 PHILODENDRON SCANDENS
Climbing philodendron

Family Araceae.
Origin Central America.
Description The genus comprises many plants, most of which are climbers with aerial roots and highly decorative foliage. The leaf shape varies from species to species and from young to adult plant. *P. scandens* is a climber with thin stems up to 1.5 m (5 ft) long, with pointed, heart-shaped leaves, dark green, 10 cm (4 in) long and up to 8 cm (3 in) wide. As with all members of the genus, the plant seldom flowers when grown indoors.
Care Easy to grow as a house plant, it resists fumes and smoke and requires bright, indirect light. Does well at normal room temperatures all the year round. While growing, water so as to wet the soil thoroughly but let it dry out before repeating; during winter rest period simply prevent soil from drying out entirely. Give liquid fertilizer fortnightly from April to October. Growing medium made up of 1 part organic soil, 2 parts peat and 1 part sand. Repot in alternate years in spring. The plant can be induced to climb up moss-covered poles kept permanently moist or used as a trailing specimen in hanging baskets. Pinch the growing tips to maintain within bounds.
Propagation In spring take 10 cm (4 in) tip cuttings, removing lowest leaves, and plant in moist mixture of peat and sand in equal proportions. Set in greenhouse at 21–24°C (70–75°F) or in plastic bag, exposing cuttings to bright, indirect light.
Pests and diseases Aphids; root rot if overwatered.

187 PHILODENDRON 'BURGUNDY'

Family Araceae.
Origin Horticultural hybrid.
Description This is a hybrid derived from the crossing of diverse species. It is a hardy climber, slow-growing – 10–15 cm (4–6 in) a year – with a height of 2 m (6 ft). The stem bears aerial roots and shiny, arrow-shaped leaves 25–30 cm (10–12 in) long; these are initially pink, then olive-green above and dark red below. The stalks are 30 cm (12 in) long, set horizontally and, like the stems, colored red.

Care General requirements and growing techniques are as for other philodendrons; bright, indirect light and temperature of 18–22°C (64–71°F) throughout the year. Since it is a climbing plant, it needs a support to which it can either be tied or attached by means of its aerial roots. A moss-covered pole, kept moist by daily spraying, is the usual method. The soil should be well watered at regular intervals but the surface must be allowed to dry out before a fresh application. During winter, when growth slows down, reduce watering. Give liquid fertilizer fortnightly from April to October. Medium formed of 1 part organic soil, 2 parts peat and 1 part sand. Repot April–May when roots have filled container.

Propagation From tip cuttings according to method described for *P. scandens,* but difficult to get good results indoors.

Pests and diseases As a rule plant resists attacks by parasites quite well, but prone to attack by aphids or scale insects; liable to root rot if overwatered.

---

188 PHOENIX CANARIENSIS
Canary Islands date palm

Family Palmae.
Origin Canary Islands.
Description Belongs to the same genus as the common date palm but is more ornamental and is thus more frequently cultivated as a house plant. It grows fairly slowly and, in a pot, can reach a height of 3 m (10 ft). It normally has a short stem with persistent dark green, feathery fronds, initially stiff, then arching, up to 1 m (3 ft) and more in length. The stiff pinnules are shorter towards the base and tip of the frond, and longer in the middle. The flowers, in long clusters, appear in April. The fruits are similar to dates but only ripen in favorable climatic conditions. The plant is dioecious and to obtain fruits you must have specimen of both sexes. House plants rarely produce flowers or fruits.
Care The plant is easy to cultivate, responding to direct sun and preferring to be placed outdoors in summer. Indoors it can be kept at normal room temperatures of 18–22°C (64–71°F) and it is advisable to give it a winter rest period at 10–12°C (50–53°F). In spring–summer water to keep mixture always moist but without letting it collect; during dormancy reduce watering, allowing upper half of soil to dry out between successive applications. Give liquid fertilizer while plant is growing. Potting medium should consist of loam, peat and sand in equal proportions. Repot smaller plants every other year. Give older plants fresh soil. Use pots of up to 30 cm (12 in) diameter, or bigger tubs.
Propagation From seed, but the procedure is lengthy.
Pests and diseases Scale insects.

189 PHYLLITIS SCOLOPENDRIUM
Hart's tongue fern

Family Aspleniaceae.
Origin Subtropical Europe, Madeira.
Description Species of fern much cultivated as a house plant. It has an upright, half-buried rhizome, covered with pale brown scales. From this grow the strap-shaped fronds on stalks of variable length, 5–25 cm (2–10 in). The stalks are black at the base and green at the joint with the fronds. In specimens raised indoors the fronds are up to 25 cm (10 in) long and 6–7 cm (about 3 in) wide. The blades are lobate and often wavy at the margins, pointed at the tip, and pale green.
Varieties *P. scolopendrium* 'Capitatum,' very wavy leaves, crested at the tip; 'Crispum,' deeply incised or crinkled leaf margins; 'Cristatum,' crinkled edges and crested tips.
Care Like all ferns, this species requires bright light but cannot stand direct sun. It can be kept all year round at room temperature without becoming dormant, but if the surroundings are above 18°C (64°F) it must have a high level of humidity, entailing placing the pots on layers of wet gravel and spraying daily. Water the mixture sparingly with lime-free water, letting the surface dry out before repeating. Give liquid fertilizer fortnightly to less fertile plants potted in peat, monthly to plants in soil. Recommended potting mixtures (always lime-free) are: peat, sand and vermiculite in equal amounts, or 2 parts leafmold, 1 part each organic soil, peat and sand. Add a teaspoonful of charcoal to every 2 liters of mixture.
Propagation Indoors by dividing the rhizome in spring.
Pests and diseases Thrips, scale insects, mealy bug.

190 PILEA CADIEREI
Aluminum plant, watermelon pilea

Family Urticaceae.
Origin Vietnam.
Description Herbaceous perennial grown for its ornamental foliage. It takes the form of a many-branched evergreen shrub up to 30 cm (12 in) in height. The ovate-oblong leaves, set opposite, are up to 8 cm (3 in) long and are dark green with silvery patches among the veins of the upper surface, pale green below. The insignificant flowers may bloom at any time of year.
Varieties *P. cadierei* 'Minima' resembles species plant but is not taller than 15 cm (6 in), leaves up to 4 cm (2 in) long.
Care During winter it needs a well-lit position, even in direct light, but in summer it must be given indirect light. It does well at room temperatures, 18–22°C (64–71°F), all year round, and requires plenty of humidity, so pots should be placed on layers of damp gravel. Water moderately, letting two-thirds of the soil mixture dry out between successive waterings. Give diluted liquid fertilizer fortnightly from June to September. Potting medium consists of 3 parts leafmold, 3 parts peat and 2 parts sand. Repot every spring in containers of up to 10 cm (4 in) diameter or in shallow bowls. Pinch out shoots to encourage bushy habit. After several years the plant tends to lose its basal leaves and it is a good idea to replace it with a younger specimen.
Propagation In spring take 8–10 cm (3–4 in) tip cuttings, treat with a root-stimulating preparation and plant in mixture of 1 part sand and 2 parts peat. Keep warm and shaded, just keeping the soil moist.

191 PITTOSPORUM TOBIRA

Family Pittosporaceae.
Origin Japan, China, Taiwan.
Description Small tree or evergreen shrub with many branches which, as a house plant, does not usually grow to more than 1.5 m (5 ft) in height. It has woody stems and glossy, leathery, obovate leaves. The highly scented creamy yellow flowers bloom from May to July.

Varieties *P. t.* 'Variegata,' leaves with white streaks.
Care The plant enjoys bright light and needs direct sun for at least 3–4 hours a day. It prefers to be kept in surroundings that are not too warm, 15–18°C (59–64°F) but will tolerate higher temperatures. It needs a period of winter dormancy at 9–10°C (48–50°F). Water plentifully during growth, but in winter rest period simply water sufficiently to prevent soil from drying out. Give liquid fertilizer fortnightly, except when plant is dormant. Growing medium should consist of organic soil, peat and sand in equal proportions.

Propagation In May–June take 8 cm (3 in) cuttings, treat with rooting hormone and plant individually in pots with slightly damp mixture of peat and sand in equal parts. Wrap in plastic bags, exposing to indirect light. Appearance of new shoot indicates that roots have taken. Uncover cuttings and start watering moderately, letting surface dry out between applications. Gradually increase exposure to light to a maximum in about 2 weeks. Begin giving a little food and transplant into growing medium when roots fill pot. Also propagated from seed.

Pests and diseases Very prone to attacks by scale insects, mealy bug, aphids.

192 PLATYCERIUM BIFURCATUM
Staghorn fern, elkshorn

Family Polypodiaceae.
Origin Tropical Australia, Papua New Guinea.
Description Species of stolon-bearing, epiphytic fern notable for having 2 types of frond, sterile and fertile. A single sterile frond enfolds the base of the plant; in time it becomes dry and papery and is replaced by a new frond. The spores develop at the tip of the lower side of the fertile fronds. The stolon produces new individuals.

Varieties *P. bifurcatum* 'Majus,' vigorous variety with fronds less divided than those of original species.
Care The plants like bright, not direct, light provided this is not too intense. They do well at temperatures of 18–24°C (64–75°F), optimum 21°C (70°F), and need plenty of humidity. Spray with rain water every day. To get a plant to grow on bark, pack the roots with coarse-grained peat and sphagnum, bind them to the support with twine or wire and keep both bark and roots moist until they adhere to the support. This is the best method of cultivation. Water by plunging the pot in deep water and leaving the roots in water for 15 minutes during growing season and for 3 minutes during dormancy. Allow almost all the soil to dry out before repeating the operation. Also plunge the roots 2–3 times a year, while plant is growing, in a low-concentrate fertilizing solution.

Propagation From seeds of spores, in March, but this is a method for specialists.
Pests and diseases Scale insects, mealy bug, aphids.

193 PLECTRANTHUS COLEOIDES 'MARGINATUS'
Candle plant

Family Labiatae.
Origin Cultivated form of an Indian species.
Description Graceful trailing plant consisting of fleshy, almost square herbaceous stems; the heart-shaped leaves, 6–7 cm (3 in) long, are soft and hairy with roughly toothed margins. The original green-leaved species is not, apparently, cultivated, but its cultivar, *P. coleoides* 'Marginatus,' with white-bordered green leaves, is freely available. When touched, the plant gives out a distinctive smell. Clusters of small, inconspicuous, pale lavender, tubular flowers, are produced in summer.

Care This plant is very suitable for growing in hanging baskets. It needs bright light with at least 3–4 hours daily of direct sunshine. It can be kept at average room temperatures all year round; the ideal is 18–21°C (64–71°F), and if higher place the pots on layers of moist gravel. Winter rest period at 14–15°C (57–59°F), which will improve growth. Water abundantly throughout the year or in growing period only if plant is allowed to rest; feed with liquid fertilizer from April to October. Potting medium formed of organic soil, peat and sand in equal parts. Repotting is not as a rule necessary; the plant can be kept for 2–3 years and then discarded.

Propagation From 6–8 cm (about 3 in) tip cuttings from April to August. Plant them in normal potting mixture and keep in bright, indirect light, watering moderately. After rooting, transplant 3–4 cuttings into a hanging basket.
Pests and diseases Little prone to disease.

---

194 PLUMBAGO AURICULATA
Cape leadwort

Family Plumbaginaceae.
Origin South Africa.
Description More frequently known as *P. capensis,* this is a climbing shrub which can grow to a height of about 1.5 m (5 ft) as a house plant, its stems guided on supports. The elliptic leaves tend to roll up at the base. Racemes of some 20 light blue flowers bloom from April to October.
Varieties *P. auriculata* 'Alba' has white flowers.

Care The plant needs plenty of light and at least 3–4 hours of daily sunshine while growing. It lives at room temperatures but should be given a short winter rest period at around 10°C (50°F). Water regularly from spring to autumn and apply a standard liquid fertilizer every fortnight. In winter simply keep the compost from drying out entirely. Increase amount of water when first shoots appear. Mixture formed of 1 part organic soil, 1 part peat and 1 part sand. Repot every spring, increasing the diameter of the pot to a maximum of 20 cm (8 in). At the end of winter prune the stems to about one-third of their length. The flowers develop on the new shoots.

Propagation In June–July take 10 cm (4 in) cuttings which are neither too soft nor too woody and plant in pots filled with equal parts peat and sand. Wrap the pots in plastic bags and expose them to filtered light. When rooting occurs, uncover and begin watering. Fertilize once a month.
Pests and diseases Young shoots liable to attack by aphids.

195 PODOCARPUS MACROPHYLLUS
Buddhist pine, Japanese yew

Family Podocarpaceae.
Origin China, Japan, Taiwan.

Description When cultivated indoors as a small tree reaches a maximum height of 2 m (6 ft). The upright stems bear numerous lateral branches with a horizontal or drooping habit. The narrow leaves have central veining which is prominent on both surfaces; they are firm, sometimes wavy or folded near the tip. Flowers do not appear in indoor plants.

Care Prefers exposure to bright but slightly filtered light, or to several hours of daily sunlight, provided this is not too strong. It does not require a defined rest period and can therefore be kept at room temperature, 18–22°C (64–71°F) all year round; in winter there is simply a slowing down of growth. If the temperature drops to around 13°C (55°F) the plant does become dormant. Water regularly but not excessively from spring to autumn and let the surface of the mixture dry out before repeating. In winter watering can be reduced but not suspended, particularly if the plant is not dormant. Give liquid fertilizer fortnightly from April to October. Potting medium made up of organic soil, peat and sand in equal parts. Repot in spring, using containers of up to 30 cm (12 in), only if roots have filled pot. It is advisable to tie main stems to supports.

Propagation In spring take 10 cm (4 in) tip cuttings from beneath a node and after treatment with root-stimulating hormones plant them in groups of 2–3 in mixture of equal parts peat and sand. Enclose in plastic bag and place pot in filtered light without watering. Will root in about 2 months.

Pests and diseases Prone to root rot. Do not overwater or allow water to collect in pot.

---

196 POLYSCIAS BALFOURANA
Dinner plate aralia

Family Araliaceae.
Origin New Caledonia.

Description Erect, much branching shrub which, when grown as a house plant, does not normally exceed 1 m (3 ft) in height. The stems are green, spotted gray, and the glossy green leaves vary in shape according to whether they are young or adult. Young shrubs have single, almost upright, rounded leaves, 5 cm (2 in) wide, whereas adult plants have leaves composed of 3 larger and longer leaflets, with more deeply incised margins.

Varieties More common than the original species are the cultivars *P. balfourana* 'Marginata,' white-bordered leaflets; 'Pennockii,' yellow stripe down the central vein, bigger leaflets.

Care Likes exposure to bright light but not to direct sun. Thrives in medium and high temperatures, minimum 18°C (64°F) throughout the year; keep atmosphere moist by placing pots on layers of wet gravel. Watering should be regular but not excessive; let the surface of the mixture become dry before repeating. Give liquid fertilizer fortnightly from spring to autumn. Medium should consist of organic soil, peat and sand in equal parts. Repot every spring.

Propagation From tip cuttings. Take 10 cm (4 in) sections from beneath a node and plant them in mixture of equal parts peat and sand. Wrap in plastic bag and place in filtered light, keeping warm. At beginning of summer transplant into standard mixture.

Pests and diseases Scale insects, red spider if air is too dry.

197 POLYSTICHUM TSUS-SIMENSE
Tsus-sima holly fern

Family Aspidiaceae.
Origin Japan, Korea, China, Taiwan.
Description A fern with bipinnate, triangular-shaped fronds on stalks covered by brown scales. The fronds are 20 cm (8 in) long and 6 cm (about 2 in) wide at the base, and are formed of pairs of pinnules in their turn composed of pairs of leaflets 1 cm (½ in) long and 5 mm (¼ in) wide, oval in shape, with a pointed tip. Numerous round, dark brown spore-cases are present on the underside of the leaflets. The young fronds, still closed, are covered with silver scales. The fronds develop from a rhizome half-buried in the soil.

Care The fern needs bright or medium light, always filtered. It tolerates a wide range of temperatures, from 13°C (55°F) upwards. In excess of 18°C (64°F) increase humidity by placing pots on layers of wet gravel and spraying foliage daily with water at room temperature. It does not become dormant in winter but growth slows down. Water abundantly, always keeping the soil mixture damp; under 15°C (59°F) reduce watering. Feeding depends on substratum: if this consists largely of peat, feed every fortnight all year round; if it contains loam, feed only once a month. Growing medium can be made up of 3 parts coarse-grained peat, 3 parts leafmold, 2 parts sand, or equal amounts of organic soil, leafmold, peat and sand. Repot in spring in containers of up to 25 cm (10 in).

Propagation By dividing the rhizome in early spring.
Pests and diseases Scale insects, mealy bug.

---

198 PRIMULA MALACOIDES
Fairy primrose

Family Primulaceae.
Origin China.
Description This is a very free-flowering plant, suited for cultivating indoors. It has sturdy, fleshy flowering stalks which bear early flowers (January–February) in large clusters, each bloom being up to 4 cm (2 in) wide. There are various varieties. The leaves are rounded and hairy.

Care The plants are discarded after initial flowering. Growing requirements and techniques are as described for *P. obconica*.

Propagation From seed up to end-July in greenhouse at 16°C (61°F). The procedure is not easy to achieve indoors.
Pests and diseases Yellowing leaves may indicate lack of magnesium; apply sulfate of magnesium in measure of 7 g to 1 liter of water. Also vulnerable to many parasites which cause the tissues to rot or die (gray mold, bacteria, viruses); red spider if surroundings too dry.

199 PRIMULA OBCONICA
Poison primrose

Family Primulaceae.
Origin China.

Description Herbaceous perennial plant generally cultivated as an annual. It forms tufts of basal leaves from the center of which grows a stem 20–25 cm (8–10 in) tall bearing clusters of flowers. The rounded, heart-shaped leaves are rough and hairy; the numerous flowers differ in color according to variety. Flowering is from winter to summer.

Varieties 'Coerulea,' blue flowers; 'Giant White,' white flowers; 'Salmon King,' salmon flowers; 'Fasbender Red,' bright red flowers; 'Wyaston Wonder,' crimson flowers.

Care As a rule the plant is discarded after flowering, though it may be kept for a second year if it is put in an airy, shaded spot during summer and watered sufficiently to prevent the soil from drying out. At the beginning of autumn remove dead leaves and repot in fresh soil, gradually increasing amount of water. The plants need plenty of light and sunshine in the morning and evening. Flowering can last a long time if the plants are kept at temperatures of 10–15°C (50–59°F) and all dead flowers removed. Higher temperatures shorten flowering season, so in this case spray plants every day and place pots on layers of wet gravel. Water plentifully, keeping soil mixture always moist. Give liquid fertilizer every fortnight. Medium formed of organic soil, peat and sand in equal parts.

Propagation From seed up to end-July in greenhouse at 16°C (61°F). Method not easy to realize indoors.

Pests and diseases Gray mold, red spider.

---

200 PSEUDERANTHEMUM ATROPURPUREUM

Family Acanthaceae.
Origin Polynesia.

Description A small shrub cultivated for its colorful, highly decorative foliage. The stiff stems, up to 50 cm (20 in) tall, bear pairs of opposite, elliptic leaves, 10 cm (4 in) long and 5 cm (2 in) wide. The leaf color is reddish-purple and green. Adult plants flower in spring.

Varieties P. o. 'Tricolor,' reddish-purple and green leaves patched white and pink; more commonly cultivated than original species.

Care To maintain its colors the plant needs bright light but cannot stand direct sunshine. It does well at room temperatures, minimum 15°C (59°F) throughout the year, and does not become dormant in winter. It requires high atmospheric humidity and pots should therefore be set on layers of wet gravel. Water regularly but moderately all year round, letting the soil surface dry out between successive waterings. In spring–summer apply liquid fertilizer every fortnight. Potting medium formed of organic soil, peat and sand in equal parts. Repot whenever roots fill container, up to maximum diameter of 16 cm (6 in).

Propagation In spring take 7–8 cm (3 in) tip cuttings from immediately beneath a node. Dip the base of the cutting (removing the lower leaves) in a root-stimulating hormone and plant in a pot filled with a damp mixture of peat and sand in equal amounts. Place in greenhouse at 21–24°C (70–75°F) or in plastic bag, exposing it to filtered light.

Pests and diseases Red spider.

201 PTERIS CRETICA
Cretan brake, stove fern

Family Pteridaceae.
Origin Old World Tropics, Subtropics.
Description Species of rhizomatous fern including fertile specimens with a row of spore-cases on the edges of the undersides of the fronds, and sterile specimens with no spore-cases on the fronds. Each plant has only one type of frond, fertile or sterile. The frond, about 30 cm (12 in) long and up to 20 cm (8 in) wide, consists of 2–4 pairs of opposite, ribbon-shaped pinnules, up to 10 cm (4 in) long and 2 cm (1 in) wide, on a black stalk.
Varieties *P. cretica* 'Albolineata,' popularly called ribbon fern, a white band along the central vein of each pinnule.
Care The species, like the majority of ferns, needs bright light but cannot stand direct sun. It does well at room temperatures of 18–22°C (64–71°F); if above 18°C (64°F) you need to place the pots on layers of moist gravel and spray the plants daily. Minimum temperature 13°C (55°F). Water plentifully, keeping the soil constantly damp but not allowing water to collect. If the temperature drops below 16°C (61°F) reduce watering and let soil surface dry between successive applications. Feed every fortnight with liquid plant food. Medium formed of 1 part loam, 1 part sand, 3 parts peat. Repot in spring if roots have filled container, up to 25 cm (10 in) diameter. Cut off old fronds when they lose their beauty; the plant will form new ones.
Propagation In spring divide the rhizomes into sections, each with fronds and roots, and plant each portion in growing mixture, treating as adult. Alternatively seeds from spores.
Pests and diseases Scale insects, mealy bug, aphids.

202 PUNICA GRANATUM
Pomegranate

Family Punicaceae.
Origin Southeast Europe to the Himalayas.
Description In the wild this is a tree or shrub of considerable size. Only the variety *P. granatum* 'Nana' is suitable for growing indoors. This is a slow-growing shrub up to 1 m (3 ft) tall, with persistent glossy leaves 2–3 cm (1 in) long and wide. They are opposite in pairs or in whorls of 3–4. The orange-red, bell-shaped flowers are 3 cm (1 in) long and appear singly or in groups at the tips of lateral branches. The flowers, from May to September, are followed by orange or yellow fruits.
Care The plant needs bright light and several hours of direct sunshine daily while growing. During the dormant period it prefers medium light and temperatures of 12–13°C (53–55°F). From spring to autumn it does well at average temperatures and needs plenty of water which must not be allowed to collect. During winter simply avoid letting soil dry out entirely. Give liquid fertilizer fortnightly from April to October. Growing medium formed of organic soil, peat and sand in equal proportions. Repot every other year.
Propagation In July take 8 cm (3 in) cuttings with portion of bark, treat base with rooting hormone and plant each portion in pot filled with damp mixture of peat and sand in equal parts. Place in unheated greenhouse or in plastic bag and in bright, filtered light. After rooting (in about 2 months) uncover and water moderately. Transplant into standard soil mixture the following spring.
Pests and diseases Fairly resistant to parasites.

203　RHAPIS EXCELSA

Large lady palm, ground rattan cane

Family Palmae.
Origin Japan, China.
Description Also known as *R. flabelliformis,* this is a small, bushy palm which as a house plant does not grow higher than 1.5 m (5 ft). Its dark green fan-like leaves are cut lengthwise into 5–8 almost separate segments with blunted tip, 20–25 cm (8–10 in) long and up to 5 cm (2 in) across.

Varieties The cultivar *R. excelsa* 'Zuikonishiki' has variegated yellow leaves and is smaller than the original species, maximum 60 cm (2 ft).
Care From spring to autumn it prefers to be exposed to screened light, but during winter it benefits from a few hours of sunshine every day. It does well at medium room temperatures of 18–22°C (64–71°F) all year round, or even cooler; in latter case it grows more slowly and rests in winter. Watering should be moderate and the surface of the soil mixture must be left to dry out before repeating. Reduce amount of water if plant is dormant. Give liquid fertilizer monthly while growing. Medium formed of organic soil, peat and sand in equal proportions. Use small pots in relation to size of root mass, maximum 30 cm (12 in), and repot every other year.
Propagation Easily done in spring by removing basal shoots, preferably with some roots, and planting them in 10 cm (4 in) pots containing recommended mixture. Place in bright, filtered light, keeping warm, and water with moderation. When new shoots appear, treat plants as adults.
Pests and diseases Mealy bug, scale insects.

204　RHODODENDRON INDICUM

Family Ericaceae.
Origin Japan.
Description Evergreen shrub which grows to a height of 2 m (6 ft). The leaves are lanceolate-elliptic, dark green and hairy. The shoots are covered with fine down. The funnel-shaped flowers are bright red or pink, single or in pairs. They bloom May–June.
Varieties *R. indicum* var *balsaminaeflorum,* double, salmon-red flowers.

Care While in flower, the plant enjoys bright light but not direct sun. When not flowering, place in average light. To prolong flowering period, keep the pots in cool positions, at 8–16°C (46–61°F); in warmer surroundings at more than 21°C (70°F) both flowers and leaves quickly drop. The plant needs a high measure of humidity; keep the soil permanently moist, set the pots on beds of wet gravel and spray flowers and leaves daily if air is dry. Like most azaleas, the species hates lime, so both the water and the potting medium must be lime-free. Feed with a liquid fertilizer made for azaleas, fortnightly from May to September. After flowering, put the plant outside in a cool, semishaded place, keeping the soil damp. At the onset of the first frosts, in September–October, bring it indoors, but do not give it too much heat. The acid growing medium should consist of 1 part lime-free organic soil, 2 parts peat and 1 part sand. Repot every 2–3 years after flowering.
Propagation See *R. obtusum.*
Pests and diseases See *R. obtusum.*

205 RHODODENDRON OBTUSUM
Japanese azalea

Family Ericaceae.
Origin Horticultural hybrid of Japanese species.
Description The genus *Rhododendron* comprises a very large number of species, including the house plants commonly known as azaleas. The many hybrids obtained are divided into 11 groups; *R. obtusum* is a parent of the Kurume group and is itself probably derived from crosses of Japanese species including *R. kaempferi*. It is a small evergreen tree with small, shiny leaves and slightly woody stems. The funnel-shaped flowers are 2–4 cm (1–2 in) wide and normally appear April–May, but can be forced to bloom in winter. The flowers come in white, pink or red.
Varieties The many varieties are differentiated by color of the flowers and by a single or double corolla; 'Kirin,' pink flowers; 'Amoena,' magenta-pink; 'Kure-no-yuki,' white; 'Princess Beatrix,' semi/double deep pink flowers.
Care The same as for *R. simsii*.
Propagation Both *R. obtusum* and *R. simsii* are propagated from tip cuttings. Take cuttings 5–8 cm (2–3 in) long from young branches in June–August and plant them individually in 8 cm (3 in) pots filled with a moist mixture of 1 part peat and 2 parts coarse sand or perlite. Enclose in plastic bag and set in shade, or get to root in greenhouse at 21–24°C (70–75°F). After rooting has occurred, repot the young plants in growing medium and treat as adult individuals. About 2–3 months are needed from the time propagation commences.
Pests and diseases Azalea moths, scale insects feed on leaves; tortrix caterpillars spin webs that curl young leaves. The plant prone to root rot and fungal rust; yellowing leaves indicate chlorosis due to lack of iron if grown in lime soil.

206 RHODODENDRON SIMSII

Family Ericaceae.
Origin China, Taiwan.
Description This is the common azalea sold in florist shops. It is a woody shrub with ovate, leathery leaves which are fairly glossy. The flowers appear in May.
Varieties There are many varieties with single or double corollas and flowers of diverse colors.
Care In flower, the plants like bright but not direct sun; when not flowering, they prefer medium light. It is usual to buy plants with flower buds already formed, and to prolong flowering it is best to keep pots in cool surroundings, at 8–16°C (46–61°F); both flowers and leaves are likely to drop quickly in rooms where the temperature exceeds 21°C (70°F). In summer the plants can be set outdoors in a cool, half-shaded position, with the soil always kept moist. They need a high measure of humidity, so indoors the pots should be put inside bigger containers filled with damp peat; watering should be plentiful but flooding is to be avoided. Because azaleas dislike lime, both water and soil must be lime-free. From May to September feed with liquid azalea fertilizer every fortnight. Growing medium made up of 1 part lime-free organic soil, 2 parts peat and 1 part coarse sand; alternatively grow in pure peat. Repot every 2–3 years after flowering, before placing plant outdoors.
Propagation As for *R. obtusum*.
Pests and diseases See *R. obtusum*.

207 RHOICISSUS RHOMBOIDEA (CISSUS ANTARCTICA)
Grape ivy

Family Vitaceae.
Origin Australia.
Description Vigorous climbing plant which in a pot may grow to over 2 m (6 ft). The stems are furnished with curling tendrils; the leaves are ovate, leathery and lustrous bright green, paler beneath.
Care This species is very suitable for growing in hanging baskets or as a climber with supporting stakes. It is easy to cultivate, enjoying medium or bright light but not direct sunshine. The plant is unaffected by polluted air and smoke. While growing, it should be kept at average temperatures of 18–24°C (64–75°F); in winter it is best to give it a period of dormancy at 10–13°C (50–55°F). Water regularly, wetting the soil thoroughly without flooding it. If the plant is kept in cool surroundings in winter, water just enough to prevent the soil from drying out. Give liquid fertilizer every fortnight from March to October. Potting mixture formed of organic soil, peat and sand in equal parts. Repot annually in April, in containers of up to 20–25 cm (8–10 in). Stop the tips of shoots periodically to encourage branching. It is a good idea to prune in early spring, cutting back the main stems by one-third and the side ones to a node.
Propagation In April–May take 8–10 cm (3–4 in) cuttings from lateral shoots and plant them in a pot filled with a mixture of peat and sand in equal parts. Wrap the pot in a plastic bag and put it in a warm place, in bright, indirect light.
Pests and diseases Red spider if surroundings too dry.

---

208 ROSMARINUS OFFICINALIS
Rosemary

Family Labiatae.
Origin Mediterranean regions.
Description Erect, evergreen, slow-growing shrub which as a house plant will reach a height of 1 m (3 ft). The narrow leaves are strongly fragrant, dark green above, whitish below. Groups of blue flowers bloom from February right through the summer.
Varieties *R. officinalis* var. *prostratus* has a creeping habit; *R. o.* var. *albiflorus*, white or very pale blue flowers.
Care Needs bright light and sun. During winter it is best to keep it in cool surroundings, at 10–14°C (50–57°F), at least for a short while; for the rest of the year medium temperatures of 18–22°C (64–71°F) are recommended. In summer it can go outdoors in the sun. Water regularly during growth period, allowing the surface of the mixture to dry out before repeating. Give liquid fertilizer fortnightly from spring to autumn. Growing medium consists of 1 part organic soil, 1 part peat and 1 part sand. Provide the pot with good drainage by using crocks to avoid water collecting. Repot in spring only when the plant has filled the container.
Propagation In July-August take 10 cm (4 in) cuttings and plant them in mixture of peat and sand. Wrap the pot in plastic bag and place in filtered light.
Pests and diseases Fairly resistant to parasites.

209   RUELLIA DEVOSIANA

Family Acanthaceae.
Origin Brazil.
Description Bushy evergreen species of modest dimensions. It has glossy dark green, elliptic leaves with paler veining. The flowers grow in the upper leaf axils during winter and spring. The tubular corolla opens into 5 pink lobes.
Care In winter it needs exposure to bright, even direct, light; in summer it prefers semishaded positions. To get it to flower in winter, keep pots at 13–16°C (55–61°F), but for the remainder of the year normal room temperatures are suitable. Always keep the soil moist during flowering and until end-summer. Reduce watering towards autumn, as this is the plant's dormant period. Give liquid fertilizer every fortnight from October to July. Medium formed of organic soil, peat and sand in equal parts. Repot in September. Replace the plant every couple of years as it loses its beauty as time passes. After flowering, if necessary, prune branches that are too long.

Propagation In April–May take 5–8 cm (2–3 in) cuttings and plant them in mixture of equal parts peat and sand. Wrap the pot in plastic bag, exposing it to filtered light at temperature of 18–20°C (64–68°F). After rooting, transplant into standard medium.

Pests and diseases Aphids on leaves, flowers and young shoots.

---

210   SAINTPAULIA HYBRIDS
African violet

Family Gesneriaceae.
Origin Cultivated derivatives of a Central African species.
Description Most African Violet varieties are derived from *S. ionantha*. They are small herbaceous perennial plants, growing at most to a height of 15 cm (6 in). The fleshy leaves are arranged in a rosette. The heart-shaped, hairy leaves are green, sometimes with reddish tints on the underside. Flowering may occur at any time of year.
Varieties There are many varieties, all hybrids, divided into 3 groups: Diana, Ballet and Rhapsody, which differ in flower color and in corolla form, single or double.

Care In order to produce an abundance of flowers, the plants require bright light, even artificial light, for the whole year round, but not direct sunlight, especially if very strong. Ideal temperatures are 18–24°C (64–75°F) but should be stable because even slight temperature fluctuations are likely to arrest growth. Increase humidity by placing pots on beds of moist gravel. Watering should be sufficient just to dampen the soil and the surface should be allowed to dry out before repeating. Reduce amount of water still further if the temperature falls below 16°C (61°F). Overwatering may rot the roots. Use lime-free water. Give diluted liquid fertilizer every fortnight from March to September. Acid mixture composed of sphagnum moss and perlite in equal proportions or 3 parts peat and 1 part lime-free organic soil.

Propagation From leaf cuttings, in greenhouse at 18–24°C (64–75°F).
Pests and diseases Aphids, mealy bug, mites.

211 SANSEVIERIA TRIFASCIATA 'HAHNII'
Mother-in-law's tongue, snake plant

Family Agavaceae.

Origin Tropical Africa.

Description The original species is not normally cultivated indoors but its varieties are among the best known and easiest house plants to grow. Some of these have long, upright leaves, whereas others, such as *S. trifasciata* 'Hahnii,' are dwarf varieties with rosette-type leaves. The stiff, pointed and spiny leaves grow directly from a rhizome emerging just above the surface of the soil; they are green with yellow and gray marbling.

Varieties In addition to *S. trifasciata* 'Hahnii,' the variety 'Golden Hahnii,' leaves edged with golden-yellow bands; 'Silver Hahnii,' silver-green leaves with dark green patches.

Care The species and its varieties are fairly tolerant in respect to light; they prefer bright light and direct sun but can also thrive in dimmer surroundings, although not for too long, as this may arrest growth. This transition from well-lit to shadier areas and vice-versa should be made gradually. Temperature for cultivation is 18–27°C (64–80°F) all year round; the minimum is 10°C (50°F) but the plants can even survive at 6–7°C (43–44°F) so long as the soil is dry. Water with moderation because the roots rot easily; in winter, particularly, allow at least half of the soil to dry out before watering again. Do not let any water collect in the rosette. Feed very little; a liquid fertilizer applied once a month in spring–summer is sufficient. Growing medium is made up of 1 part loam, 1 part peat and 2 parts sand. Drain the pot thoroughly. Repot only occasionally.

Propagation See technique for *S. trifasciata* 'Laurentii.'

Pests and diseases As for *S. trifasciata* 'Laurentii.'

212 SANSEVIERIA TRIFASCIATA 'LAURENTII'
Mother-in-law's tongue

Family Agavaceae.

Origin Tropical Africa.

Description *S. trifasciata* 'Laurentii' is a variety with lanceolate, stiff, upright leaves, up to 1 m (3 ft) or more in length. Each leaf has a pointed tip which must not be allowed to break, otherwise it will not grow any more, and is sometimes slightly twisted. The color is dark green with broad, golden-yellow margins. The leaves grow from a large rhizome lying just below the surface of the soil. It is a slow-growing plant which produces only a few new leaves each year.

Care The same as for *S. trifasciata* 'Hahnii.'

Propagation Can be propagated by rhizome division or from basal shoots, from May to August. In the first case, pull up the plant and, with a sharp knife, cut this into 2–3 sections, each with a leaf, perhaps a rosette, and some root. Pot each piece in growing mixture. If the portion has few roots pot it in a moist mixture of peat and sand in equal proportions; when the roots are stronger, transplant into growing medium. In the second case, detach the basal shoots from the parent plant and pot them in standard soil mixture if there are roots, and in a damp mixture of equal parts peat and sand if there is none, transplanting into standard growing medium when these have formed.

Pests and diseases Subject to weevils which gnaw the leaf edges and do irreparable harm to the plant's appearance.

213 SAXIFRAGA STOLONIFERA
Mother of thousands, magic carpet, strawberry geranium, Aaron's beard, roving sailor

Family Saxifragaceae.
Origin China, Japan.
Description Stemless plant with kidney-shaped leaves. The upper surface of these is dark green with silvery veins; the underside is purple-red. Long, creeping stolons produce new plantlets that can be used for propagation. White flowers appear in July–August.

Varieties *S. stolonifera* 'Tricolor' (magic carpet) smaller than the original species, has variegated yellow and pink leaves.
Care Bright light including at least an hour of daily sunshine (3 hours for the 'Tricolor' variety), but not fierce midday heat. The plant prefers cool temperatures of 10–15°C (50–59°F) but can also thrive at higher levels provided the surrounding humidity is high. Above 18°C (64°F) set pots on beds of moist gravel or place a dish of water beneath the hanging basket. During the growth period water plentifully but avoid flooding, reduce after flowering, and during rest period simply make sure the soil does not dry out. Liquid fertilizer once a month from spring to autumn. Growing mixture: organic soil, peat and sand in equal parts. Drain bottom of pot.

Propagation Detach the plantlets that have formed on the stolons and pot them individually in 6–7 cm (3 in) pots filled with equal parts peat and sand. Place in filtered light in warm position, barely wetting the soil. After a few weeks transplant into standard medium.
Pests and diseases Mealy bug, red spider.

214 SCHEFFLERA ACTINOPHYLLA
Queensland, umbrella tree, octopus tree

Family Araliaceae.
Origin Queensland, Papua New Guinea, Indonesia.
Description Also called *Brassaia actinophylla*. Sturdy shrub growing up to 2 m (6 ft) as a house plant and cultivated for its decorative foliage. The leaves are palmately divided and comprise several oval-elongate, leathery leaflets which radiate from a central point. The number of leaflets may vary from 3 to 5 in young leaves, and from 7 to 15 in adult leaves. Each leaflet is up to 30 cm (12 in) long. The color is bright green above and lighter green below. Plants raised indoors do not normally produce flowers.

Care It is an easy plant to cultivate indoors, thriving on bright light but not direct sun. The ideal growing temperature is 15–18°C (59–64°F) throughout the year, but can be higher provided there is adequate humidity. It cannot withstand drafts. Water with moderation, allowing the surface of the soil to dry out before repeating. Apply a liquid fertilizer fortnightly from March to October. Potting medium formed of 1 part organic soil, 1 part peat and 1 part sand. Repot in spring. It is advisable to give the main stem a supporting prop.

Propagation In spring from tip cuttings or piece of stem treated with hormone rooting preparation. Plant in pot filled with damp mixture of equal parts peat and sand; place in greenhouse at 18–24°C (64–75°F) or in plastic bag, exposing it to filtered light. After about 1 month, when rooted, acclimatize the plant gradually to growing conditions.

Pests and diseases Prone to attack by aphids.

215   SCHLUMBERGERA TRUNCATA

Thanksgiving cactus, crab cactus

Family   Cactaceae.
Origin   Brazil.
Description   This is an epiphytic succulent which lives in detrital soil rich in humus. The stems are formed of flattened joints with a few prominent teeth. The flowers, which appear in winter, bloom for 3–4 days. The color may be white, pink or violet-red according to the variety.
Care   The plant does not like direct sun and prefers exposure to medium light throughout the year. Because the buds appear in autumn, when hours of daylight are decreasing, an abundance of flowers can best be encouraged by ensuring that the plant is not kept under artificial light for lengthy periods at this season. It will do well at room temperatures all the year round but likes to be set outdoors in a shady spot during the summer. Water plentifully, keeping the soil moist but not flooding it in spring, autumn, winter and when in flower. When flowering is over, reduce amount of water without ever letting the mixture dry out, and resume as before when the stem begins to grow. Spray the plant with lime-free water. Apply a fertilizer with a high potassium content fortnightly all year round except during the period after flowering. Growing medium formed of 3 parts peat, 3 parts leafmold and 2 parts sand. Repot after flowering if roots have filled container.
Propagation   In spring–summer take cuttings composed of 2–3 joints and, having let the surface of the cuttings dry, plant them in growing medium. Also set other cuttings around the edge of a pot. Rooting occurs within a few weeks.
Pests and diseases   Scale insects, mealy bug.

---

216   SEDUM RUBROTINCTUM

Christmas cheer

Family   Crassulaceae.
Origin   Mexico.
Description   Shrubby succulent formed of stems that are branched at the base, thickly covered, with fleshy, stalkless leaves. In cool, wet environments these are bright green, but in warm, dry surroundings and in sunlight, they turn red. The creeping basal stems root as they make contact with the ground. Rarely flowers indoors.
Varieties   'Aurora,' gray-green leaves with red tints.
Care   Thrives on bright light and sunny positions. During growth it does well at room temperatures of 18–22°C (64–71°F); in winter it needs to be kept at 10°C (50°F). In summer, if possible, place it outside in the sun. Water it sparingly; during growth just wet the soil and allow one-third of it to dry out prior to repeating, and during dormancy simply avoid letting it dry out completely. Do not feed it too much but apply a liquid preparation of low concentration every 3–4 weeks in spring–summer. Potting mixture should be made up of 1 part organic soil, 1 part peat and 2 parts sand.
Propagation   Between April and September take 5–8 cm (2–3 in) stem cuttings. Remove lower leaves to about 2 cm (1 in) and let the cuttings dry for a couple of days; then plant them in normal mixture, treating them as adults. The species can also be multiplied from seed in March–April at 18°C (64°F) and subsequently pricked out.
Pests and diseases   Aphids, scale insects; rotting of roots, stem and leaves.

217 SEDUM SIEBOLDII
October plant

Family Crassulaceae.
Origin Japan.
Description *S. sieboldii* is a species with creeping, fleshy stems up to 20–25 cm (8–10 in) long. The rounded, succulent leaves have palm toothed edges, about 2 cm (1 in) across; they are gray-blue and are arranged in groups of 3 or more. The pink, star-shaped flowers are in clusters 5–8 cm (2–3 in) across; they bloom at the stem tips in autumn.
Varieties *S. sieboldii* 'Mediovariegatum,' green, pink-tinged leaves with a creamy patch in the middle.
Care An easy house plant which is very suitable for cultivation in hanging baskets. It needs to be exposed to the sun; if not the colors fade and the stems become bare. During growth it does well at room temperatures; in winter it must have a brief rest period at around 10°C (50°F). Water with moderation while growing, letting the top part of the mixture dry out before watering again; reduce amount of water during dormancy. In summer give a low-concentrate liquid fertilizer once a month. Potting medium made up of 1 part organic soil, 1 part peat and 2 parts coarse sand or perlite. Repot every spring, increasing size of containers (shallow pots or bowls) up to 18–20 cm (7–8 in). If plants get bigger, it is better to replace them with young specimens.
Propagation In spring–summer take cuttings and plant them in standard growing mixture, treating them as adults.
Pests and diseases Root rot.

218 SELAGINELLA MARTENSII
Resurrection plant, club moss, rose-of-Jericho

Family Selaginellaceae.
Origin Mexico.
Description A graceful plant cultivated for its ornamental foliage. The branched stems are erect at the base and then droop downwards. The sturdy roots and the leaves which cover the entire stem to about 1 cm (½ in) from the tip grow from the lower part of the stem. The fleshy, light green leaves are arranged in rows of 4 around the stem.
Varieties *S. martensii* 'Variegata,' a white leaf tip with silvery tints; 'Watsoniana,' pale green leaves.
Care The plant should be placed in shady, moderately light positions. It thrives on warm, humid surroundings, otherwise the leaves turn yellow and dry; so the plant should be sprayed with tepid water at least once a day and kept at average room temperature of 18–24°C (64–71°F) all year round. Water plentifully at all seasons, keeping the soil permanently damp, though not flooding it. Apply a low-concentrate liquid fertilizer every 2–3 weeks throughout the year. Acid soil mixture formed of 1 part leafmold, 2 parts peat and 1 part coarse sand. Repot every spring; after that change the mixture but not the container. If the plant grows too fast, prune up to half the branch length if necessary.
Propagation In spring, while pruning, take 7–8 cm (2–3 in) cuttings and plant them in normal moist soil. Keep warm and in filtered light. Rooting occurs within a few weeks and after that the plant should be handled as an adult specimen.
Pests and diseases Mites, aphids.

219 SEMPERVIVUM ARACHNOIDEUM
Cobweb hen-and-chicks, cobweb house leek

Family Crassulaceae.
Origin Mountains of southern Europe.
Description Succulent plant with leaves in tight rosettes, more or less rounded, up to 4 cm (about 2 in) across. The elliptic leaves are green, often tinted red, the tips being covered by a layer of whitish down similar to cobweb. The plant is stoloniferous, producing many lateral rosettes that form dense carpets. In June–July some rosettes produce flowering stems 8–15 cm (3–6 in) tall bearing pinkish-red flowers measuring 1 cm (½ in) in diameter. After flowering, the rosette dies.
Care Likes bright light and very sunny positions. Does well at room temperature but prefers a period of winter dormancy at around 10°C (50°F). In summer the plant should be placed, if possible, out in the sun. Water with moderation, preferably by plunging, since the rosette will easily rot if water is left to stand. In any event, the plant can withstand dry conditions. During the winter rest period merely make sure that the soil does not dry out completely. Feed very sparingly with a low-concentrate liquid fertilizer; every 3–4 weeks is sufficient. Mixture formed of 1 part organic soil, 1 part peat and 2 parts sand. Repot every spring in slightly larger containers.
Propagation In March–April or September–October cut off lateral rosettes with roots and plant in ordinary medium, handling as adult plants. The plant can also be propagated from seed, by sowing in unheated greenhouse in March and then pricking out.
Pests and diseases Aphids, scale insects, mealy bug, red spider.

220 SENECIO X HYBRIDUS
Cineraria

Family Compositae.
Origin Cultivated hybrids derived from Canary Islands species.
Description The genus *Senecio* comprises a very large number of species that differ greatly from one another; some are herbaceous plants with big leaves, others are succulents that much resemble cacti. The plants are therefore often commonly known by other names, as here, where the old botanical name of cineraria is applied. Plants of *Senecio x hybridus*, which have *S. cruentus* in their parentage, are herbaceous plants cultivated for their splendid flowers – hybrid varieties growing to a height of 30–50 cm (12–20 in) which flower in late winter or spring. The daisy-like blooms are red, blue, lilac, violet or white, often bicolored and arranged in such a way as to form 2 concentric rings, the inner one white. The leaves are heart-shaped, thick and hairy with toothed margins. Sometimes the underside has reddish-purple tints.
Care The plants are bought and kept indoors while in flower, a period of several weeks, after which they are discarded. Keep in filtered light in cool surroundings of 14–16°C (57–61°F). Water plentifully and allow the soil to remain damp at all times. Place the pots on layers of moist gravel to increase atmospheric humidity. Do not feed.
Propagation Sow seed in early summer and grow plants under glass at temperature of 8–12°C (46–53°F).
Pests and diseases Very prone to attack by whitefly and aphids; the latter concentrate on the growing tips and buds.

221 SETCREASEA PALLIDA var. PURPUREA
Purple heart

Family Commelinaceae.
Origin Mexico.
Description Trailing herbaceous plant notable for its deep purple stems and leaves. The oblong-lanceolate leaves are stalkless and their base enfolds the stem. Each leaf is 10–15 cm (4–6 in) long and covered with a thin layer of down. In summer the species produces small pink flowers from the leaf axils.

Care The plant is ideal for hanging basket arrangements alongside green trailing species. It needs full light and direct sun for 3–4 hours daily. It grows well, without a rest period, at temperatures that are not too low, around 13–18°C (55–64°F), all year round. Water regularly but let the soil surface dry out between successive applications. Feed once a month all through the year. Growing mixture formed of organic soil, peat and coarse sand in equal proportions. The plant grows fast and needs to be transplanted into bigger pots twice a year. Because it tends to grow ugly with age, it is best to discard it after about 18–24 months and replace it with newly propagated specimens. Stems that have borne flowers should be cut off after flowering.

Propagation From April to July take 8–10 cm (3–4 in) tip cuttings and after removing the lower leaves plant them in normal soil mixture. Place in bright but filtered light and water moderately, keeping the soil barely moist. After rooting, in 2–3 weeks, treat the plant as adult specimen.

Pests and diseases Scale insects, mealy bug, aphids.

222 SINNINGIA SPECIOSA
Gloxinia

Family Gesneriaceae.
Origin Brazil.
Description Herbaceous plant with tuberous roots, short stems and large, hairy leaves, ovate with toothed margins, bright green with lighter veining above, red underneath. The pink or purple flowers bloom in the original species from May to August.
Varieties 'Emperor Frederick,' scarlet flowers, white edges; 'Mont Blanc,' white flowers; 'Tigrina Red,' red flowers.

Care While growing, the plant needs light but not direct spring–summer sunshine. During its winter dormancy light is unimportant. It does well at room temperature, 18–24°C (64–75°F), but needs plenty of humidity so pots should be set in bowls filled with wet gravel. The air around the plant should also be sprayed, but not the plant itself. Water plentifully during growth but without letting it collect; if temperature is below 18°C (64°F) water with moderation. Reduce watering by stages towards the end of growing period and keep tuber dry when plant is dormant. Give special liquid flower fertilizer weekly throughout flowering season. When this is over, reduce fertilization and suspend it entirely at the end of summer. Highly organic soil of 3 parts leafmold, 3 parts peat and 2 parts sand. In spring the tubers should be potted in fresh mixture. At the start of germination water sparingly, then gradually increase amounts.

Propagation From seed October–March by dividing clumps in March and taking leaf cuttings in June–July.

Pests and diseases Aphids, scale insects, thrips.

223 SOLANUM CAPSICASTRUM
False Jerusalem cherry

Family Solanaceae.
Origin Brazil.
Description Shrubby species up to 40 cm (16 in) tall, grown for its very decorative fruits. The elliptic-lanceolate, wavy-edged, densely hairy leaves are up to 8 cm (3 in) long and 3 cm (1 in) wide. The white, 5-petaled flowers, single or in groups of 2–3, grow from the leaf axils in June–July. From the flowers, around October, inedible oval berries develop; these are initially green, then orange-red.
Varieties *S. capsicastrum* 'Variegatum,' creamy-yellow streaked leaves.
Care These plants are often thrown out when they lose their fruits. When fruiting, the plant should be given as much sun as possible. When the berries drop, let the plant rest for about a month and, if fruiting is desired for a second year, prune vigorously and place pots outside, protecting them from really strong sun in late spring and summer. To get the fruits to last a long time, keep the plants at a temperature of 14–16°C (57–61°F) and set pots on layers of moist gravel. Water abundantly, without flooding, during growth period and spray plants when in flower. During the short winter dormancy after fall of berries simply keep the soil from drying out. Give liquid fertilizer every fortnight, except during dormancy. Repot in spring in organic soil, peat and sand in equal parts.
Propagation Sow seeds at beginning of spring and wrap pot in plastic bag; then prick out. The plant will bear fruit the same year.
Pests and diseases Loses its fruits if air too dry.

224 SPARMANNIA AFRICANA
African hemp

Family Tiliaceae.
Origin South Africa.
Description Resembles a small linden tree of bushy habit. The original species, if grown indoors, may reach a height of over 3 m (10 ft) but there is a dwarf variety more suitable for cultivating as a house plant. The hairy, heart-shaped leaves are light green, up to 20 cm (8 in) long, on stalks which are equally long. When young, the stem and branches are green, but as they grow older they turn brown. The inflorescence, consisting of groups of 4-petaled white flowers with yellow stamens, appears early in the spring.
Varieties *S. africana* 'Flore Pleno,' double flowers; 'Nana,' smaller than the original species.
Care The plant requires bright light but does not enjoy direct sun. The ideal temperature for cultivation is 10–15°C (50–59°F); if the surroundings are too warm, place the pot in a bowl on a layer of moist gravel. Water regularly, allowing the surface of the soil mixture to dry out before repeating. During dormancy reduce amount of water still more. Give liquid fertilizer every fortnight from spring to autumn. Medium formed of 1 part organic soil, 1 part peat and 1 part sand. Repot once or twice a year, in spring–summer only, because the plant grows rapidly.
Propagation In spring take 15 cm (6 in) tip cuttings and root them in water or damp mixture of peat and sand, keeping them in warmth and light. Then transplant into growing medium and treat plants as adults.
Pests and diseases Aphids, red spider.

225 SPATHIPHYLLUM WALLISII

Family Araceae.
Origin Colombia, Venezuela.
Description Bushy plant cultivated for both its decorative foliage and its unusual flowers. The leaves, on stems 15 cm (6 in) long, are oblong-lanceolate, leathery, 15 cm (6 in) long and 8 cm (3 in) wide, with sheathed stalks. In spring–summer perfumed flowers appear from the center of the clustered leaves; they consist of a spadix enveloped inside an inward-curving spathe that is initially white and then green. Each flower is 10 cm (4 in) long and blooms for several weeks.
Varieties The many hybrid varieties cultivated include *S. wallisii* 'Clevelandii,' smaller than the species, and 'Mauna Loa,' which flowers abundantly for a long period.
Care It likes bright positions but not direct sun. Does well at room temperature throughout the year, but in winter growth slows down. Water moderately, allowing surface of soil to dry out before repeating; if temperature drops, reduce watering. Keep the surrounding air moist by putting pots on layers of wet gravel. Spray foliage, especially the underside, once a week. Give liquid fertilizer fortnightly from spring to autumn. Growing mixture formed of organic soil, peat and sand in equal parts. Repot every spring in containers of up to 20 cm (8 in).
Propagation In spring divide clumps that are too dense and plant individually in growing medium.
Pests and diseases Red spider on underside of leaves if surroundings too dry.

226 STAPELIA VARIEGATA (ORBEA VARIEGATA)

Carrion flower star flower

Family Ascepiadaceae.
Origin South Africa.
Description Succulent species with thick stems, branched at base, then drooping, characterized by 4 incised ribs, giving the overall effect of a dense clump. The star-shaped flowers develop at the base of the stems at the end of summer or beginning of autumn; they are light brown with purple streaks and give out an unpleasant smell.
Care Like almost all the plants of the genus *Stapelia, S. lepida* is not easy to cultivate indoors. It likes direct sun both in winter and summer. During winter it prefers moderate temperatures of 10–14°C (C50–57°F), and for the rest of the year medium temperatures of 18–24°C (64–75°F). Water regularly during spring-summer, but very little in winter, simply making sure that the soil does not dry out completely Feed once a month from April to September. Growing medium formed of 1 part organic compost, 1 part peat and 2 parts sand. Repot in early spring.
Propagation From seed in March-April at temperature of 18–20°C (64–68°F); alternatively by dividing clumps at time of repotting or by taking cuttings in June-July.
Pests and diseases Root rot if overwatered. Scale insects, mealy bug.

227 STEPHANOTIS FLORIBUNDA
Wax flower, Madagascar jasmine

Family Asclepiadaceae.
Origin Malagasy Republic (Madagascar).
Description A vigorous and highly decorative climbing shrub. The stems bear opposite, ovate leaves 10 cm (4 in) long; glossy and persistent, they are dark green with a paler central vein. The plant produces fragrant, waxy white flowers which grow in clusters of 10 or thereabouts from the leaf axils. The tube-shaped corolla opens into 5 ovate lobes with pointed tip. The flowers appear in spring and may continue throughout the summer.
Care The plant can be made to climb upwards on supports to a height of 4 m (17 ft) or trained round a wire hoop set at the edges of the pot. It likes bright light but not direct sun. It does well at medium-high temperatures of 18–24°C (64–75°F), provided the air is moist and there are no extreme temperature fluctuations. The best position is on an east-facing windowsill or in a terrarium. Water plentifully, always keeping the soil wet and spray the plant daily if the temperature rises above 21°C (70°F). Reduce watering in winter, but do not let the mixture dry out. Apply liquid fertilizer fortnightly from April to October. Growing mixture formed of organic soil, peat and sand in equal parts. Repot in early spring in containers of up to 20 cm (8 in).
Propagation Take tip cuttings between April and June, rooting them in peat and sand and wrapping pot in plastic bag.
Pests and diseases Scale insects which normally infest underside of the leaf, along the main vein.

---

228 STRELITZIA REGINAE
Bird of Paradise

Family Musaceae.
Origin South Africa.
Description This plant, of considerable size in the wild, will, when cultivated indoors, reach a height of 1 m (3 ft) or slightly more. It is a tufted species, formed of leathery, ovate or oblong leaves, 30–40 cm (12–16 in) long, on sturdy stalks 35–70 cm (14–28 in) in length. The plant flowers from about the age of 6 years. In spring a long stalk develops; at its tip is an inflorescence of most peculiar form, consisting of a green, keel-shaped bract, 20 cm (8 in) long, in an almost horizontal position, from which grow bright orange, erect flowers, each with a violet tongue, measuring 20 cm (8 in) in length. The flowers develop in the course of a few weeks and give the inflorescence the likeness of a crest.
Care It needs bright light, with at least 3–4 hours of sunshine daily. Does well at room temperature but in winter must spend some months at 13°C (55°F). It can go outside in the summer, but sheltered from the wind and not in full sun. Water during growth period and let the surface of the soil mixture become dry before repeating. During dormancy avoid letting soil dry out. Give liquid fertilizer every fortnight while growing. Potting medium should consist of 1 part organic soil, 1 part peat and 1 part sand. Repot young plants every spring, increasing size of container.
Propagation In spring divide clumps that are too dense or cut off side shoots with some leaves and roots; plant in growing medium, giving filtered light and little water.
Pests and diseases Prone to attack by scale insects.

229 STREPTOCARPUS HYBRIDS
Cape primrose

Family Geseneraceae.
Origin Hybrids of horticultural origin.
Description The *S. hybrids* comprise a group of stemless, bushy varieties with rough, hairy leaves in a rosette. Flowers, variously colored according to cultivar, bloom from May to October.
Varieties *S.* 'Constant Nymph,' best-known cultivar, with blue flowers; *S.* 'Wiesmoor' has given rise to hybrids of various colors: red, blue and white, propagated from seed.
Care The plants should not be placed directly in the sun but in a position with constant light, ideally facing northeast or northwest. They can be kept all year round at room temperature, but if this rises above 24°C (75°F) the pots should be placed on beds of moist gravel. Below 13°C (55°F) the plants become dormant. Water regularly with tepid water, letting the surface of the soil dry out before repeating. If the plant becomes dormant, reduce amount of water. Give liquid fertilizer fortnightly from April to September. Porous growing medium with plenty of organic soil, as, for example, sphagnum moss and large-grained perlite or coarse peat and perlite in equal proportions. The roots are not deep, so it is best to use shallow pots or bowls with a diameter of maximum 15 cm (6 in). Repot after flowering.
Propagation 'Constant Nymph' cultivar is propagated in spring from leaf cuttings; 'Wiesmoor' is propagated from seed at end-January for summer flowering or end-June for flowering the following spring.
Pests and diseases Powdery mildew if air too dry; mealy bug.

230 SYNGONIUM PODOPHYLLUM
African evergreen

Family Araceae.
Origin Mexico.
Description Climbing species characterized by a marked difference in the form of its leaves. The leaves of the adult plant are ovate, divided into 5–11 sections, whereas those of the young plant are arrow-shaped and scarcely divided; both forms are glossy and persistent. The flowers are shaped like lilies.
Varieties *S. podophyllum* 'Emerald Gem' is a more compact cultivar than the original species; its leaves are dark green, with lighter areas along the veining; *albolineatum* has young leaves attractively patterned with grayish stripes.
Care Needs bright but filtered light. It does well at room temperature throughout the year and is vulnerable to sudden fluctuations. At 18°C (64°F) and above, place the pot in a bowl filled with wet gravel. Spray the foliage. Water with moderation during the growing season, letting the soil surface dry out between applications. In the winter period of dormancy, should the temperature drop below 15°C (59°F), merely ensure that the soil does not dry out. Use soft water. Give liquid fertilizer every fortnight, except during rest period. Potting mixture should consist of 1 part organic soil, 2 parts leafmold, 1 part peat and 1 part sand. Repot every spring.
Propagation In spring–summer take 10 cm (4 in) cuttings and plant them in mixture of equal parts peat and sand. Keep in the greenhouse or in a plastic bag in filtered light.
Pests and diseases Scale insects.

231 THUNBERGIA ALATA
Black-eyed Susan

Family Acanthaceae.
Origin Tropical Africa.
Description Perennial climbing herbaceous plant with thin stems which twist spirally around supports. The leaves, 8 cm (3 in) long and wide, are generally triangular with toothed margins, on slender stalks. Flowers appear in summer–autumn. The tubular flowers, 5 cm (2 in) across, have a corolla which opens into 5 lobes, with a dark central eye; the tube is dark purple, and there are 2 green bracts at the base.

Varieties *T. alata* 'Aurantica,' the commonest variety, orange flowers; 'Alba,' white; 'Lutea,' bright yellow.
Care Very suitable for rooms, balconies and gardens, usually grown as an annual and discarded after flowering. They are either bought as ready-grown plantlets in spring or obtained by propagation and induced to climb round stakes set in the pot. For an abundance of flowers the plants need bright light and at least 2–3 hours of sunshine every day. They do well at normal room temperature down to a minimum of 10°C (50°F). Water sparingly when growth begins, increasing amounts when in flower, keeping soil moist. Give liquid fertilizer every fortnight. Growing medium formed of loam, peat and sand in equal parts. Repot if necessary during summer. Remove dead flowers to prolong flowering period.

Propagation From seed in spring, in potting mixture, placing 3 seeds in an 8 cm (3 in) pot and exposing to heat and light. Keep mixture wet. Germination occurs in about 4 weeks. Gradually acclimatize plants to partially shaded positions and repot separately when 15 cm (6 in) tall.
Pests and diseases Aphids.

232 TIBOUCHINA URVILLEANA
Glory bush

Family Melastomataceae.
Origin Brazil.
Description Shrub grown for its very beautiful flowers. The herbaceous stems of young plants are covered in reddish down and become woody in adult plants. The downy ovate leaves, set opposite, are 5–10 cm (2–4 in) long and 2–3 cm (1 in) wide; they have prominent lengthwise veins and finely toothed margins. The flowers grow singly or in groups of 2–3 at the branch tips, usually in winter. Each flower measures 8 cm (3 in) across, flat, with 5 pinkish-purple or dark purple petals and a group of purple stamens in the center.

Care From spring to autumn the plants should stand in bright, indirect light; in winter they need a few hours of sunshine daily. During spring and summer they live at normal room temperature; in winter it is best to keep them cooler, at 10–15°C (50–59°F). Water plentifully, avoiding flooding, from spring to autumn, and place pots in bowls filled with moist gravel. Keep the soil barely damp in winter. Give liquid fertilizer every fortnight from April to October. Growing medium formed of loam, peat and sand in equal parts. Repot in spring, increasing container's diameter. In spring cut the main branches by a half and the side ones to a single pair of leaves.

Propagation Take tip or stem cuttings in spring, treating them with hormones, and plant them in mixture of equal parts peat and sand. Put in unheated greenhouse or in plastic bag, with filtered light.
Pests and diseases Mealy bug, scale insects in general.

233 TILLANDSIA CYANEA
Pink quill

Family Bromeliaceae.
Origin Ecuador.
Description An apiphytic species with very few roots, and therefore grown on tree trunks, absorbing food and water mainly through the leaves. The plant consists of a rosette of thin, pointed leaves, 30–40 cm (12–16 in) long and 1–2 cm (up to 1 in) across; they are gray-green with long reddish bands on the underside. The inflorescence grows from the center of the rosette and consists of a flowering stalk and a flat, stiff flower head, formed of smooth, overlapping, pink bracts. Single blue or violet flowers, protrude among the bracts. After flowering, the rosette dies and is replaced by lateral shoots.
Care Exposure to bright, filtered light. The plants can be kept all year round at average room temperatures without becoming dormant. Place the pots in bowls filled with wet gravel and spray plants 2–3 times a week. As a rule it is unnecessary to water the soil (or only rarely by immersion), for the water sprayed on the leaves is sufficient. This water must be lime-free and once a month a liquid fertilizer can be administered with the spray. The growing medium should be highly porous and lime-free, as, for example, leafmold and peat in equal parts. Alternatively pieces of wood can be used as supports and the plantlets attached to them after wrapping their base in sphagnum.
Propagation Lateral shoots can be taken from the parent plant at any time of year, when leaves are 8 cm (3 in) long, and planted individually in equal parts peat and sand. Place them in unheated greenhouse.
Pests and diseases Highly resistant to parasites.

234 TOLMIEA MENZIESII
Piggy-back plant, youth-on-age, thousand mothers

Family Saxifragaceae.
Origin United States.
Description Tufted evergreen plant. The stalked leaves develop from a rhizome. Each leaf is rounded and slightly lobed, the surface hairy and the margins toothed. New plantlets form at the base of the leaves, their weight serving to bend the stalks so that the plant appears to droop. The spikes of green-white flowers appear in June.
Care Suitable for cultivation in hanging baskets, it can be kept both in medium light and sunny positions. It will adapt to average temperatures of 18–24°C (64–75°F) and also cooler conditions, down to a minimum of 10°C (50°F). Water abundantly during period of growth, wetting the soil thoroughly. In the winter rest interval, however, avoid letting the soil dry out. Give liquid fertilizer fortnightly from April to October. Potting medium formed of organic soil, peat and sand in equal parts. Place different plants in a pot or hanging basket and repot in spring–summer. Change the plants every couple of years or so because young ones are far more decorative.
Propagation In spring–summer cut off a leaf with plantlet and 2–3 cm (1 in) of stalk. Pot in moist mixture of equal parts peat and sand, burying the stalk and stretching the leaf out on the surface. Place in bright, filtered light and water sparingly. In 2–3 weeks the plant will root and can be treated as an adult. After 5–6 weeks transplant into normal soil. Can also be multiplied by layering.
Pests and diseases Scale insects.

235   TRADESCANTIA ALBIFLORA
Spiderwort

Family Commelinaceae.
Origin South America.
Description Fast-growing herbaceous plant with prostrate stems and elliptic, pointed, stalkless leaves, 5 cm (2 in) long. The leaf color is green with a purple-red tip and underside. In spring–summer small flowers with 3 triangular white or pink tepals grow from the stem tips.

Varieties *T. fluminensis* 'Variegata,' leaves streaked creamy yellow; 'Quicksilver,' vigorous, fast-growing cultivar, leaves striped silver-white, without pink shading underneath and bearing more flowers than 'Variegata.'

Care An easy species to cultivate indoors and extremely decorative in hanging baskets. It needs a lot of light and, if possible, a few hours of sunshine daily. Does well at temperatures of 21–24°C (70–75°F), in humid surroundings; it is advisable, therefore, to place pots on layers of wet gravel. Water the soil regularly during growth, allowing the surface to dry out before watering again. In winter the plant may become dormant – when temperature falls below 15°C (59°F) – in which case reduce watering to the point of keeping the soil barely moist. Give liquid fertilizer fortnightly from spring to autumn. Potting medium made up of 1 part organic soil, 1 part peat and 1 part sand. Repot in spring in containers of maximum diameter 15 cm (6 in). Because the plants tend to shed their lower leaves, they are often replaced by younger specimens.

Propagation Take tip cuttings from April to September and root them in water or in compost.
Pests and diseases Resistant to attacks from parasites.

---

236   TULIPA HYBRIDS
Tulip

Family Liliaceae.
Origin Hybrids of horticultural origin.
Description The tulip varieties most suitable for indoor cultivation are early-flowering hybrids, low in size with small leaves and large flowers on short stems. The bulbs are oval, 3–5 cm (1–2 in) wide, and covered by a brown tunic.

Varieties Cultivars include: *T.* 'Bellona,' golden-yellow; 'Diana,' white; 'Brilliant Star,' bright red; 'Pink Beauty,' bright pink with white stripes, 'Electra,' light purple with pale pink borders.

Care Tulips can be grown indoors for flowering from December to March, but for one year only. In the following autumn the bulbs can be planted outdoors for flowering in subsequent years, but they will never give flowers again indoors. The bulbs should initially be planted in October (staggered to obtain a succession of flowers) in a mixture of loam, peat and sand in equal parts, leaving the tips just protruding. The mixture must always be kept damp. Place the pots in a dark place at around 10°C (50°F) or cover with black plastic until the leaves are 5–6 cm (2 in) in length (about 8–10 weeks). After that expose the plants gradually to higher temperatures and to the light. Keep them at below 16°C (61°F) until the buds appear; even afterwards it is better to maintain the temperature at around that level in order to get flowers to bloom for 3–4 weeks. They do not need feeding. The bulbs can also be planted in bowls full of water, following the same procedure.

Pests and diseases Highly resistant to disease.

237 VALLOTA SPECIOSA
Scarborough lily

Family Amaryllidaceae.

Origin South Africa.

Description A bulbous plant. Strap-shaped leaves grow from the bulb; they are green, often with a bronze base. A single flowering stem, develops from the center of the leaf, bearing 3–10 flowers at its tip. The bright red flowers bloom in August–September.

Varieties *V. speciosa* 'Alba,' white flowers; 'Delicata,' salmon-pink flowers.

Care The species flowers in bright light and can even stand direct sun provided not exposed to intense midday heat. It grows at medium temperatures of 18–24°C (64–75°F) but during winter the bulbs should be given a rest period at 10–12°C (50–53°F). Plant the bulbs singly in late spring and early summer, in 10–12 cm (4–5 in) pots filled with a mixture consisting of organic soil, peat and sand in equal parts. Water sparingly at the start, allowing the surface of the mixture to dry out between successive waterings. When shoots appear, increase amount of water, but still with moderation. During winter dormancy simply avoid letting the soil dry out. Give liquid fertilizer fortnightly from April to August; after that, while flowering, give fertilizer with high potassium content.

Propagation The principal bulb produces a number of offset bulbs. When the plant has filled the pot, divide into several sections, each with offset. The larger ones of around 3 cm (about 1 in) should be planted individually; the smaller ones should be repotted every spring.

Pests and diseases Bulb rot if overwatered.

238 VRIESEA SPLENDENS
Flaming sword

Family Bromeliaceae.
Origin Venezuela, Guiana.
Description Species cultivated for its highly decorative foliage and showy flowers. It has stiff, sword-shaped leaves, 40 cm (16 in) long, in an open rosette. At the center of the rosette the leaves form a tube that holds water. The leaves are dark green with prominent dark red or purple transverse stripes. Flowers are produced only by adult plants. A central flowering stem, up to 1 m (3 ft) long, develops with a flattened inflorescence formed of bright red, overlapping bracts, from which the yellow flowers appear. The bracts remain decorative for many months.
Care Needs exposure to bright light with several hours of direct sun morning and evening. Can be kept at normal room temperature all year round, but in winter growth stops for a short time. Water regularly during growth season and refill central tube. Place pots on layers of wet gravel. In winter merely prevent soil mixture from drying out. Give low-concentrate liquid fertilizer once a month from spring to autumn, applying it both to the soil and the central well of the rosette. Lime-free soil formed of equal parts leafmold and peat or 1 part organic soil, 1 part sand and 2 parts peat. Repot every 2–3 years in spring, using containers of up to 12 cm (5 in).
Propagation The plant produces lateral shoots which can be detached when about 10 cm (4 in) long and planted in growing medium. Enclose in plastic bag and keep in filtered light until rooting in about a month.
Pests and diseases Highly resistant to disease.

---

239 WASHINGTONIA FILIFERA
Washington palm, desert fan palm, petticoat palm

Family Palmae.
Origin California, Arizona.
Description Palm originating in the California desert. In the wild it may grow to over 20 m (65 ft) but as a house plant it does not normally exceed 2.5 m (8 ft). It comprises a mahogany-brown stem with palmate fronds on thorny stalks 50 cm (20 in) long. Each frond is 60 cm (24 in) wide and divided to about halfway into some 20 segments. Thin fibrous threads hang from the edges of the leaf segments.
Care A fairly easy plant to cultivate indoors. It needs bright light all year round and benefits from a few hours of daily sunshine, especially in summer; so it is best to stand it outside from June to September. It does well at temperatures of 20–24°C (68–75°F) and although it tolerates dry air larger and greener fronds are produced if the pot is kept on layers of wet gravel. Minimum temperature 10°C (50°F). Water abundantly from spring to autumn, keeping the soil wet; in winter, because growth stops or slows down, amounts of water should be reduced and the surface allowed to dry out between successive waterings. Liquid fertilizer should be applied fortnightly from March to October. Growing mixture formed of 1 part organic soil, 2 parts peat and 1 part sand. Drain the bottom of the pot thoroughly, letting no water collect. Repot seldom, using small containers and pressing the mixture down firmly. The plant has fragile roots and is sensitive to shock.
Propagation From seed but difficult indoors.
Pests and diseases Scale insects, mealy bug.

240 YUCCA ALOIFOLIA
Dagger plant, Spanish bayonet

Family Agavaceae.
Origin United States, Mexico, West Indies.
Description A species with a shape that varies greatly depending on variety and according to the conditions in which it is grown. As a house plant it generally develops a woody, unbranched stem, with tufts of stiff leaves. These are sharply pointed and have finely toothed margins. As a rule, does not flower when cultivated indoors.
Varieties *Y. aloifolia draconis,* a many-branched variety with tufts of soft leaves; 'Quadricolor,' leaves with green, white, yellow and reddish longitudinal stripes; 'Tricolor,' yellow and white stripes in the central part of the leaf.
Care Easy to cultivate indoors provided it is placed in bright light and receives at least 3 hours of direct sunshine daily. Can be kept at room temperature throughout year without any rest period; but if there is insufficient light in winter it is advisable to keep it for a while at temperatures of 10–15°C (50–59°F) so that growth can be halted temporarily. It tolerates dry air and likes to go outside in the summer, in the sun. While growing it needs plenty of water, and the mixture must always be moist, without flooding. Should it become dormant, merely make sure the soil does not dry out entirely. Administer a liquid fertilizer fortnightly throughout the growth period. Potting medium formed of organic soil, peat and sand in equal proportions. Repot in spring only if roots have filled pot.
Propagation In spring detach lateral shoots produced by plant and root them in mixture suitable for cuttings. Repot these in the following year in standard growing medium.
Pests and diseases Very resistant to parasites.

241 YUCCA ELEPHANTIPES
Spineless yucca

Family Agavaceae.
Origin Mexico, Guatemala.
Description The plant consists of a woody, branched stem, 1–1.5 m (3–5 ft) high, often with a swollen base. Tufts of shiny, dark green leaves, over 1 m (3 ft) long, form at the tips of the branches. The leaves are strap-shaped, with toothed margins, curving outwards and softer than in *Y. aloifolia,* especially at the tip.
Varieties *Y. elephantipes* 'Variegata,' creamy-white leaf margins.
Care An easy plant to cultivate indoors provided it is given at least 3 hours of direct sunshine daily. It can be kept all the year round at medium temperatures of 18–22°C (64–71°F) without becoming dormant, but if there is insufficient light in winter it is well to set it for a while in cool surroundings, at 10–15°C (50–59°F) in order to slow down its growth. In summer it thrives outdoors in the sun. During the growth period give it plenty of water, but should it be allowed to rest, simply ensure that the soil does not become completely dry. Give liquid fertilizer every fortnight except when resting. Growing medium formed of organic soil, peat and sand in equal proportions. Repot, if necessary, in spring.
Propagation Detach future side shoots in spring and root them in mixture suitable for cuttings.
Pests and diseases Highly resistant to parasites.

242 ZANTEDESCHIA AETHIOPICA
Arum lily, calla lily, white calla, pig lily

Family Araceae.
Origin South Africa.
Description Stemless species consisting of a thick, fleshy underground rhizome from which sprout the roots and the broad, arrow-shaped leaves, up to 50 cm (20 in) long and 20–25 cm (8–10 in) wide; they are dark green and borne on stalks up to 1 m (3 ft) long. The very showy flower is formed of a golden-yellow spadix encompassed by a white spathe, and blooms in winter or early spring.

Care The species grows naturally in swampy areas which dry out completely in the summer, so these are the months when the plant rests. In plants cultivated indoors, the growing period, similarly, is winter–spring. In summer the plants wither; only the rhizome survives and this should be kept outdoors in the sun until late autumn, without being watered. In October the rhizomes can be brought indoors and kept in bright light, with several hours of sunshine daily, and when growth recommences they should be kept at temperatures of 10–14°C (50–57°F) for about 3 months, with little water at the start but gradually more as growth continues. Subsequently the optimum temperature is 16°C (61°F); the plants will live at higher temperatures but flowering will be shorter. During full growth always keep the soil moist and place the pot in a bowl of water. Feed with liquid fertilizer fortnightly while plant is growing, and weekly when in flower. Growing medium should consist of organic soil, peat and sand in equal proportions.
Propagation By dividing the rhizomes in autumn, taking care that each portion has at least one shoot.
Pests and diseases Sometimes attacked by scale insects.

243 ZEBRINA PENDULA
Wandering Jew

Family Commelinaceae.
Origin Mexico.
Description Also known by the name of *Tradescantia zebrina,* this is a fast-growing species with drooping stems that bear decorative ovate, pointed leaves. In spring and summer the plant produces small, 3-petaled, purple-pink flowers.

Varieties *Z. pendula* 'Discolor,' narrower leaves than original species, with thinner silvery stripes and a bronze central band; 'Purpusii,' larger leaves, bronze without a silvery stripe; 'Quadricolor,' the most difficult to cultivate, leaves irregularly streaked in pink, green, cream and silver.

Care The plant maintains its colors only if exposed to bright light. It grows normally at room temperatures of 18–22°C (64–71°F). Water with moderation even in growing season, and very little during rest period. Give liquid fertilizer every fortnight from April to October. Growing medium formed of organic soil, peat and sand in equal parts. As a rule repotting is unnecessary; it is better to keep the plants for several years and to replace them frequently because they shed their basal leaves as they age. Get rid of old stems in early spring.
Propagation From April to June take tip cuttings about 7 cm (3 in) long, plant them in mixture of peat and sand, and set in bright, filtered light. After about a month transplant into standard growing medium, placing a few rooted cuttings in each pot.
Pests and diseases Aphids.

GLOSSARY

Acid As applied to soil gauged on the pH scale from 1 to 14. Below 7 the soil is acid, above 7 alkaline. Acidity denotes absence of lime.

Aerial root Root that grows from the stem of a plant. In house plants it can remain loose, be trained on a support or embedded in the soil.

Agamic Form of vegetative propagation whereby plant may be multiplied by division or by cuttings, as opposed to seminal propagation from seed.

Air-layering Method of vegetative propagation whereby a cut is made in a stem of a growing plant, wrapped in a moist medium such as sphagnum moss until roots form, and then cut off and separately planted.

Alkaline As applied to soil; above 7 on the pH scale. Alkalinity denotes the presence of lime.

Alternate Arrangement of leaves which are placed at different heights alternately on either side of the stem.

Annual Plant that grows, fruits, flowers and produces seeds in the course of a single year.

Anther Thickened tip of the stamen which contains the pollen, often brightly colored.

Aphid Small insect that sucks the sap of plants, causing wilting, distorted growth etc.

Areole Typical organ of succulent plants from which spines, hairs, flowers, etc. grow.

Axil Angle formed by a leaf and its stalk on a stem from which an axillary bud sometimes grows.

Berry Spherical fleshy fruit containing seeds enveloped in pulp.

Bilobate Divided into two lobes, as of a plant organ, such as a leaf.

Bipinnate Doubly pinnate, as of a leaf consisting of a central axis with lateral axes to which the leaflets are attached.

Blade Flattened part of a leaf at the end of the stalk.

Bract Modified leaf, often brightly colored, which subtends a flower, or which enfolds an inflorescence.

Bulb Swollen underground stem covered in fleshy scales and terminating in a growing tip or flower bud. Each bulb gives rise to a single flowering stem.

Bulblet Small bulb, also known as bulbil, which forms on a parent bulb and can be removed for the purpose of vegetative propagation.

Calcareous Applied to soil containing a high measure of lime.

Calcifuge Plant that does not thrive in alkaline or chalky soil.

Calyx Outer part of flower surrounding the corolla, formed of sepals, usually green, which may be separate or fused together, serving to protect the flower when in bud. Sometimes the calyx is colored similarly to the corolla.

Chlorosis Yellowing of leaves as a result of unsuitable environmental conditions, such as poor light, etc., or of attacks by parasites.

Clump Closely compact group of roots, etc. which can be divided for purposes of vegetative propagation.

Compost Soil, usually one rich in organic matter.

Cordate Heart-shaped.

Corolla Ring of petals, which may be separate or fused together, usually brightly colored for attracting insects, protecting the reproductive organs of a flower.

Corona Crown-like appendage on inner side of a corolla, common to certain plants such as narcissus.

Corymb Inflorescence, with flowers in a flat or convex cluster, in which the outer flowers open first.

Crocks Fragments of clay flower pots or pottery placed in bottom of pot to improve drainage.

Cultivar Horticulturally produced variety of plant.

Cutting Portion of stem, root or leaf which is cut off and planted under suitable conditions to produce a new plant virtually identical to the parent.

Deciduous The loss of parts of a plant such as leaves, at certain seasons or stages of growth.

Dentate Toothed, as of leaf margins.

Dioecious Having male and female organs on separate plants.

Division Technique of propagation whereby a growing plant is uprooted and divided into sections, each with roots and leaves, and individually planted to produce several smaller ones.

Dormancy Phase when a plant is said to be dormant or resting, its growth slowed down or suspended.

Double Applied to a flower with two or more layers of petals, the innermost of which derives from a modification of the stamens.

Drupe Pulpy fruit with hard internal shell, usually enclosing a single seed.

Edible Plant or part of plant, such as fruit or seed, which can be eaten.

Epiphyte Plant that lives on another plant, without behaving like a parasite, using it merely as a support; characteristic of most bromeliads.

Family Wide group of plants which contains a number of genera, often including forms that are very dissimilar.

Fertilizer Substance, often one chemically prepared to enrich soil by supplying nutrients, thus stimulating plant growth, commercially available in form of liquid, powder, granules, etc.

Filament Slender stalk of the stamen which supports the anther.

Flower Part of a seed plant comprising the reproductive organs (stamens, pistil, etc.), usually brightly colored and sometimes scented to attract pollen-carrying insects.

Forcing Specialized procedure designed to anticipate certain natural phases of a plant's development, such as flowering, fruiting, rooting of cuttings, germination, etc., usually practiced in order to bring it into bloom outside its normal season.

Frond Finely divided leaf, simple or compound, of ferns and certain palms.

Fungus Plant organism without chlorophyll which reproduces by spores and can parasitize other plants, causing many ailments.

Genus Group of closely related plants, forming a subdivision of a family, itself further subdivided into species; the first word of the Latin or scientific name denotes the plant's genus.

Germination Sprouting of a seed to produce a new plant.

Gray mold Plant disease, characterized by gray, furry growth on affected parts.

Growing tip Terminal part of a stem, branch or root from which plant growth occurs.

Habit Characteristic bearing or appearance of a plant.

Herbaceous Plant with soft, non-woody stems and branches, generally applied to perennials that die down in winter and develop again in spring.

Hormones Organic substances either produced by living things themselves, or of synthetic origin, which condition certain vital processes of the plant, speeding them up or slowing them down; there are, for example, hormones that stimulate the rooting of cuttings, others that inhibit plant development, producing dwarf forms, etc.

Hybrid Plant created by crossing two species of the same genus, denoted in the scientific name by the symbol x.

Hydroculture Method of growing plants in water, into which fertilizing elements have been introduced.

Inflorescence Flowering part of a plant, on which individual flowers are arranged in various ways on the axis, in spikes, corymbs, racemes, panicles, etc.

Lanceolate Lance-shaped.

Lateral Positioned at side; an extension of a branch or shoot.

Latex Opaque or milky liquid exuded by certain plants such as species of Euphorbiaceae.

Layering Method of vegetative propagation whereby part of a stem or branch is inserted in soil until roots form and then cut off to continue development as independent plant.

Leaf Organ of plant, usually flat and green, growing from branch or stem, provided with chlorophyll, through which photosynthesis takes place. The leaves of some species are transformed into needles, spines, etc.

Leaflet Part of a compound leaf.

Lip Portion of the corolla which in certain flowers is large and brightly colored.

Lobe Division of a leaf or petal.

Mealy bug Plant-sucking insect of family Coccidae.

Node Joint that occurs at intervals along stem of a plant, from which a leaf or bud develops.

Opposite Arrangement of leaves, situated at the same level on opposed sides of the axis, sprouting from a single node.

Osmunda Type of fern, the rhizomes of which are used as a soil for the cultivation of orchids.

Palmate Applied to the lobing of leaves radiating outwards like fingers of an outstretched palm.

Panicle Compound flower structure or inflorescence, with groups of many flowers on short stalks.

Parasite Living organism (virus, bacterium, fungus, insect or plant) that draws sustenance from another organism; many house plants are susceptible to attack either by animal or plant parasites.

Peat Partially decomposed vegetable matter from marsh or bog regions, treated and sold commercially, useful as ingredient in potting soil.

Perennial Plant that lives for two years and more, generally dying down in late autumn or winter, regrowing in spring.

Persistent Continuous or permanent, as applied to leaves.

Petal Modified leaf, as a rule brightly colored, forming part of a flower corolla.

pH The hydrogen ion concentration in the soil or water. The pH scale, which goes from 0 to 14, is used to measure acidity or alkalinity.

Pinch out To remove tip of a growing plant in order to stimulate development of lateral shoots and encourage bushy habit.

Pinnate Compound leaf with leaflets, usually paired, on either side of the stalk.

Pinnule Subdivision of compound pinnate leaf or frond of fern.

Pistil Female reproductive parts of flower, comprising ovary, style and stigma.

Prick out Transplant seedling or cutting to larger container or into pot.

Propagation Method of multiplying plants, either from seed (seminal) or by means of cutting, division, layering, etc. (agamic).

Prostrate Habit of a plant with branches that creep along ground.

Pruning Seasonal or periodic cutting back or removal of branches and stems, especially when dead, diseased or overcrowded, to improve health and general appearance, restrict excessive growth and promote flowering.

Pseudobulb Swollen stem of an epiphytic orchid often developing at intervals from an underground rhizome and bearing leaves and flowers.

Raceme A simple inflorescence bearing flowers on an elongated axis.

Red spider Small mite inhabiting and often causing damage to house plants, often present when surroundings are too dry.

Repotting Procedure, carried out annually or more frequently, whereby the plant is lifted and replanted, with fresh soil, in bigger pot or container, in order to provide more room for roots, consistent with plant's dimensions.

Rest period Phase of plant's development, also called dormancy, usually occurring in winter, when growth is slowed down or temporarily arrested.

Rhizome Modified stem which develops horizontally underground or at surface, usually bearing roots in the lower part, and leaves and flowering stems in the upper part.

Root Part of the plant which usually grows downward into the soil, supporting it and absorbing nutriment and moisture.

Rosette Cluster of leaves arranged at same level around stem.

Runner Slender stem, also called stolon, which grows horizontally on surface of soil and puts down roots at every node, where a new plant may form.

Scale insect Small insect of family Coccidae whose young sucks plant juices.

Seed Fertilized ovule capable of developing into new plant.

Sepal Leaf-like structure forming part of the calyx of a flower, sometimes more prominent than the petal.

Sheath Basal portion of leaf enfolding the stalk.

Shrub Woody perennial plant with branches spreading from ground level, smaller than a tree.

Single Applied to a flower whose corolla is formed of a single whorl of petals.

Spadix Spike of flowers with a fleshy axis, usually enfolded by a spathe.

Spathe Bract or pair of bracts enclosing a spadix.

Species Group of related plants belonging to a single genus; the second word of the Latin or scientific name denotes plant species.

Sphagnum Type of moss from damp zones used as potting medium to retain moisture.

Spike Inflorescence consisting of an elongated axis along which stalkless flowers are arranged at intervals.

Spore Microscopic reproductive propagule of ferns and other lower plants, formed of one or several cells.

Stalk Part of plant, also known as petiole or peduncle, bearing leaf or flower.

Stamen Male organ of flower, consisting of filament and anther, containing pollen.

Stem Part of plant above ground level, developing from roots, bearing branches, leaves, flowers, etc.

Stigma Enlarged terminal part of pistil on which pollen is deposited.

Stolon Alternative name for runner or modified stalk from which new plants grow.

Stopping Alternative name for pinching out, removing growing tips.

Style Elongated part of pistil between ovary and stigma.

Succulent Plant with swollen, fleshy leaves and stems capable of absorbing and retaining water and thus withstanding long periods of drought.

Tendril Thread-like extension of stem or leaf of climbing plant that wraps itself around stakes, trellises, etc. as a support.

Terminal At or close to tip, as of branch or leaf.

Thrip Minute insect with mouthparts for sucking juices of plants.

Throat Opening of the tube of a flower corolla or calyx, often of a contrasting color.

Transplant Move a growing plant to a new location when sufficiently developed.

Tuber Swollen underground stem which stores food and produces shoots from which new stems develop.

Umbel Inflorescence comprising a branch of flowers all stemming from one point.

Variegated Of a leaf marked in two or more colors.

Variety Subdivision of species which, when produced by special horticultural techniques is known as a cultivar; the third word of the Latin or scientific name denotes the variety concerned.

Vein Element of the vascular tissue that forms the framework of a leaf.

Whorl Three or more leaves or flowers arranged around a point on an axis, also known as a verticil.

INDEX

Picture sources

All the photographs are by Enzo Arnone except for those illustrating the following entries: 204, 237: Eric Crichton, Bruce Coleman Ltd; 11 (below), 14, 133, 200, 230: Giuseppe Mazza, Montecarlo; 37, 38 (above and below), 44, 61, 88, 139, 219, 234: Harry Smith, Horticultural Photographic Collection, Chelmsford; 97, 125, 127: Warren, Photos Horticultural, Suffolk.